Modern World History
FOR AQA SPECIFICATION B

$8/12

CORE

David Ferriby • Jim McCabe
David Hansom • Tony Hewitt
Alan Mendum • Steve Waugh

Heinemann Educational Publishers
Halley Court, Jordan Hill, Oxford, OX2 8EJ
a division of Reed Educational & Professional Publishing Ltd
Heinemann is a registered trademark of Reed Educational & Professional Publishing Ltd

OXFORD MELBOURNE AUCKLAND
JOHANNESBURG BLANTYRE GABORONE
IBADAN PORTSMOUTH NH (USA) CHICAGO

© David Ferriby and Jim McCabe 2001, 2002

First published 2001
Revised edition 2002
10-digit ISBN: 0 435312 06 5
13-digit ISBN: 978 0 435312 06 0
05
10 9 8 7

Designed and illustrated by Ian Foulis and Associates

Printed and bound in China by China Translation & Printing Services Ltd.
Picture research by Geri May

Photographic acknowledgements
The authors and publisher would like to thank the following for permission to reproduce
photographs:

AKG: 42E, 182A, 187E, 191K, 192A, 196G, 197H, 199C, 208D, 210F; AKG London: 186D,
189H; Associated Press: 32G; Corbis: 22F, 58C, 64J, 72A, 235C, 236E, 248F; Corbis/Sygma:
79B, 83D; Daily Mirror: 277D; Daily Mirror/Centre for the Study of Cartoon and Caricature:
11C, 276A; David King: 153J, 155L, 156M, 158B, 161E, 166D, 168I, 175I, 176J; David
Low/Solo Syndication: 29E, 31F, 202G; e.t. archive: 135D, 137H; Hulton Getty: 14A, 20A, 37C,
74E, 85F, 127F, 138J, 140N, 144A, 151E, 159D, 162A, 170A, 188G, 239C, 250A, 251B,
252C, 253E, 267A, 269B, 278F, 280H, 284G; Hulton Getty/Archive Photos: 86A; Imperial War
Museum: 97B, 103K, 110W, 111X, 123C, 125D, 133J, 135C, 143U; Imperial War
Museum/London Express: 105N, 105O; Jean-Loup Charmet: 53E; Krauze: 90C; Les Gibbard:
82B; Magnum: 73C; Mary Evans: 256; Nebelspalter: 45S; New Statesman: 63I; PA News: 261C;
Peter Newark: 39H, 77I, 134A, 218A, 224C, 225E, 226F, 230L, 231A, 237A, 243F, 247E;
Popperfoto: 59D, 71D, 80D, 126E, 148A, 154K, 167F, 201F, 204A, 233B, 263F, 279G; Public
Record Office: 136F, 137G, 140O; Punch: 25I, 51H; Royal Army Museum Collection, Brussels:
16E; Scholastic: 262D; School of Slavonic Studies: 62G; Simplissimus: 190I; Solo Syndication:
129H; Solo Syndication/Centre for the Study of Cartoon and Caricature: 54B, 69D; Source
unknown: 9B, 12E, 16D, 28D, 41D, 48C, 54A, 54B, 69D, 77J, 78A, 84E, 95A, 99D, 100G,
101I, 103K, 104M, 105N, 105O, 106P, 107Q, 108R, 109T, 112B, 113D, 114F, 115, 116H,
117I, 118K, 119B, 122A, 123C, 133J, 135D, 136F, 137G, 137H, 139L, 140O, 141P, 143U,
143V, 143W, 145C, 162A, 172D, 184C, 194D, 208D, 222B, 230L, 237B, 240D, 242E, 244G,
247D, 254F, 256G, 262D, 271D, 271E, 282C; Süddeutscher Verlag Bilderdienst: 214B; The
Hoover Institution: 178B; The Press Association: 257H; Topham: 130I, 228I, 273H

With thanks to John and Andrew Frost at John Frost Historical Newspapers for the loan of the
newspapers used in 264G and 265H

Cover photograph: © Hutton Getty

Written source acknowledgements
The authors and publisher gratefully acknowledge the following publications from which
written sources in the book are drawn. In some sentences the wording or sentence has been
simplified:
Daily Express, 30 September 1938: 44G; *Daily Herald*, 16 April 1921: 260B; *Daily Mail*, February
1903: 12D; *Deutsche Zeitung*, 28 June 1919: 25J; *Peking Peoples Daily*, 1 January 1980: 82C; *The
Guardian*, 11 November 1989: 88B; *The Times*, 23 February 1968: 73B, 22 August 1968: 74D,
23 March, 1972: 80C, 3 January 2000: 91D, 27 December 1979: 92C, 18 April 1922: 215C,
October 1936: 272G; *Washington Daily News*: 62H; *Yorkshire Post*, December 1938: 44K

Contents

Chapter 1

International History 1900-91

INTRODUCTION

Option V: 1900–49

At the beginning of the twentieth century there was much tension between the Great Powers. Europe was divided into two rival alliances: the Triple Alliance and the Triple Entente. Both sides built up their armed forces because they feared an attack from the other alliance. The alliances opposed each other in disputes in Morocco and Bosnia but managed to solve these until 1914, when the assassination of the heir to the throne of Austria-Hungary at Sarajevo led to the outbreak of the First World War. Germany's use of the Schlieffen Plan to attack France through Belgium ensured that Britain joined the war in 1914.

The First World War ended in 1918 and the Great Powers met in Paris in 1919 to reach a peace settlement with Germany. The French wanted to weaken Germany so much that she would be unable to invade France again. The USA had entered the war in 1917 and their President, Woodrow Wilson, wanted to set up the League of Nations to prevent any future war. The Treaty of Versailles, which the Germans were forced to sign in 1919, satisfied none of the powers. Germany was weakened, but was left strong enough to seek revenge in the future. Wilson obtained his League, but the USA refused to join it. There was some co-operation with the League in the 1920s, but it proved to be too weak to resist the challenges of the military dictatorships during the 1930s.

Hitler made use of the weaknesses of the Treaty of Versailles to gain concessions for Germany in the 1930s. Britain's policy of appeasement attempted to solve Germany's grievances and avoid a war. But Hitler's aims were not limited to righting the wrongs of Versailles, and his aggressive policies in Czechoslovakia and Poland led to the outbreak of the Second World War in 1939 which ended in the defeat of Germany in 1945.

This option ends with another period of tension, this time between the two new superpowers: the democratic USA and the communist USSR. These two powers had combined to defeat Germany but they began to argue at the end of the war. The USSR took control of Eastern Europe and the USA responded with the Truman Doctrine and Marshall Aid, which were to help democratic countries resist communism. This rivalry between the two superpowers is known as the Cold War because it was a war of words with no direct fighting between the two powers.

1904	Entente Cordiale
1905–6	First Moroccan Crisis
1907	Anglo-Russian Agreement
1908–9	Bosnian Crisis
1911	Agadir Crisis
1914	Assassination at Sarajevo
1919	Treaty of Versailles
1929	Wall Street Crash
1931	Manchurian crisis
1935	Abyssinian crisis
1938	*Anschluss* Munich Conference
1939	Invasion of Czechoslovakia Nazi-Soviet Pact Invasion of Poland
1945	End of Second World War – Yalta and Potsdam Conferences
1946	Churchill's Iron Curtain speech
1947	Truman Doctrine and Marshall Plan
1948	Berlin Blockade and Airlift
1949	Formation of West Germany and NATO

Option W: 1919–63

The Treaty of Versailles, which Germany was forced to sign in 1919 at the end of the First World War, was intended to prevent another war. It failed because there was no agreement at the Peace Conference. Germany was excluded; France wanted revenge; while the President of the USA, Woodrow Wilson, wanted to establish a new, fairer world in which all disputes would be settled by the League of Nations, without the need for war. The final treaty satisfied no one: Germany lost land but was left strong enough to recover in the future. The League of Nations was set up, but the USA never joined and Germany was not allowed to join until 1926. There were some early successes for the League in the 1920s, but the League was too weak to resist the military dictatorships during the 1930s.

Hitler took full advantage of the situation in Europe during the 1930s. He used the criticisms of the Versailles Treaty to obtain support for his expansionist policies and took advantage of Britain's policy of appeasement to make territorial gains for Germany. It was only in 1939 that Britain began to realise that his aims were more than correcting the faults of Versailles and that he intended to expand Germany at the expense of other countries. His occupation of the whole of Czechoslovakia in 1939 and the invasion of Poland in September 1939 led to the outbreak of the Second World War.

After the Second World War, there followed a new war, the Cold War, which was a war of words between the two superpowers: the communist USSR and the democratic USA. These two powers had co-operated to defeat Germany in World War Two, but became opponents afterwards. The Soviet Union's takeover of Eastern Europe was answered by the USA's Truman Doctrine and the provision of Marshall Aid to help countries to recover from the war and to keep them democratic. The USA set up NATO in 1949. The Soviets responded with the Warsaw Pact. The dispute between the powers spread worldwide, starting with the Korean War in 1950. The development of nuclear weapons meant that each crisis between the superpowers could involve the destruction of the world, but the Cold War consisted of tension, provocation and a nuclear arms and space race, as each side tried to outdo the other. The nearest that the superpowers came to direct fighting was the Cuban Crisis of 1962. The peaceful solution of this crisis led to an improvement in relations between the USA and USSR and the end of the option is marked by the beginning of a period of co-operation between the superpowers.

1919	Treaty of Versailles
1929	Wall Street Crash
1931	Manchurian crisis
1935	Abyssinian crisis
1938	*Anschluss* Munich Conference
1939	Invasion of Czechoslovakia Nazi-Soviet Pact Invasion of Poland
1945	End of Second World War – Yalta and Potsdam Conferences
1946	Churchill's Iron Curtain speech
1947	Truman Doctrine and Marshall Plan
1948	Berlin Blockade and Airlift
1949	Formation of West Germany and NATO
1950	Start of Korean War
1953	End of Korean war – death of Stalin
1955	Warsaw Pact
1956	Hungarian Rising
1957	Soviet Union launches Sputnik
1960	U2 spy plane incident
1961	Building of Berlin Wall
1962	Cuban Missile Crisis
1963	Nuclear Test Ban Treaty

Option X: 1945–91

The Second World War was followed by a period of tension and rivalry between the two superpowers: the USSR and the USA. These two powers had worked together to defeat Germany in the Second World War, but became intense rivals afterwards. The Soviets took control of Eastern Europe so the USA showed their opposition by stating the Truman Doctrine and helping countries to recover from the war by providing them with Marshall Aid. The USA set up an alliance of the western powers, NATO, to which the USSR replied by setting up the Warsaw Pact. This tension and rivalry is known as the Cold War because there was no direct fighting between the two superpowers. Instead it took the form of provocation, propaganda and a nuclear arms race and space race in which both countries tried to gain an advantage. It was the development of nuclear weapons which made the Cold War so frightening: any dispute between the superpowers could result in the end of the world.

The Cold War spread worldwide, involving the Korean War in 1950 and the Cuban Missile Crisis in 1962. This latter crisis was the nearest the powers came to a nuclear war, but its solution led to a new period of improved relations between the USA and the USSR. It resulted in the setting up of the 'hot line' direct communication link between the USA and USSR and the signing of a Nuclear Test Ban Treaty. This was followed by a period of relaxation in the tension, known as Détente, in which attempts were made to control the arms race through SALT 1, and the Soviet Union and USA signed the Helsinki Agreement in 1975. Superpower leaders visited each other and there was co-operation in space, culture and sport.

Détente was threatened by the Soviet intervention in Czechoslovakia in 1968, but a 'second Cold War' broke out in 1979 when the Soviet invasion of Afghanistan was opposed by the Americans who protested by withdrawing from the Moscow Olympics and refusing to agree to the SALT 2 agreement. The Soviets became increasingly wary of the American increase in defence spending and the development of the Strategic Defense Initiative which would prevent Soviet missiles reaching their targets in the USA. The Soviet Union was virtually bankrupt and the cost of the arms race had become too much for both superpowers. The new Soviet leader, Mikhail Gorbachev, agreed to further arms reductions and withdrew Soviet troops from Afghanistan. His introduction of reforms in the USSR led to protests throughout Soviet-controlled Eastern Europe. The communist governments were overthrown and the Iron Curtain was torn down. The Soviet Empire disintegrated in 1989 and the Cold War came to an end.

1945 End of Second World War – Yalta and Potsdam Conferences

1946 Churchill's Iron Curtain speech

1947 Truman Doctrine and Marshall Plan

1948 Berlin Blockade and Airlift

1949 Formation of West Germany and NATO

1950 Start of Korean War

1953 End of Korean War – death of Stalin

1955 Warsaw Pact

1956 Hungarian Rising

1957 Soviet Union launches Sputnik

1960 U2 spy plane incident.

1961 Building of the Berlin Wall

1962 Cuban Missile Crisis

1963 Nuclear Test Ban Treaty

1968 Prague Spring and the invasion of Czechoslovakia

1972 SALT 1

1975 Helsinki Agreement

1979 Soviet invasion of Afghanistan

1980 USA boycott of Moscow Olympics

1981 USSR imposes martial law in Poland

1984 Soviet boycott of Los Angeles Olympics

1985 Mikhail Gorbachev becomes leader of Soviet Russia

1989 Disintegration of the Soviet Empire – Berlin Wall pulled down

1991 End of communist rule in Russia

1.1 Why did tension increase in Europe between 1900 and 1914?

The Great Powers in 1900

Germany

In 1871, the German state, Prussia, had defeated France in war. This victory led to Prussia joining all the German states together to form the German Empire with the Prussian leader becoming Kaiser (Emperor) of Germany. France was forced to accept a humiliating peace settlement at the Treaty of Frankfurt in 1871. By this treaty, the Germans took the two French provinces of Alsace and Lorraine and the French were forced to pay 200 million francs in war damages to the Germans.

By 1900, Germany was rapidly overtaking Britain as the most important industrial country in Europe. The Germans' modern steel works produced enough steel for the munitions factories to make enough weapons for their army. They needed a strong army to prevent the French from trying to win back Alsace and Lorraine.

The Kaiser of Germany in 1900 was Wilhelm II, the grandson of Queen Victoria of Britain. Like many other Germans he wanted his country to have an overseas empire to match that of Britain. He talked of Germany having its 'place in the sun'. To achieve this Germany needed a strong navy and the Kaiser announced his intention to build one.

France

The French could not forgive the Germans for the loss of Alsace and Lorraine in 1871 and were looking for an opportunity to take revenge. They had built up their industry and their army and had been trying to make alliances with other Great Powers since 1871. France had a large overseas empire and felt threatened by the ambitions of Kaiser Wilhelm.

Britain

Britain was a trading nation whose wealth depended on its overseas empire. To protect this wealth Britain needed a strong navy to keep the trade routes open. As an island, Britain felt safe from invasion as its navy was greater than that of any other state. It had no need of help from other powers, so it chose to

Source A

Germany has gone beyond her rights as a civilised nation in forcing defeated France to give up Alsace and Lorraine which contains one and a half million of her people. It was with a knife at her throat that France, bleeding and exhausted, signed us away. Give us our freedom. Give us justice.

A deputy from Alsace-Lorraine speaking to the German Parliament in 1874.

THINGS TO DO

1 If you were a politician living in one of the following countries in 1900, which country would you say was your main rival? Explain why.

   (a) France;
   (b) Austria-Hungary;
   (c) Great Britain.

2 How does **Source A** help you understand why there was rivalry between France and Germany?

be isolated, a policy known as 'splendid isolation'. At the beginning of the 20th century, however, Britain felt threatened by the growing power of Germany.

Austria-Hungary

This was a large Empire made up of many different nationalities, including Germans, Hungarians, Czechs, Poles and Serbs. It faced problems trying to keep all these different peoples, who each had their own language and customs, together as one country. Its leaders were particularly worried about the growth of Serbia as they feared that the Serbs of Austria-Hungary would want to join Serbia.

Russia

This was the largest but by far the most backward of the Great Powers. Its people were poor and there was little modern industry. The Russians believed that they should have influence over the Slav people, who included the Serbs, so they supported them against Austria-Hungary. This meant that there was great rivalry between Russia and Austria-Hungary in the area known as the Balkans. Russia also wanted to extend its influence in this area to gain access to the rich trade in the Mediterranean.

Italy

This was a relatively new country, formed in 1861. Before then the country had been a collection of small states. By 1900, Italy was allied with Austria-Hungary and Germany in the Triple Alliance, but was also in dispute with Austria-Hungary over land on the borders of the two countries. This meant there was a conflict of interests within the alliance.

Source **B** Kaiser Wilhelm II drawn by a French artist. Note that the Kaiser is shown as the centre of attention with his place in the sun. The Kaiser had a withered left arm and this is clearly shown in the picture.

THINGS TO DO

1 What message do you think the French artist was trying to portray in **Source B**? Use the detail in the picture to support your answer.

2 What problems do you think a historian would have using **Sources A** and **B** as evidence of relations between France and Germany at the beginning of the twentieth century?

The Alliance System, 1900–14

The Alliance System, which involved the Great Powers of Europe, is often seen as a major cause of the First World War. This was because of the build-up of tension between the Great Powers. As relations between rival countries worsened their allies would often support them, and so the tension would increase. In 1900 Germany was allied to Austria-Hungary and to Italy in what is known as the Triple Alliance. Under this alliance these countries agreed to help one another if they were attacked by any other power. France was allied to Russia by a treaty made in 1894, under which both countries agreed to help each other if Germany attacked them. In 1904 Britain signed the Entente Cordiale (Friendly Agreement) with France. The two countries agreed to be on good terms and not to quarrel over ownership of colonies. Britain also reached a friendly agreement with Russia, in 1907, and so the Entente Cordiale became the Triple Entente. The Great Powers of Europe were now divided into two opposing alliances.

But the treaties were defensive. Countries agreed to help one another only if they were attacked. So how could they cause a war? One reason is that they were secret treaties, so the rival powers did not know that the alliances were defensive and feared that they were directed against them. This led to each alliance trying to get the better of the other in a series of disputes between 1900 and 1914. This had the effect of increasing the tension between the powers, strengthening the alliances and creating a situation in which one incident could lead to war. This is exactly what happened when Archduke Franz Ferdinand of Austria-Hungary was assassinated in 1914.

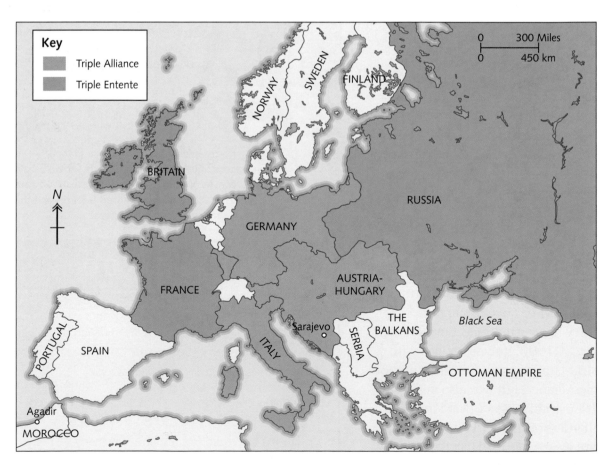

The countries in the Triple Alliance and Triple Entente.

Rivalry increases

Between 1905 and 1914 the Great Powers were involved in a series of crises in Morocco (in North Africa) and the Balkans (Eastern Europe) and they were involved in a race to build up their arms and navies. The effect was that the rival alliances grew stronger and more aggressive and this eventually led to war in 1914.

Events in Morocco, 1905-6

In 1905 when on a visit to Morocco Kaiser Wilhelm II promised to support Morocco's independence. This upset the French, who were interested in occupying Morocco as a colony. Wilhelm was also testing the strength of the new friendship between Britain and France. In a conference held at Algeciras in 1906 Britain and Russia stood by France and it was agreed that Germany should have no say in Morocco. This strengthened France's alliance with Britain who shortly afterwards made a colonial agreement with Russia, in 1907, so forming the Triple Entente with France. The Germans sensed they were being surrounded and the Kaiser became even more resentful.

The Bosnian crisis, 1908-9

Bosnia was a Slav state in the Balkans. In 1908 it was annexed by Austria-Hungary and became part of the Austrian Empire. This was opposed by Serbia, which was also a Slav state and had ambitions to include the Slavs of Bosnia within it. But Serbia was too small to do anything about it on its own, so it looked to Russia for support. Russia supported Serbia but in 1909 backed off going to war to help Serbia gain Bosnia when Germany made it clear that if Russia declared war on Austria, Germany would declare war on Russia.

The crisis was important because Austria-Hungary now felt confident that it could rely on German support. This helps explain why Austria-Hungary acted as it did in 1914

(see pages 14–15). Russia had backed down in 1909, but by 1914 had built up its armies and was determined not to back down again when the next crisis came. Serbia had to accept that Bosnia was part of Austria-Hungary, but now looked for an opportunity to get its own back on Austria-Hungary. Italy had been concerned by Austria-Hungary's action in the Balkans and feared that it could get drawn into a war, so became less enthusiastic towards the Triple Alliance.

Source C A British cartoon of 1905 of the Entente Cordiale.

THINGS TO DO

1 Explain how Europe had become divided into two different groups by 1907.

2 Why were events in Morocco (1905–6) and Bosnia (1908–9) so important in the period leading up to the First World War?

3 How reliable is **Source C** to an historian writing about the Entente Cordiale?

Morocco again – the Agadir crisis 1911

In 1911 there was a rebellion against the Sultan of Morocco which was put down with French help. This was an opportunity for the French to take Morocco. They were prepared to grant compensation to countries such as Germany and Spain who were concerned by the French action. But the Germans sent a gunboat, the *Panther*, to Agadir, a port on the Atlantic coast of Morocco, to challenge the French. The Kaiser hoped to force the French into giving Germany a share of Morocco. The British were alarmed that Germany was going to set up a naval base in Agadir to challenge Britain's naval supremacy.

Germany's aggressive action in Morocco confirmed Britain's worst fears: Germany was aiming to dominate Europe. Britain's response was to support France over Morocco. The British and French also made a naval agreement by which Britain promised to defend the north coast of France if it was attacked from the sea. The French took over Morocco as a protectorate, that is they governed the country without it becoming part of the French Republic. Germany was given 100,000 square miles of the French Congo in compensation, but the land was mostly swamp and jungle. The Agadir crisis was a clear victory for France and the Entente. The Kaiser was determined not to be the loser in the next crisis.

Modern World History for AQA

Source D

While great naval power in the hands of Britain cannot constitute a menace, in the hands of Germany it will be a great peril to the world. This is even more so as the recent history of German policy of daring aggression and the lack of space at home compels Germany to conquer the colonies of others or perish.

A comment from a British newspaper, the Daily Mail, *February 1903.*

Source E
A Dreadnought battleship.

The naval race, 1906–14

As an island with a large overseas empire, Britain needed to have a powerful navy, particularly since the British army was very small. In 1900 Britain had the largest navy in the world. When the Germans began to build their navy in 1898, the British thought that it was an attempt to challenge Britain and its colonies. These British fears were partly responsible for Britain entering into agreements with France and Russia.

The German navy only became a real threat to Britain after 1906, when both sides began building Dreadnoughts, a new battleship that could easily destroy any of the older type battleships. Britain's naval supremacy was in the older ships, so the race was on to build the most Dreadnoughts.

The naval race reached its peak in 1909. The Germans refused to agree on the number of Dreadnoughts they would build. The Liberal government in Britain only planned to build four Dreadnoughts in 1909–10. Many in Britain believed that the German fleet build-up was aimed at challenging British naval superiority. Public pressure demanded the government spend more money building Dreadnoughts, under the slogan 'we want eight and won't wait'. The government gave way and increased spending on the fleet to maintain Britain's naval superiority over Germany.

The naval race did much to make the British resent the Germans and lead Britain into better relations with France. However, this was not a main cause of Britain going to war in 1914, as by then Britain had far more Dreadnoughts than the Germans.

The build-up of armies, 1900–14

The existence of large armies in Europe was another threat to peace. Military leaders argued that the only way to ensure peace was to have a strong enough army to prevent an invasion from another country. This view was supported by the manufacturers of arms who made vast profits from the arms race.

Apart from Britain all the Great Powers increased the size of their armies during this period (see diagram below). Britain was the only power that had not introduced conscription (compulsory military service) before 1914. In 1913 the French raised the period of compulsory military service from two years to three and the Russians raised theirs from three to three-and-a-half years. This meant that both countries would have more trained men. By 1913 the German army was very powerful and only Russia had more men in arms.

Though the Russian army was the largest it was badly equipped and much inferior to that of Germany. The Germans took pride in their armed forces and this was encouraged by the Kaiser who enjoyed being photographed in military uniform (see Source B on page 9).

THINGS TO DO

1 Why do you think **Source D** opposes Germany having a powerful navy?

2 How did (a) the Agadir crisis and (b) the naval race affect relations between the Great Powers in the period 1905–14?

3 Which was the greater threat to the peace of Europe, Morocco or Bosnia? Explain how you made your choice. (You will need to look back at pages 10 and 11.)

4 Does the fact that the Great Powers increased the size of their armies in the period 1900–14 mean that they thought war was inevitable? Explain your answer.

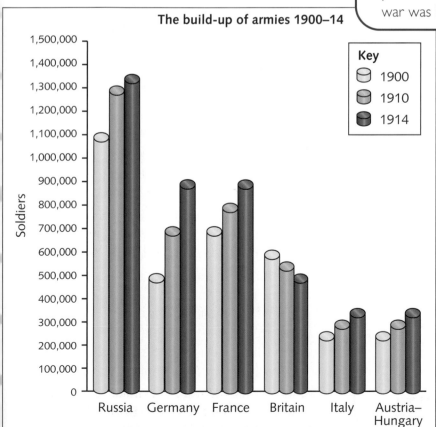

The build-up of armies 1900–14

Key
1900
1910
1914

SUMMARY

Relations between the Great Powers

1904 Entente Cordiale.

1905 First Moroccan crisis.

1906 Launch of the Dreadnought – the naval race begins.

1907 Triple Entente.

1908 Bosnian crisis.

1911 Agadir crisis.

Assassination at Sarajevo

On 28 June 1914, the heir to the throne of Austria-Hungary, the Archduke Franz Ferdinand, visited the Bosnian capital of Sarajevo. A group of Serbian terrorists planned to kill him to publicise their opposition to Bosnia being part of Austria-Hungary. There were two attempts. In the first a bomb was thrown at the Archduke but he deflected it so that it fell behind the car, exploded and injured several people in the following car. The Archduke continued the visit but insisted on visiting the injured in hospital. On leaving the hospital the driver of the car took a wrong turning. As he stopped to reverse, one of the waiting assassins, Gavrilo Princip, fired two shots: the first one hit the Archduke, the second hit his wife. The Archduke's wife died immediately and he died on the way to hospital.

Such a murder would normally have been a matter for the two countries involved alone.

Source A An artist's impression of the assassination of the Archduke Franz Ferdinand. This was drawn in 1914.

THINGS TO DO

1 How accurate a picture of the assassination do you think is given in **Source A**? Explain your answer.

2 Do you agree with what the Kaiser says in **Source B**? Look back at pages 8–13 to help you answer the question.

3 Do you think the person who drew **Source C** approved of the German invasion of Belgium? Explain your answer.

4 Why did the assassination of the Archduke Franz Ferdinand lead to war?

But relations between the alliances of Great Powers were so strained in 1914 that it led to the outbreak of the First World War. Some politicians in Austria-Hungary saw the assassination as an excuse for attacking Serbia and solving the problem of the Serbs within the Austrian Empire (see page 9). The Austrians issued an ultimatum to Serbia to comply with ten conditions, even though they had no proof that the Serbian government had anything to do with the assassination. Serbia replied very favourably to the ultimatum, accepting nine of the ten points. But the Austrians were not satisfied and declared war on Serbia on 28 July 1914.

From assassination to war

The Serb reply to the Austrian ultimatum indicated they did not want a war. They were prepared to accept help from Austria-Hungary in getting rid of all the societies in Serbia engaged in propaganda against Austria-Hungary, but could not accept one of the points because it involved delegates from Austria-Hungary taking part in the inquiry against those involved in the murder of the Archduke and his wife. This would mean the Serbian courts would be influenced by a foreign country, and this would be a threat to Serb independence. Although it did not accept this point, the Serbian government stressed it was prepared to refer the matter to an international court. Serbia did not want war in 1914 as it was recovering from the Balkan Wars which had been fought between 1912 and 1913. The Black Hand Group, which was responsible for the assassination, was not associated with the Serb government. Serbia could therefore see no reasons for Austria-Hungary to declare war on it in 1914. It was the determination of the war party in Austria-Hungary to take this opportunity to deal with Serbia that caused it to reject the Serb reply and declare war.

The Austrian declaration of war on Serbia was the first step towards general war in 1914. After the Bosnian crisis of 1908 Russia felt it had let down its Slav allies in the Balkans, so was determined not to back down again. On 30 July the Russians mobilised their army and prepared for war.

Source B

I no longer have any doubt that Britain, Russia and France have agreed among themselves to wage war to destroy us. The encirclement of Germany has already been achieved.

Kaiser Wilhelm II speaking in 1914 before the outbreak of the war.

BRAVO, BELGIUM!

Source C This British cartoon, published in August 1914, shows Belgium being bullied by Germany.

They did this without consulting Britain or France. Germany supported its ally Austria-Hungary by declaring war on Russia on 1 August and two days later went to war with France. At this stage the British were not keen to join the war and the British Foreign Secretary, Sir Edward Grey, said Britain would remain neutral unless Germany attacked the north coast of France. If Germany did, then Britain would offer assistance to the French.

On 3 August 1914 the Germans launched the Schlieffen Plan. This was an attack on France from the north through Belgium. To the surprise of the Germans, their invasion of Belgium brought the British into the war. Britain and most other European countries had guaranteed Belgium's neutrality by the Treaty of London in 1839. Britain now stood by that agreement and the Kaiser was astonished that the British had joined the war over 'a scrap of paper' which seemed to have so little relevance to Europe in 1914.

In August 1914 all members of the rival alliance systems, except Italy, declared war on each other. The outbreak of war was the result of a series of crises and mistakes. Events before 1914 had pushed the Great Powers towards war; events after Sarajevo sparked off the war.

Britain and the war

In 1914 Britain was allied to France and Russia in the Triple Entente, but this did not automatically mean that they would join them in a war. The building of the German navy had annoyed the British but, by 1914, Britain had far more Dreadnoughts than the Germans, so the fear had died down and was unlikely to cause a war. Grey appeared to want to support France but only if the German navy attacked the north coast of France. On 2 August, the British cabinet stated that they would only go to war if the neutrality of Belgium was violated. This was seen as a victory for those in Britain who wanted Britain to remain neutral as it was felt that if Germany attacked France it would be a direct attack as it had been in 1870 when the neutrality of Belgium had been upheld.

Why was Belgium so important to Britain? It is partly because the neutrality of Belgium had been guaranteed by Britain and other states, including Prussia, in 1839. Treaties that had been agreed had to be kept. The invasion of Belgium by Germany was against international law. But there is more to it than that. Britain did not want the whole of Europe to fall under the control of one power and in particular wanted to prevent the coastline opposite Britain from falling into the hands of a possible opponent. Belgium and the north coast of France could be used to launch an attack on Britain. It is possible that Britain would have eventually entered the war to prevent Germany from becoming too strong in Europe; the invasion of Belgium ensured that Britain entered at the beginning and the breaking of Belgian neutrality made sure that Britain was united in going to war.

Source D — British postcard published in 1914.

THINGS TO DO

1 Why did the British government publish **Sources D** and **E**?

2 What were the advantages and disadvantages of the Schlieffen Plan for Germany?

3 Do you think the Germans were wise to use it in 1914?

THE "SCRAP OF PAPER"

These are the signatures and seals of the representatives of the Six Powers to the "Scrap of Paper"—the Treaty signed in 1839 guaranteeing the independence and neutrality of Belgium. "Palmerston" signed for Britain. "Bülow" for Prussia.

The Germans have broken their pledged word and devastated Belgium. Help to keep your Country's honour bright by restoring Belgium her liberty.

ENLIST TO-DAY

Source E — The signatures and seals guaranteeing Belgian neutrality on the treaty signed in 1839. The treaty is shown on a British poster with the heading 'The Scrap of Paper'.

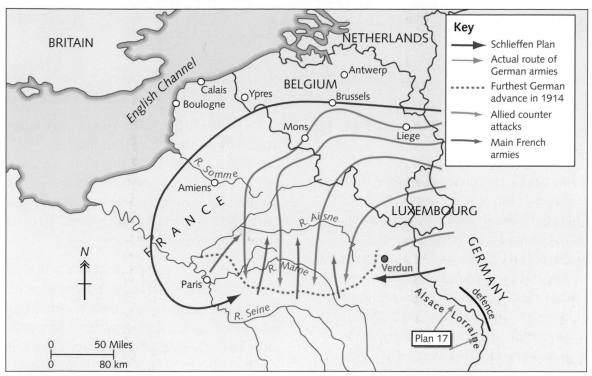

The Schlieffen Plan.

The Schlieffen Plan

Germany had the problem of what to do if there was a war with both France and Russia, who had been allies since the Franco-Russian Treaty of 1894 (see page 10). The German answer to this war on two fronts was to attack France first before Russia was ready. The German Head of General Staff was Count Alfred von Schlieffen, and he devised a plan to defeat France within six weeks by attacking through Belgium. Once the French were defeated the Germans could then turn to the east and defeat Russia. Von Schlieffen believed that it would take the Russians at least six weeks to be ready for war because of the size of the country and its poor transport.

The plan depended on the right wing of the German forces attacking France through Belgium and Holland, leaving only a few troops to hold the French attack on Germany in Alsace and Lorraine. The plan was changed in 1914 by General Moltke: he only attacked through Belgium and strengthened the forces in Alsace and Lorraine at the expense of the right wing. The plan involved moving large armies quickly over great distances, which would be difficult. The Germans also failed to foresee the effect that the invasion of Belgium would have on Britain, or perhaps they felt that the British army was too weak to cause them any problems.

SUMMARY

Events leading to war

28 June	Assassination of Franz Ferdinand.
23 July	Austrian ultimatum to Serbia.
28 July	Austria-Hungary declares war on Serbia.
1 August	Germany declares war on Russia.
3 August	Germany declares war on France.
	German troops enter Belgium.
4 August	Britain declares war on Germany.
5 August	Austria-Hungary declares war on Russia.

The First World War, 1914–18

In 1914 the Great Powers of Europe went to war. Britain, France and Russia (the Allies) found themselves in conflict with Germany, Austria-Hungary and Turkey (the Central Powers). By 1917 both Italy (joined the war in 1915) and the USA had joined the war on the Allies' side. Although there was fighting worldwide, the main campaigns took place in Eastern Europe (the Eastern Front) and in France and Belgium (the Western Front).

The last stages of the First World War, 1917–18

The main focus of the war was on the Western Front. Both sides poured millions of men into this area in a desperate bid to win the war. The names of the major battles, such as Ypres, Verdun and the Somme, are famous in history for their huge numbers of casualties. But by 1917 there still seemed no end in sight. When the British attacked the Germans at Passchendaele in that year, they lost 250,000 men in gaining just 750 metres of waterlogged land.

However, 1917 can be seen as a turning point for the war. In April the USA declared war on Germany. President Woodrow Wilson had persuaded the US Congress that 'the world must be made safe for democracy'. The British and French were about to get huge supplies of equipment and troops. Germany would have to win the war quickly before the balance tipped against it.

It appeared at the end of 1917 that Germany had a good chance of success. A communist revolution in Russia in November 1917 led to

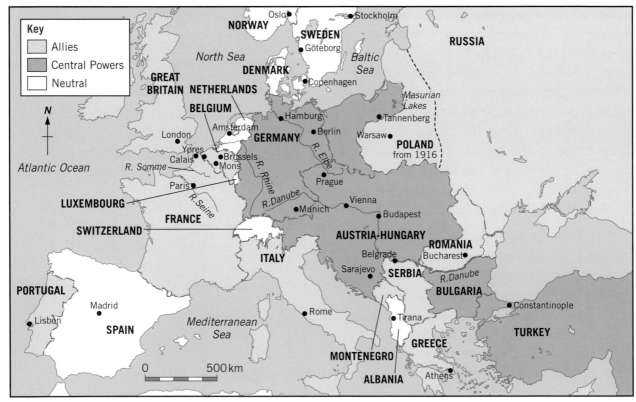

The alliances of the First World War.

Russia leaving the war. In the Treaty of Brest-Litovsk in March 1918 Russia signed a peace agreement, and gave Germany land that included a quarter of Russia's population, farming land and three-quarters of its iron ore. Germany could now concentrate on fighting on the Western Front.

Germany's gamble fails

In March 1918, the Germans threw all their resources into one final major attack on the Western Front. They attacked where the Allies were weakest and, after years of stalemate, they made great gains. However, the Allies managed to stop the advance and then in late July counter-attacked. By now US soldiers were beginning to arrive in France in substantial numbers, and these fresh troops gave great heart to the Allied soldiers fighting against exhausted German troops.

At the same time, conditions in Germany were becoming desperate. A blockade of German ports by the Royal Navy was preventing food entering Germany and thousands were starving. Many more were dying in a huge influenza outbreak. Soon Munich and Berlin were in the hands of revolutionaries who wanted the German government overthrown. In October 1918 the German navy mutinied in Wilhelmshaven and some soldiers on the Western Front refused to fight.

The German Emperor, Kaiser Wilhelm II, and his government ministers realised that they had to end the war, particularly as Germany's allies (Bulgaria, Turkey and Austria-Hungary) had all surrendered by early November. So on 9 November 1918 the German Kaiser stood down to allow his government to surrender. Germany surrendered at 11 a.m. on 11 November 1918. The Kaiser fled to Holland and a new government was set up in Germany.

The impact of the war

Casualties in the war had been huge. Nearly two million Russian soldiers had been killed in the fighting. Germany had lost almost as many. France and Austria had lost over a million each, and Britain nearly a million. In addition, at least 20 million soldiers had been wounded – many of them were still suffering the consequences of their wounds long after the war had ended.

France

Most of the fighting in western Europe had taken place in France, destroying 750,000 homes and leaving 2 million people homeless. Many roads, railways and places where people had worked, such as factories, were destroyed, as were large tracts of farmland. There was also the constant danger of unexploded shells.

Belgium

The Germans had occupied most of Belgium for four years, taking the country's resources, such as machinery and crops, to help their own war effort. The area not occupied by the Germans had been the scene of bitter fighting and widespread devastation. For example, Ypres was left in ruins.

Britain

The British had not suffered serious damage at home, although air attacks had killed over 1000 people. Many families had lost relatives or friends. Life would be totally different after the war compared with before 1914. Also the country was very heavily in debt because of the war, and owed nearly £1 billion to the Americans.

Germany

There had not been much fighting inside Germany's borders, but the country was suffering very badly by the end of 1918. There was widespread starvation, made worse by the British blockade of German ports. Many German people could not believe that they had lost – and so quickly. German politicians had told the German people of military successes in the spring of 1918; the retreats had not been so well publicised!

Some Germans suspected their leaders of treachery.

Russia

The Russians suffered very heavy casualties in the war, even though they had ceased to fight after the new Bolshevik (communist) government took over in November 1917. This new government signed the Treaty of Brest-Litovsk with the Germans in March 1918. Russia gave up huge areas of land on its western borders, in Finland, Poland and the Ukraine, and on the Baltic coastline. What should happen to these areas after the war?

Source **A** Destruction of the city of Ypres, Belgium.

Source **B**

We must not let any sense of revenge, any spirit of greed, any grasping desire override the fundamental principles of righteousness. The mandate of this government at the next election will mean that the British Government will be in favour of such a peace.

Lloyd George speaking to Parliament on 12 November 1918.

Source **C**

If I am returned, Germany is going to pay restitution, reparation, and indemnity, and I have personally no doubt that we will get everything out of her that you can squeeze out of a lemon and a bit more.

A speech by Eric Geddes made in Cambridge on 9 December 1918 as part the general election campaign.

THINGS TO DO

1 What would be the effect of damage such as that shown in Source A on the peacemakers?

2 **Sources B, C** and **D** are from British politicians. Explain what they mean. How are they different? Can you explain their differences?

Source **D**

We propose to demand the whole cost of the war from Germany.

Lloyd George speaking in the same election campaign on 11 December 1918 in Bristol.

The main personalities and their attitudes to the defeated countries

1n January 1919 people from the Allied countries met in Paris. The leaders of America, France and Britain dominated the detailed discussions. Each had his priorities, and they did not always agree. Yet they were under pressure to reach a peaceful settlement to Europe's problems. The defeated countries were not allowed to join them, nor was Russia, as the Western allies did not trust communism.

Woodrow Wilson, President of the USA

The American President was an idealist – he believed in finding perfect solutions. He had great plans to make sure that war never happened again. To achieve world peace in the future, nations would have to co-operate. He made his views clear in January 1918, before the end of the war. His Fourteen Points set out principles that he believed should guide peacemaking once the war had finished. The most important was self-determination – people of different national groups had the right to rule themselves.

Some of these points were easy to argue in 1919. Others were acceptable in theory, but were difficult to apply in practice, such as self-determination of peoples. The peoples of Eastern Europe were scattered across wide areas. Some people were bound to end up being ruled by people from another group who had a different language and culture.

Wilson believed that Germany should be punished, but not too harshly. If the peace treaty was too harsh, Germans would be resentful and demand revenge. Instead Wilson wanted all countries to join a League of Nations, which would resolve disputes peacefully. He believed that Germany should lose some territory, but should not be made to pay the cost of war damage.

It was easy for him to take this lenient attitude as the USA had not suffered much from the war. After all, it did not join until April 1917, and American soldiers did not reach Europe until late 1917. Americans could take a more detached attitude than Europeans, who had suffered the full horrors of the war.

Some of the Fourteen Points

1. No secret treaties

2. Free access to the seas in peacetime and wartime

3. Free trade between countries

4. Disarmament

5. Colonies to be able to have a say in their own futures

6. German troops to leave Russia

7. Independence for Belgium

8. France to regain Alsace-Lorraine

13. Poland to become an independent state with access to the sea

14. A League of Nations to be set up to keep the peace

Source **E**

I consider it a distinguished privilege to be permitted to open the discussion in this conference on the League of Nations. We have assembled here for two purposes – to make the peace settlements, and also to secure the future peace of the world. The League of Nations seems to me to be necessary for both of these purposes.

From a speech by President Woodrow Wilson to the Paris Peace Conference, January 1919.

David Lloyd George, Prime Minister of Britain

David Lloyd George had been involved in politics for nearly thirty years and was very experienced. He understood that there would have to be many compromises in the peace talks, otherwise a settlement would never be reached.

He wanted Germany to be punished, but not too harshly – like Wilson, he did not want Germany to seek revenge in the future. This conflicted with the view of most British people. Indeed, Lloyd George's government had won an election in December 1918 promising to 'squeeze the German lemon until the pips squeak'.

Lloyd George also wanted to protect British interests at sea, and therefore disliked Wilson's idea of 'freedom of the seas'. He was keen for Germany to have only a limited navy. Yet at the same time he knew that Britain was primarily a trading nation, and it was important that Germany was not crippled too much, so that the two countries could start trading again.

Source **F** David Lloyd George, Georges Clemenceau and Woodrow Wilson.

Georges Clemenceau, Prime Minister of France

Georges Clemenceau had had a long career in French politics, and he was aged 77 when the peace talks began. He had become Prime Minister in November 1917, promising to win the war for France and to ensure that Germany could never do the same to France again. After all, Germany had invaded France before in 1870, and had taken Alsace-Lorraine. Now this must be restored to France.

Clemenceau was under great pressure from the French people to make Germany pay for the suffering that they had endured. They argued that this should take the form of money and land. If Germany lost land on the French–German border, this would help to make the French feel more secure from possible future attack. With Clemenceau as their leader, the French people had a tough politician who would argue their case strongly.

THINGS TO DO

1 What did Clemenceau want France to get from the peace settlement?

2 Did Lloyd George want the same for Britain?

The Treaty of Versailles, June 1919

On 28 June 1919 the Treaty of Versailles was signed by the victorious countries at the Palace of Versailles near Paris. It dealt only with Germany, but it contained over 400 clauses and ran to more than 200 pages. Two representatives of the new German government were summoned. The Germans had been allowed no say in the discussions; they were simply invited to sign in humiliating circumstances. They had no choice.

Territorial changes

The map shows the main changes that Germany was forced to accept at Versailles.

- Alsace and Lorraine were returned to France. (They had been French before 1871.)
- Eupen and Malmédy went to Belgium.
- North Schleswig went to Denmark.
- Germany lost land to the recreated Poland including West Prussia, Posen and part of Upper Silesia. (East Prussia was separated from the rest of Germany by Polish land.)
- Memel was taken over by the League of Nations and went to Lithuania in 1923.
- The League of Nations was to control the Saar for 15 years but France controlled the coalfields.
- Danzig was made a free city under League of Nations control. Poland could use its port for trade and had a corridor of land to the sea.
- Germany lost all the land taken from Russia in the Treaty of Brest-Litovsk in 1918. (Estonia, Latvia and Lithuania became independent states.)
- Germany was forbidden to unite with Austria.
- Germany lost all its colonies. The League of Nations gave them to victorious countries as mandates.

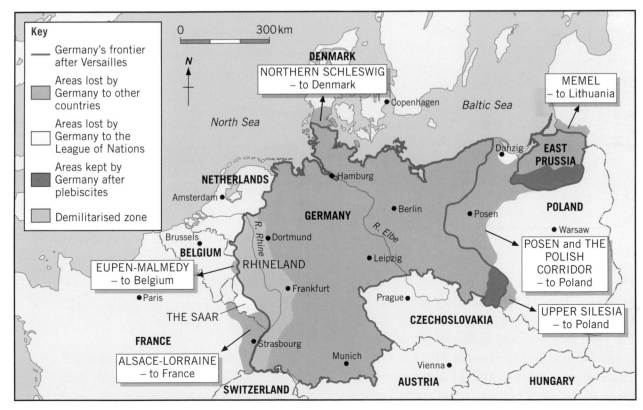

The territorial terms of the Treaty of Versailles.

Military restrictions

The Treaty of Versailles restricted Germany's armed forces to a level far below what they had been before the war.

- The army was limited to 100,000 men.

- Conscription was banned; all soldiers had to be volunteers.

- Germany was not allowed tanks, submarines or military aircraft.

- The navy could have only six battleships.

- The Rhineland became a demilitarised zone. This meant that no German troops were allowed into this area near the French border. It included all the land west of the River Rhine and an area 50 km wide on the east bank. The Allies were to keep an army of occupation on the west bank for fifteen years.

War guilt

The War Guilt Clause (Clause 231) forced Germany to accept responsibility for the war.

This provided the reason for punishing the German people in the peace settlement.

Source G

> The Allied governments affirm, and Germany accepts, the responsibility of Germany and her allies for causing all the loss and damage to which the Allied governments and their peoples have been subjected as a result of the war.
>
> ***The War Guilt Clause.***

Reparations

The Allied powers agreed that Germany had to pay for the damage caused by the war. These payments were called reparations. The sum was not fixed in the Treaty of Versailles, but was later set in 1921 at the huge figure of £6600 million. Germany was supposed to pay a certain amount each year – originally for 42 years. (In fact, the amounts

were modified during the 1920s and then, in 1930, Germany stopped paying altogether.)

Source H

> It is a people's treaty because it achieves the liberation of peoples. Not one foot of territory is demanded by the conquerors. The time has come when the peoples of Europe will not consent to live under masters, but to live under governments that they choose themselves. This is the fundamental principle of this great settlement.
>
> ***From a speech by President Woodrow Wilson at Pueblo, Colorado, on 25 September 1919. This was part of his campaign to get US support for the Treaty of Versailles. The next day he collapsed through exhaustion.***

The League of Nations

The League of Nations was set up to keep international peace in the future. The Covenant (binding agreement) was included at the beginning of each of the peace treaties. It meant that the League was made responsible for maintaining the details of the peace settlement as the central part of its job. (For details on the League of Nations, see pages 26–34.)

THINGS TO DO

1 Which terms of the Treaty of Versailles would Clemenceau be happy with? And which would he not be?

2 Would Lloyd George's views be the same?

3 Look at **Source H**. Do you think that the Treaty of Versailles reflects what Wilson was claiming?

Modern World History for AQA

Reasons for resentment and bitterness in Germany

Germans were horrified when they discovered the terms of the Treaty of Versailles. They did not believe they had started the war, and saw no reason why they should be blamed. They did not even believe they had lost the war. The Germans had agreed to an armistice – a ceasefire – but expected there to be negotiations. Many Germans were outraged when Germany was not even represented at the discussions to sort out a peace settlement. The Allies blamed Germany for the war, but the person who could be held responsible, Kaiser Wilhelm II, had fled the country, which now had a new democratic government (known as the Weimar Republic). Surely the Allies would want to support this, especially with the possible threat of communism spreading from Russia.

November Criminals

Many Germans did not want their new government to sign the peace settlement. They believed they had been stabbed in the back by the 'November Criminals' – those who had agreed to end the fighting in November 1918. They were happy to believe their country had been betrayed by cowards or those whom many thought might be disloyal to the country, like the Jews.

Land and population

Under the terms of the treaty, Germany was to lose 10 per cent of its land, all its overseas colonies, 12.5 per cent of its population; 16 per cent of its coalfields, and half of its iron and steel industry. The losses in land were made worse by what Germans saw as the unfair way the Fourteen Points were applied to Germany. There were millions of Germans living in other countries. But the way the principle of self-determination was applied was always to Germany's disadvantage. The loss of all its colonies was not justified by the Fourteen Points at all; it was all determined by the attitudes of other victorious countries that

THE FINISHING TOUCH.

Source A cartoon from *Punch*, 1919.

had empires themselves. It seemed disarmament was only for defeated countries.

Germans ignored the fact that Austria-Hungary and Turkey were later treated even more harshly. They also overlooked how harshly Germany had treated Russia when it signed a peace treaty at Brest-Litovsk in March 1918.

War guilt

The losses in land and materials were made even worse by the War Guilt Clause. Germans felt that this took away their pride and left them humiliated. This was reflected in a patriotic German newspaper, the *Deutsche Zeitung*, published on the day that the treaty was signed (see Source J). Its front-page comment appeared surrounded by a black mourning band.

Source J

Vengeance! German Nation!

Today in the Hall of Mirrors at Versailles a disgraceful treaty is being signed. Never forget it! On the spot where, in the glorious year of 1871, the German Empire in all its glory began, today German honour is dragged to the grave. Never forget it! There will be vengeance for the shame of 1919.

From the front page of the Deutsche Zeitung, 28 June 1919.

The League of Nations was formed in 1919–20 as part of the peace treaties. Indeed, the Covenant setting out the aims of the League was included in each of the treaties. The League was the idea of Woodrow Wilson, who had included such a body in his Fourteen Points. It would, he believed, ensure that there was no repeat of the First World War. In fact, almost everyone wanted no repetition. The only question was whether the League of Nations would work. Most people thought (or hoped) that it would, with the USA taking a leading role. Even those who had doubts had nothing else to offer as an alternative.

The powers, membership and peace-keeping role of the League

The Covenant was a set of 26 Articles or laws that all members agreed to follow. These encouraged countries to co-operate in trade and in improving social conditions. They also encouraged nations to disarm. However, the most important Article was Article 10, which said that members of the League would act together to ensure any member threatened with war was protected by the other members. This became known as collective security.

Initially, 42 countries joined – by the 1930s this had become 59. However, defeated countries were not invited to join; nor was Russia because it was communist. This gave the League the appearance of being a club for the victorious countries.

The USA fails to join

Woodrow Wilson confidently expected the USA to join the League of Nations. But many Americans hated the idea. Many had been

Source A

We have interests of our own in Asia and in the Pacific which we must guard. The less we play the part of umpire in Europe, the better for the United States ... I must think of America first. I love only one flag, and cannot give affection for that mongrel banner invented for a league. The United States is the world's best hope, but if you tie her in the interests and quarrels of other nations, if you tangle her in the intrigues of Europe, you will destroy her power for good.

From a speech made in August 1919 by the US Senator Henry Cabot Lodge, a leading opponent of Woodrow Wilson's arguments.

against US involvement in the war, and they certainly did not want the USA to get entangled in European affairs after 1919. They did not want to be involved in what they saw as petty squabbles in Europe that could cost Americans a lot of money. Also, within the USA there were millions of recent immigrants from many European countries, including Germany and the Austro-Hungarian Empire.

Woodrow Wilson campaigned vigorously for Congress (the US parliament) to support him. In spite of poor health (leading to a stroke), Wilson toured the country by train and spoke

Source B

If America does not join the League I can predict with absolute certainty that within a generation there will be another war.

Woodrow Wilson.

in many cities and towns. However, when the vote was taken, American politicians voted for the USA to be isolated. When Americans voted for their next President to take office in 1921, they voted for a leader, Warren Harding, who promised a return to 'normalcy'. In other words, he promised a policy of isolationism to keep Americans out of European political affairs. This greatly weakened the League of Nations.

The structure of the League of Nations

THE ASSEMBLY

Every country in the League sent a representative to the Assembly. It could recommend action to the Council and could vote on the budget, admitting new members, and so on.

It met once a year at the League's headquarters, Geneva in Switzerland. Decisions made by the Assembly had to be unanimous – that is, they had to be agreed by all members of the Assembly.

THE COUNCIL

This was a smaller group that met several times a year and for emergencies. It included permanent members. (In 1920 these were Britain, France, Italy and Japan. The fifth was meant to be the USA.) It also included non-permanent members, elected by the Assembly for three-year periods.

Each of the permanent members had a veto. That meant that one vote against could stop action being agreed.

If persuasion did not work against a wrongdoer, the Council had powers to act (see page 28).

THE SECRETARIAT

This was like an international civil service. It kept records of meetings and prepared reports. Many of its staff were linguists. English and French were the main languages used.

THE PERMANENT COURT OF INTERNATIONAL JUSTICE

This was intended to help settle disputes peacefully. The Court was based at The Hague in the Netherlands. It was made up of judges from the member countries. However, it had no way of enforcing its rulings.

Source C

Should any member of the League resort to war, all other members of the League shall immediately break off all trade and financial relations with it. The Council will recommend what effective military, naval, or air force the members of the League shall contribute to protecting the Covenant of the League.

Article 16 of the Covenant of the League of Nations.

THINGS TO DO

1 Read **Source A**. Explain why the arguments used by Henry Cabot Lodge would appeal to many Americans.

2 How does **Source B** differ? Why?

3 Can you see any weaknesses in Article 16 (**Source C**)?

Source A British cartoon from 1920.

Powers of the League

The Covenant of the League set out three ways in which the League could act to settle disputes:

- A hearing by an impartial, neutral country.
- A ruling by the International Court of Justice.
- An inquiry by the Council.

If these did not work, and a country ignored the League's decision, then the League could take action:

- It could put pressure on the guilty country, bringing world opinion against it (moral pressure).
- Members of the League could refuse to trade with the guilty country (economic sanctions).
- The armed forces of member countries could be joined together and used against an aggressor (military force).

Strengths of the League

When the League was set up in 1919–20, there was almost total goodwill towards it from ordinary people and from most governments. People genuinely wanted to avoid conflicts like the one just ended, and they believed that this could be done. Most of the major countries had joined; others would surely do so, and defeated countries would be allowed to enter later on. Better communications by the 1920s (including international flights and the telephone) seemed to make it easier to act when conflict threatened.

Weaknesses of the League

Yet the League had a number of weaknesses. The USA's unwillingness to join undermined the League from the start. The organisation of the League relied on goodwill and persuasion; it had very little real power and did not have a permanent army. In addition, disarmament was still a hope, not a reality. The Disarmament Commission tried, but found it impossible to achieve success. For example, the French regarded disarmament as a threat to their security, while the failure of other nations to disarm enabled the Germans to claim that they had a right to rearm to protect themselves. There was still a lot of hatred left over from the war. International suspicion and traditional rivalries remained.

It is therefore all too easy to blame the League of Nations for its 'failure' to prevent the

Second World War. It is also easy to forget that the League did solve some political disputes in the 1920s. These attracted little attention at the time simply because they were solved. In 1921 there was a dispute between Sweden and Finland over the Aaland Islands. Then, following an incident in 1925 on the border between Bulgaria and Greece, the Greeks reacted by invading Bulgaria. In both cases the League of Nations restored order.

However, the very treaties that created the League of Nations also contained the explosive issues that later destroyed it. In the 1930s, the League proved to be powerless to act against the dictatorships of Japan, Germany and Italy. Goodwill on the part of the League of Nations was not enough in itself to keep the peace.

Japanese expansion into Manchuria and China

Effects of the Wall Street Crash

In the 1920s the world economy was thriving. There was a boom in world trade, centred on the USA. Japan benefited as well as Europe. But in 1929 economic disaster struck. In the USA, in October 1929, there was a spectacular collapse of the New York Stock Exchange (known as the Wall Street Crash), as a result of which millions of people lost their jobs. In the USA, many banks went bankrupt. As confidence disappeared, world trade was very badly affected. Countries put up tariffs (trade barriers) to try to protect their own industries. The USA did this against Japanese goods, and with less trade Japan could not afford to import food. Japanese industrial production and employment fell by 30 per cent between 1929 and 1931.

THINGS TO DO

1 Explain the meaning of **Source D**. How accurate was this view?

2 **Source E** and **Source F** (page 31) are by the same cartoonist. What are his views on the League of Nations? Did they change between 1920 and 1933? Explain your answer.

" KEEP THE HATE-FIRES BURNING "

  Source **E** A cartoon from the *London Star*, November 1920.

The Japanese army

The depression gave Japan's army leaders the chance to voice their opinions to a sympathetic people. They were not happy with the way Japan was treated by the other powers. Japan had not gained as much as it had hoped in the Paris peace settlement. It also appeared that its government allowed itself to be pushed around by the western world leaders. For example, in the Washington Naval Agreements (1922), Japan had agreed to have only three ships to every five built by Britain and the USA. Now it appeared that the Japanese government was unable to act effectively against the results of the Wall Street Crash. Japanese army leaders believed that the only possible policy to show Japan's strength and solve its economic problems was territorial conquest.

Manchuria

Manchuria was an area over which Japan already had some influence. It was a province of China and had raw materials, such as coal and iron ore, that Japan lacked. China was weak at the time. The last Emperor, aged six, had been overthrown in a revolution in 1911.

China had collapsed into chaos as rival warlords divided the huge country between them and created mini-kingdoms.

Japan had already taken advantage of this. The Japanese had an army stationed in southern Manchuria to protect the territory that had been gained from Russia in 1905. The Japanese also owned the South Manchurian Railway. The Japanese military leaders saw this as the perfect opportunity to seize full control of Manchuria, while the Chinese government was in no position to act.

The Japanese takeover of Manchuria

In September 1931, an explosion occurred on the South Manchurian Railway just outside the city of Mukden. The Japanese claimed that this was sabotage by the Chinese, who wanted to be rid of the Japanese. There was a Chinese army in the area, but the Chinese claimed that all their soldiers were in their barracks at the time. Whatever the truth of the matter, the Japanese turned events to their advantage. They argued that the Chinese had sabotaged the line, which provided an excuse for Japan to take over the area. This was done within months, and the Chinese forces were forced to withdraw.

In February 1932 the Japanese set up a puppet government in Manchuria (that is, a government under the control of the Japanese). The area was renamed Manchukuo and the last Chinese Emperor, Pu Yi, was put in control.

The reaction of the League of Nations

China appealed to the League. Japan claimed it was taking control of Manchuria simply because the area was getting out of hand. China had previously agreed that Manchuria should be a Japanese sphere of interest with long-standing economic rights.

The Japanese invasion of Manchuria.

The League had to act carefully. There was some truth in Japan's arguments, and Japan was a leading member of the League of Nations with a permanent seat on the Council. On the other hand, it appeared that the Japanese army had used military aggression to get what it wanted. The League told Japan to withdraw its troops from Manchuria. Instead, the Japanese gained firmer control by taking over more territory.

The League decided to set up a Commission of Inquiry under Lord Lytton. It was sent to the area to gather information and produce a report. The slow journey by sea took months, and the report was not published until September 1932 – a full year after the initial incident.

The Lytton Report was thorough, but its conclusion was most definitely in favour of China. Japan had acted unlawfully, and Manchuria should be returned to China. All countries in the League, except Japan, accepted the report. The Japanese response was simple. They ignored the report and left the League in March 1933.

The Japanese invade China

Japan announced the intention to invade more territory. In 1933 it started to invade the Jehol province, and in 1937 it began a major invasion of China. This showed the weakness of the League. Economic sanctions would have been useless, as Japan's main trading partner was the USA, which was not a member of the League. Britain was worried about taking any further measures against Japan, in case British trade in Asia was further harmed. Although people tried to make excuses for the League, nothing could really hide the truth. When an aggressive dictator wanted to invade neighbouring territories, the League was powerless to prevent it.

THINGS TO DO

1 Was the League of Nations powerless to act against Japan in Manchuria mainly because the USA was absent from the League?

2 Why do historians consider the Manchurian incident to be so important?

THE DOORMAT.

  A cartoon from the London *Evening Standard*, 19 January 1933.

The Italian conquest of Abyssinia

The background

Abyssinia was a poor and undeveloped country in north-east Africa. It was one of very few areas of Africa not under European control, and it was next to the Italian colonies of Eritrea and Somaliland. Italy had tried to conquer Abyssinia in 1896, but the Italians had been beaten at the Battle of Adowa.

Now the Italian dictator Mussolini was keen to avenge that defeat and to gain access to the country's mineral resources and fertile lands. He wanted the glory to be gained from military victory. In spite of the treaty of friendship signed in 1928 between Italy and Abyssinia, it was clear that Mussolini was preparing for war.

Mussolini and the League of Nations, January–October 1935

The League was anxious to avoid a clash with Mussolini. Britain and France believed that he was their best ally against the growing threat of Hitler. They signed the Stresa Pact with him. Meanwhile, Mussolini hoped that Britain and France would allow him to do what he wanted in Abyssinia. The League talked of collective security to protect Abyssinia, but it had little intention of taking decisive action against Mussolini.

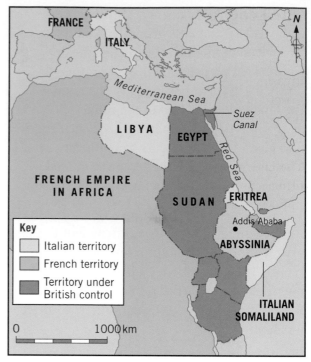

Foreign possessions around Abyssinia, 1935.

Italy attacks Abyssinia, October 1935

In October 1935 the Italians attacked Abyssinia after a clash between Italian and Abyssinian troops at the oasis of Wal-Wal in Abyssinia. The Italians used modern weapons, including tanks, planes and poison gas. The Abyssinian army was mostly infantry and cavalry and was no match for the Italians. The only hope for their Emperor, Haile Selassie, seemed to be in the size of the country, the state of the roads and an appeal to the League of Nations.

Source   Destruction caused by an Italian bombing raid on Abyssinia in December 1935.

The League's response

There seemed to be no excuse for the League not acting. This was clearly an unprovoked invasion of the weak by the strong. The Covenant of the League laid down what should happen – sanctions. A committee of the League was set up to agree what sanctions to impose.

The League banned the sale of arms and some other goods to Italy, all loans to Italy and imports from Italy. However, it did not ban oil exports to Italy because it feared that the USA would not co-operate. Neither did it ban coal exports for fear that the British mining industry would be badly affected. The Suez Canal, which was owned by Britain and France, was not closed to Mussolini's ships because they were afraid that closing it would provoke a full-scale war with Italy. This decision was important, as the canal was Mussolini's main supply route to Abyssinia.

The Hoare–Laval Pact

Behind the scenes, in December 1935 the British and French foreign ministers, Hoare and Laval, were preparing a plan that they hoped would end the fighting. They proposed to divide up Abyssinia, with Italy getting the best areas for agriculture and minerals, and Abyssinia being limited to the barren mountainous areas. The plan was never presented for discussion. It was leaked to the press and there was an outcry. Hoare and Laval were forced to resign.

This episode showed that British and French politicians were willing to put the interests of their country before that of the League of Nations. This badly damaged the League's reputation.

Mussolini triumphs

Meanwhile the Italians continued their invasion of Abyssinia. In May 1936, Italian troops entered the Abyssinian capital, Addis Ababa, in triumph. Just before this, the Emperor, Haile Selassie, fled the country and travelled to Geneva. He spoke to the League of

Source

I, Haile Selassie, Emperor of Abyssinia, am here today to claim that justice which is due to my people, and the assistance promised to it eight months ago, when fifty nations asserted that aggression had been committed in violation of international treaties.

Emperor Haile Selassie speaking to the League of Nations, 30 June 1936.

Nations on 30 June 1936. He protested against the failure of the League of Nations to protect his country from aggression.

The end of the League of Nations

This was really the end of the League of Nations. The USA was disgusted with the ditherings of the League. In March 1936, Hitler had already sent German troops into the Rhineland in violation of the Treaty of Versailles, and the League had done nothing. In October 1936, Hitler and Mussolini signed an agreement of their own, known as the Rome–Berlin Axis. Nobody took the League seriously after this, even though it existed formally until 1946.

Source

The real death of the League was in 1935, not 1939 or 1945. One day it was a powerful body imposing sanctions, seemingly more effective than ever before; the next day it was an empty sham, everyone scuttling from it as quickly as possible. Hitler watched.

The historian A. J. P. Taylor, writing in 1966.

The reasons for and the implications of the League's failure

Why did the League fail?

- The organisation of the League contained weaknesses. For example, decisions had to be unanimous, which was impractical. The League met infrequently, and so there were delays.

- Important nations were absent. The USA never joined. Germany did not join until 1926 and left in 1933. Japan left in 1933 and Italy in 1937. The Soviet Union did not join until 1934 and was expelled in 1939 after going to war with Finland.

- Sanctions were not effective, especially without the USA as a member.

- The League did not have a ready army at its disposal. Individual countries were reluctant to commit troops.

- As part of its Covenant, the League had to uphold the peace treaties of 1919–20. These were increasingly seen as unfair and in need of amendment.

- Countries were often reluctant to act unless their own interests were at stake and sometimes even acted against League decisions. For example, rather than proposing sanctions against Mussolini, Britain and France were preparing to carve up Abyssinia.

What were the implications of the League's failure?

Violence and aggression were shown to pay. Mussolini and Hitler learnt from Japan's example. Aggressive countries kept the territory gained with no penalties, except for the strongly expressed disapproval of some other countries.

The victims suffered. Manchuria and Abyssinia were occupied by foreign powers and abandoned by the League. Other weak nations came to realise that they could not expect the League to protect them.

Britain and France saw that they could not achieve success against dictators through the League. They tried to pacify Hitler by agreeing to some of his demands (the policy of appeasement), but at the same time a programme of re-armament began.

The Manchurian and Abyssinian crises showed that the League's notion of collective security did not work. The members of the League were not capable of acting firmly in the face of determined aggression. The League lost its credibility as a peace-keeping organisation.

Country		
France	1919	
Britain	1919	
Italy	1919	1937
Japan	1919	1933
Germany	1926	1933
USSR	1934	1939
USA	never joined	

The most powerful members of the League of Nations, 1919–46.

THINGS TO DO

Did the League of Nations have any chance of long-term success? Explain your answer carefully.

1.5 How did Hitler challenge and exploit the Treaty of Versailles in the period 1933 to March 1938?

The Treaty of Versailles

Section 1.3 of this chapter explained how the Treaty of Versailles had left the French dissatisfied because it had not weakened Germany enough to prevent recovery, and Germans dissatisfied because of the way they had been humiliated and the amount of land taken from them. The main problem with the treaty was that it gave the Germans legitimate grievances and left them the strongest power in Europe in terms of their economy and population. Hitler used this sense of grievance to gain support for his aggressive foreign policy in the 1930s.

Source A

What a use could be made of the Treaty of Versailles! Each one of the points of that treaty could be branded in the minds and hearts of the German people until sixty million men and women find their souls aflame with a feeling of anger and shame; they will answer with a common cry: 'We will have arms again.'

***Extract from Hitler's* Mein Kampf.**

The Germans had hoped peace would be along the lines of Wilson's Fourteen Points calling for general disarmament and countries to be divided according to nationality.

In 1921 reparations (war damages) were fixed at £6600 million, which the Germans said was too high, as their economy was in ruins. Germany was also refused entry to the League of Nations. This convinced the German people that part of the League's purpose was to keep them in check.

Hitler's aims

While he was in prison in 1924 after an unsuccessful attempt to lead a rising in Munich (see page 194), Hitler began writing *Mein Kampf*, in which he set out his aims for the future. He said that he wanted:

1 to rearm Germany and recover its lost territories;

2 to unite all German-speaking people under his control;

3 to expand in the East to gain *Lebensraum* (living space) for the German people.

To achieve all these aims Hitler argued it would be necessary to:

- destroy the power of France;
- win the friendship of Italy;
- become an ally of Britain – by agreeing on control of colonies they disputed.

Hitler's foreign policy

Although relations between Germany and other European powers improved in the 1920s, and Germany was allowed to join the League of Nations in 1926, the effects of the Wall Street Crash in the USA caused economic difficulties across Europe. Germany suffered too. In 1933 the Germans turned to Adolf Hitler in an attempt to solve their problems. Now he had a chance to put his policies into action.

German rearmament

Hitler withdrew Germany from the World Disarmament Conference in 1933 on the grounds that no other power was prepared to disarm. He claimed that Germany wanted peace and was prepared to disarm completely if its neighbours did the same. At the same time he withdrew Germany from the League of Nations. Germany was militarily very weak and Hitler could not risk opposition. There was none. He started the build-up of the German army by introducing conscription in 1935, justifying it on the grounds that other countries were increasing their arms, so Germany had to be strong enough to defend itself. This was against the Treaty of Versailles, but no power was prepared to do anything to stop it. Britain even supported Germany's right to rearm by signing a naval agreement with Hitler in 1935, allowing the Germans to build a fleet, as long as it was no bigger than 35 per cent of the British fleet. The British attitude was that if there was to be no general agreement on disarmament, then it was necessary to get an agreement in the one area that mattered to Britain – the navy.

The Saar Plebiscite, 1935

The industrial area around the Saar was removed from Germany by the Treaty of Versailles and put under the control of the League of Nations. A plebiscite among the German people was to be held after 15 years to decide whether it should be returned to Germany. In January 1935 90 per cent of the people voted in favour of returning to Germany. The result was never in doubt, but the Nazi Party celebrated it as a great victory. They presented it as the first of the injustices of Versailles to be removed.

The re-militarisation of the Rhineland, 1936

The Rhineland, the area of Germany which bordered France, was made a de-militarised zone under the Treaty of Versailles. It was still part of Germany, but the Germans were not allowed to station troops or weapons there. This was to prevent any sudden, surprise attack on France. On 7 March 1936 Hitler ordered his troops to march into the Rhineland. As this was clearly against the Treaty of Versailles Hitler feared that Britain and France would try to stop him. But nothing was done, so Hitler had his way. This action was popular with Germans and encouraged Hitler to continue pursuing his policies.

Was the Rhineland a missed opportunity?

The re-militarisation of the Rhineland is often referred to as having been the last chance to oppose Hitler without going to war. Germany's armies were too weak to take on France in 1936 and Hitler realised that he had taken a chance (see Source D). So, why was he not resisted? France had the power to drive the German army out of the Rhineland but would not act without the support of Britain. The British government did not think that Hitler was doing anything wrong – he was only 'marching into his own backyard' – so was not prepared to go to war to stop him. The French and British were more worried that Mussolini's Italian army had invaded Abyssinia and the League of Nations had done little to stop him. Hitler noticed the

Source **B**

German and Italian rearmament is proceeding more rapidly than rearmament can in England. In three years Germany will be ready.

Hitler in private conversation with Mussolini's son-in-law, October 1936.

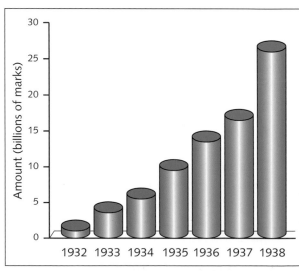

German spending on armaments in the period 1932–38.

Source C   German troops marching into the Rhineland.

reluctance of the League to act against Mussolini and correctly calculated that no action would be taken against Germany.

The League of Nations condemned Hitler's action but did nothing about it. Hitler offered to make a peace treaty that would last for 25 years. This was his way of calming those countries that wanted peace, at the same time as he was getting his way. His diplomacy had triumphed. The British government believed that the Treaty of Versailles had been unfair and that the righting of wrongs would help keep the peace with Germany in the future.

Source D

Even later, when Hitler was waging war against almost the entire world, he always termed the re-militarisation of the Rhineland the most daring of all his undertakings. 'We had no army worth mentioning. If the French had taken any action, we would have been easily defeated; our resistance would have been over in a few days.'

Albert Speer writing about how Hitler saw the re-occupation of the Rhineland by the German army.

Preparation for *Anschluss*, 1934–38

The joining together of Austria and Germany (*Anschluss*) was forbidden by the Treaty of Versailles. But it was important to Hitler who wanted to unite all German-speaking people in one country. He first tried to take control of Austria in 1934 when members of the Austrian Nazi Party murdered the Chancellor of Austria. The Nazis tried to take over the government but were prevented by the future Chancellor, Schuschnigg, and the opposition of the dictator of Italy, Mussolini. Mussolini's threats forced the Nazis to back down and prevented Hitler from interfering.

THINGS TO DO

1 List the terms of the Treaty of Versailles that would be hated by most Germans. Give reasons for your answer. (Pages 23–25 will help.)

2 Why did Britain and France not stop German rearmament in the 1930s?

3 Do you agree that the failure to stop Hitler re-militarising the Rhineland was a mistake?

When the Spanish Civil War broke out in 1936 Hitler and Mussolini supported the Spanish fascist General Franco, despite having signed a treaty not to interfere. Hitler used the war to give his new forces experience of fighting – they practised dive-bombing techniques and tank formations in Spain – and to keep Mussolini occupied so that he would not oppose *Anschluss*. The Civil War brought Italy and Germany together in 1936 and they signed the Rome–Berlin Axis, which was followed by the Anti-Comintern Pact, signed by Germany, Italy and Japan, to prevent the spread of communism. The stage was set for Hitler's next step.

The annexation of Austria (*Anschluss*), 1938

In 1938 Hitler ordered the Austrian Nazi Party to begin a campaign in Austria for union with Germany. Riots and demonstrations followed. The Austrian Chancellor, Schuschnigg, tried to arrange a plebiscite (referendum) among the Austrian people on the union with Germany. Hitler moved German troops to the border to prevent this from taking place. Schuschnigg resigned and Seyss-Inquart, a leading Nazi whom Schuschnigg had been forced to put in charge of the Austrian police, invited the Germans into Austria to restore order. This they did, imprisoning over 80,000 opponents of Hitler. Hitler then entered Austria in triumph and union with Germany was established on 14 March 1938. A plebiscite was held and 99.75 per cent agreed with the *Anschluss*.

Hitler's success was another victory for his diplomacy. Mussolini had not interfered because of the Rome–Berlin Axis and there was no opposition from Britain and France who were reluctant to take any action against Hitler which might cause war. Though the plebiscite result was influenced by Nazi pressure, many Austrians greeted the union with support. They wanted to be a part of the glory and success of Hitler's Third Reich.

Anschluss was a great success for Hitler. He now looked towards Czechoslovakia as his next target, although he told the leaders of Britain and France that he had no interest in winning land in Czechoslovakia.

Source **E**

The reunion of Germany and Austria is our life task, to be carried out by every means possible at our disposal.

This is what Hitler said in Mein Kampf.

Source **F**

Hitler finally presented an ultimatum, and threatened to march into Austria if his demands were not met. When Schuschnigg left the study to take advice, Hitler could be heard shouting behind the open door: 'General Keitel. Where is General Keitel? Tell him to come here at once.' (Keitel was Chief of the German High Command.) Keitel came hurrying up. He told us later that when he presented himself and asked for orders, Hitler grinned and said: 'There are no orders. I just wanted you here.'

Von Papen, the German ambassador in Vienna, describes an incident during the negotiations between Hitler and Schuschnigg over the plebiscite in 1938.

Source **G**

I give you my word of honour that Czechoslovakia has nothing to fear from the Reich.

Hitler speaking to Chamberlain after the Anschluss.

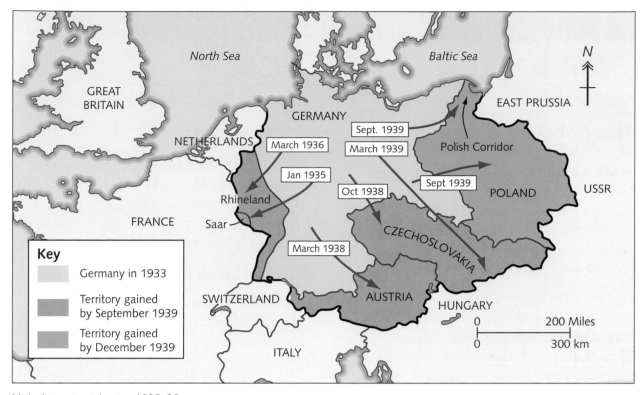

Hitler's territorial gains, 1935–39.

The people of Vienna welcome the arrival of German troops in March 1938.

THINGS TO DO

1 How did Hitler make use of the Spanish Civil War?

2 Why did Hitler take over Austria in March 1938?

3 Read **Source F**. Why do you think Hitler called Keitel? What does it tell us about his methods of negotiating?

4 Do the facts suggest that **Source H** is a reliable portrayal of the German entry into Vienna?

5 What did Hitler learn from the response of other countries and the League of Nations which helped him in the future?

1.6 Why did appeasement fail to prevent the outbreak of war in 1939?

The policy of appeasement

When Neville Chamberlain became Prime Minister in 1937, the policy of appeasement continued to be Britain's main approach to the problem of Germany. Some historians think this was the main reason why the Second World War was not prevented.

Chamberlain's approach was to find out what Hitler wanted and show him that, if his claims were reasonable, they could be discussed. Chamberlain believed that Germany had genuine grievances under the Treaty of Versailles and that if these could be solved by negotiation, Hitler would live in peace with the rest of the world. The success of appeasement, however, depended on Hitler's aims being limited and on his sincerity – he had to be trusted. France supported appeasement after 1937. The French felt safe behind their Maginot Line, a stretch of fortifications running along their border.

There was a lot of support for appeasement in Britain: people wanted to avoid another war like the First World War with its massive loss of life and damage. Also Britain had not prepared itself for a war by rearming and was in no position to resist Hitler. Some British politicians, fearing the communist Soviet Union, saw a strong Germany as a barrier to communist expansion in Europe. There had been no opposition to the occupation of the Rhineland and the *Anschluss*. The League of Nations had failed, so Chamberlain decided to use personal diplomacy instead. He dealt directly with Hitler in an attempt to solve disputes and keep the peace.

Czechoslovakia, 1938

Czechoslovakia had an army of 34 divisions, strong mountain defences in the Sudetenland, the valuable Skoda armaments works, deposits of coal and lignite and defence agreements with Russia and France. Hitler wanted Czechoslovakia as part of his policy of *Lebensraum* (living space), but he also detested the country as a democracy and a reminder of the hated peace settlement of 1919. Czechoslovakia had been formed in 1919 and its population was made up of Czechs, Slovaks and 3 million German-speakers from the old Austria-Hungary Empire. Most of the German-speakers lived in the Sudetenland, and it was they who gave Hitler the excuse he needed to invade Czechoslovakia.

The leader of the Czech Nazi Party, Konrad Henlein, was urged by Hitler to demand that the Czech government make concessions to the Sudeten Germans. Henlein kept the pressure on the Czechs by asking for more and more concessions. In April 1938, German troops began massing on the Czech border. Czechoslovakia's President, Benes, mobilised his troops to resist the Germans. Britain and France wanted to avoid war so they persuaded Benes to make further concessions to the Sudetens. It became clear that Hitler would never be satisfied with improved rights for the Sudeten Germans. What he wanted was to make the Sudetenland part of Germany.

Source

Do not misunderstand me when the government says that it is looking to our defences. I give you my word that there will be no great rearmament.

The British Prime Minister, Stanley Baldwin, in an election speech, November 1935.

Appeasement in action

On 12 September 1938 Hitler told the Sudeten Germans that he would support them. So the Sudeten Nazis began rioting but were crushed by the Czech government. On 15 September Chamberlain met Hitler at Berchtesgaden to discuss his demands. Chamberlain then persuaded the Czechs to agree to transfer to Germany those parts of the Sudetenland where the majority of the population was German. On 22 September Chamberlain met Hitler at Godesberg and informed him of the agreement. However, Hitler told Chamberlain that he wanted the whole of the Sudetenland and threatened to go to war. Chamberlain returned to Britain and prepared for war. Trenches were dug for protection from air raids, gas masks were distributed and the armed forces were put on stand-by. However, war was avoided when Mussolini persuaded Hitler to attend a four-power conference at Munich on 29 September.

The Munich Conference, September 1938

This conference was attended by four leaders: Hitler for Germany, Mussolini for Italy, Chamberlain for Britain and Daladier for France. The Soviet Union and Czechoslovakia were not invited. It was agreed at the conference that the Sudetenland would become part of Germany immediately. The Czechs were then forced by Britain and France to accept this and German armies occupied the Sudetenland on 1 October. Peace had been obtained and Hitler had gained the Sudetenland. On the day after the Munich Agreement Chamberlain signed a separate agreement with Hitler in which the two countries promised to consult in the event of any problems and never to go to war against each other. Chamberlain returned to Britain a hero. He had his critics, such as Churchill, but he had achieved what most people wanted: he had kept peace in Europe.

Source B

Hitler said that the aim of German foreign policy was to defend Germany and to enlarge it. For the improvement of our position our first objective must be to overthrow Czechoslovakia and Austria. Hitler believed that Britain and France had already written off the Czechs.

From the Hossbach Memorandum, notes of a secret meeting between Hitler and the commanders of his armed forces in November 1937.

Source C

How horrible, fantastic, incredible it is that we should be digging trenches and trying on gas masks here, because of a quarrel in a far-off country between people of whom we know nothing.

From a radio broadcast by Neville Chamberlain, 22 September 1938.

Source D A cartoon of the time, entitled 'Still hope', shows Chamberlain on his way to Munich to negotiate a settlement.

The occupation of Czechoslovakia, March 1939

Czechoslovakia had lost its strong defensive system at Munich. Moreover, the loss of the Sudeten Germans had stirred other nationalities in Czechoslovakia to demand a return to their nation states. In October 1938 Poland gained part of Czechoslovakia, as did Hungary in November. In 1939 the Slovaks were demanding more rights. The new Czech President, Hacha, appealed to Hitler for help and in the end had no choice but to invite the Germans into Czechoslovakia. On 15 March 1939 Hitler marched into Prague, the Czech capital. The state of Czechoslovakia had come to an end.

This was also the end of appeasement. The occupation of Czechoslovakia by the Germans was not opposed by Britain or France because the Germans had been invited in by the Czech government. Even so the occupation changed Chamberlain's attitude towards Hitler. Hitler could not justify the takeover by claiming that the people were German-speaking or that he was righting a wrong of the Treaty of Versailles. Hitler had broken the promise he made to Chamberlain in 1938 and was now seen as an aggressor whose aims were not limited, and who would continue to take more and more territory until he was stopped. Europe now had to take seriously Hitler's ideas on the supremacy of the Aryan race, *Lebensraum* and world domination as set out in *Mein Kampf*.

Britain began building up its arms after the Munich settlement. After the occupation of Czechoslovakia the British government brought in conscription, for the first time ever in peacetime. After occupying Prague Hitler seized the province of Memel, which was mainly inhabited by Germans, from Lithuania. The British

government expected Poland to be Hitler's next target. Poland occupied land (the Polish Corridor) which cut off East Prussia from the rest of Germany and there were German-speaking people living in Danzig, which had been taken from Germany at Versailles. In April 1939, Britain and France promised to help Poland if it was attacked by Germany. The problem was they were not in a position to defend Poland against Germany. Only the Soviet Union could do this.

THINGS TO DO

1 What was appeasement?

2 Some historians have criticised the Soviet Union for signing the Nazi–Soviet Pact. **Source F** defends the signing. Do you agree with the interpretation given in **Source F**? Explain your answer.

3 Do you think Hitler intended to remain on good terms with the Soviet Union after 1939? Explain your answer.

Source **E** German troops entering Prague in March 1939.

The Nazi–Soviet Pact, 1939

Britain and the Soviet Union (USSR) talked of forming an alliance throughout the summer of 1939. The British delayed things as much as possible. Poland was as much afraid of an invasion from the USSR as it was from Germany, so it was not prepared to accept help from the Soviets. Hitler's policy of *Lebensraum* involved conquering territory east of Germany, including the USSR. Because of his hatred of communism he would almost certainly attack the USSR. So, the world was shocked when, on 23 August 1939, the two countries signed the Nazi–Soviet Pact.

The Nazi–Soviet Pact brought war closer. Both countries agreed not to attack each other and through a series of secret clauses they divided Poland between them. Germany was to attack Poland from the west, the USSR to attack from the east. Hitler was sure Britain and France would not carry out their promise to Poland – why should they, they had backed down over Czechoslovakia? He felt free to attack Poland.

Why did the USSR sign the Pact? Their leader, Stalin, appeared to run out of patience with Britain's failure to sign an agreement with them. He had been annoyed when left out of the discussions at Munich and was suspicious that Britain and France were trying to direct Hitler's attention to the east and away from the west.

The attack on Poland, 1 September 1939

The German army invaded Poland on 1 September 1939. Chamberlain tried to get them to withdraw and hold a peace conference. This failed, and on 3 September Britain declared war on Germany, followed shortly after by France.

The Soviet Union invaded eastern Poland on 17 September. Within weeks Poland was defeated. Britain was unable to do anything to prevent it.

Source **F**

The Anglo-French plan was to direct Germany towards the east and involve Hitler in conflict with the Soviet Union. Munich and the negotiations of 1939 provided clear proof of the unwillingness of the British and French governments to form an anti-Hitler alliance. The treaty with Germany was a step which the USSR was forced to take in the difficult situation that had come about in the summer of 1939. The Soviet government realised Hitler's aims and understood that the treaty would only bring a breathing space which would give them time to carry through the political and military measures needed in order to ensure the country's security.

A Soviet historian writing in 1969 about the Nazi–Soviet Pact.

SUMMARY

1919	Treaty of Versailles.
1933	Hitler takes power.
1934	Germany begins to rearm.
1935	The Saar Plebiscite.
	Mussolini invades Abyssinia.
1936	Re-militarisation of the Rhineland.
	Spanish Civil War begins.
	Rome–Berlin Axis.
1938	*Anschluss*.
	Munich Agreement.
1939	Invasion of Czechoslovakia.
	Nazi–Soviet Pact.
	Invasion of Poland.

What are the verdicts on the Munich Agreement?

Source **G**

The Sudetenland is the last problem that must be solved and it will be solved. It is the last territorial claim that I have to make in Europe. The aims of our foreign policy are limited. Ten million Germans found themselves beyond the frontiers of the Reich – Germans who wished to return to the Reich as their homeland.

Hitler speaking in Berlin in 1938.

Source **H**

Be glad in your hearts. Give thanks to your God. People of Britain, your children are safe.

Your husbands and sons will not march into battle. If we must have a victor, let us choose Chamberlain. For the Prime Minister's conquests are mighty and enduring – millions of happy homes and hearts relieved of their burden.

Daily Express, 30 September 1938.

Source **I**

I believe that it is peace for our time ... peace with honour.

Neville Chamberlain speaking about the Munich Agreement in a radio broadcast, 1 October 1938.

Source **J**

We have suffered a total defeat. I think you will find that in a period of time Czechoslovakia will be engulfed in the Nazi regime. This is only the beginning.

Winston Churchill speaking in the House of Commons in October 1938.

Source **K**

By repeatedly surrendering to force, Chamberlain has encouraged aggression. Chamberlain's policy has always been based on a fatal misunderstanding of the psychology of dictatorship.

Yorkshire Post, December 1938.

Source **L**

The final settlement forced Czechoslovakia to give Germany 11,000 square miles of territory. Within this area lay all the vast Czech fortifications.

Czechoslovakia's entire system of rail, road, telephone and telegraph communications was disrupted. It lost 66% of its coal, 86% of its chemicals, 80% of its textiles, 70% of its electrical power, and 40% of its timber. A prosperous industrial nation was split up and bankrupted overnight.

An American historian, William Shirer, writing in 1959.

Source **M**

Hitler says he has 'No more territorial ambitions in Europe'.

Do you believe him?   Yes 7%   No 93%

Results of a public opinion poll taken in Britain after Munich.

Source **N**

Those who welcomed the Munich conference and its solution represented it as a victory for reason and conciliation in international affairs – appeasement as it was called at the time. The opponents of Munich saw in it an abdication by the two democratic powers, France and Britain; a surrender to fear; or a sinister conspiracy to prepare for a Nazi war of conquest against Soviet Russia. Munich was all these things.

From A. J. P. Taylor, The Myths of Munich, 1969.

Source O

'That fellow Chamberlain has ruined my entry into Prague.'

'Do you know why I finally yielded at Munich? I thought the Home Fleet might open fire.'

Hitler speaking in 1938 after Munich.

Source P

From the military point of view time is in our favour. If war with Germany has to come, it would be better to fight her in six to twelve months time.

Chamberlain's military advisers 1938.

Source Q

They are little worms. I saw them at Munich

Hitler's opinion of Britain and France expressed in April 1939.

Source R

The Pact of Munich is signed. Czechoslovakia as a power is out. The genius of the Führer and his determination not to avoid even a world war have again won victory without the use of force. The hope remains that the doubters have been converted and will remain that way.

A German general speaking after Munich.

Source S

Swiss comment on Munich.

THINGS TO DO

1 **Source N** gives two different views of Munich. List the sources on this page which support each view.

2 What does **Source M** tell us about the popularity of the Munich Agreement in Britain?

3 What evidence is there in the sources that
   (a) Britain could not fight in 1938?
   (b) Hitler felt defeated at Munich?
   (c) Munich affected Germany's policies after 1938?

4 Explain the the meaning of **Source S**. How reliable is this view?

1.7 Why did the USA and USSR become rivals in the period 1945 to 1949?

Communism and capitalism

The USSR and the USA had been allies during the war, but their political systems were opposed to one another. The USSR was a communist state of one-party government in which there were no free elections and the state owned industry and agriculture. The USA and Western Europe were democratic and capitalist, in which governments were elected by free elections and industry and agriculture were in private ownership to be run for profit. The Soviets believed the West wanted to destroy communism, the West believed the Soviets wanted to convert the world to communism. These fears were one of the reasons for the Cold War.

The Yalta Conference

What happened after the Second World War encouraged these fears. The three Allied leaders (Roosevelt, Churchill and Stalin) met at Yalta in February 1945 and agreed to divide Germany into four zones, with Britain, France, USA and USSR occupying a zone each. Since Berlin, the German capital, was in the Soviet zone, it too would be divided up into four Allied sectors. Stalin was to have an influence over Eastern Europe, but the countries in this part of Europe were to be allowed to hold free elections to decide who governed them. Only a framework settlement was agreed at Yalta. The details would be added later at another conference to be held at Potsdam.

Despite reaching agreement on most issues, the Allies were divided on others. The greatest source of conflict was Poland. Soviet troops had already liberated much of Poland and a communist government had been established there. Stalin insisted on the need for a 'friendly' government in Poland so that his country would have some protection from Germany. The Western Allies took this to mean a Soviet-dominated government and were not prepared to allow Stalin to get his own way in Poland. They persuaded him to agree that Polish exiles who were opposed to communism should be included in the new Polish government and that free elections would be held as soon as possible. In fact, the exiles were ignored and Stalin refused to allow democratic elections to take place.

The Potsdam Conference

By the time the Allied leaders met again at Potsdam in July 1945, after the defeat of Germany, relations between the West and East were much cooler. Roosevelt had died and was replaced by Truman, and Churchill had been defeated in a general election and Attlee was the new British prime minister. Truman and Stalin did not appear to get on well and the tension between them increased suspicions between the two nations.

Many of the decisions reached at Yalta were confirmed at Potsdam and it was agreed that Germany was to pay reparations in the form of equipment and materials, mostly to the USSR, to compensate for war losses.

Source A

The Soviet government is alarmed by the attitude of the US government. The American attitude cooled once it became clear that Germany was defeated. It was as though the Americans were saying that the USSR was no longer needed.

Stalin gives his views on the attitude of Harry S. Truman, the new American President, May 1945.

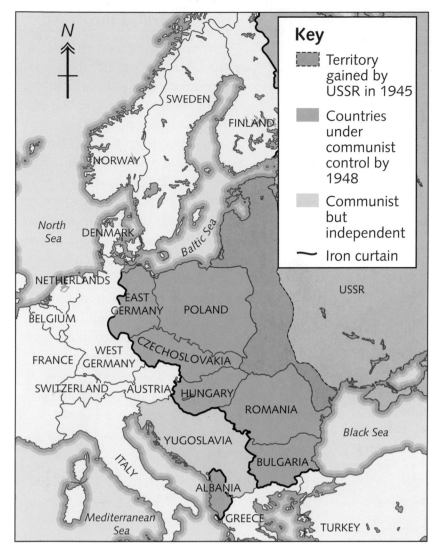

The Iron Curtain.

USSR and Eastern Europe: the Iron Curtain

The USSR's actions in Eastern Europe alarmed the Americans. After the defeat of Japan, communist governments loyal to the USSR were set up in Poland, Hungary, Romania, Bulgaria and Albania. The communists' success in gaining power in these countries was in some cases achieved only with the aid of Soviet military force, not through free elections as had been agreed at Yalta. To the Americans this proved that Stalin's plan was to spread communism throughout Europe.

In a speech to an American audience in March 1946, Churchill referred to the division between West and East as the descending of an Iron Curtain between the two sides. The Iron Curtain was not a physical division, but a political and economic division between the one-party communist states of the East and the capitalist democracies of the West. Churchill's purpose was to convince the Americans that they needed to keep a military presence in Europe to prevent the spread of communism.

Despite these agreements it soon became clear that the divisions between East and West were growing. At first the Allies had agreed that Germany was to be kept weak, but the Western allies soon realised that this was an error – a weak Germany would be prey to communist westward expansion. They began to realise that a stronger, reunified Germany would be a buffer against the spread of Soviet influence. So they decided that the German economy should be strengthened. Stalin viewed this with suspicion. He continued to weaken the Soviet zone in Germany by stripping it of all useful equipment and machinery. The West sent industrial goods to the Soviet Union as agreed at Potsdam, but Stalin failed to send back the promised food and coal. This angered the West.

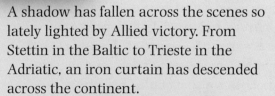

Source B

A shadow has fallen across the scenes so lately lighted by Allied victory. From Stettin in the Baltic to Trieste in the Adriatic, an iron curtain has descended across the continent.

Extract from Churchill's speech at Fulton, USA, in March 1946.

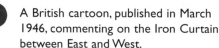

PEEP UNDER THE IRON CURTAIN

The Truman Doctrine

In 1947 communists were threatening to take control in both Greece and Turkey. The USA had no wish to stand by while communism spread to other countries. In March 1947 President Truman made a speech in which he said that the USA would help any nation threatened by communism. The USA would take the lead in the 'containment' of Soviet expansion. This 'Truman Doctrine' was based on the American belief that the countries of Eastern Europe had been forced into communism by the Soviet Union and that it was America's duty to protect other democratic countries under threat. So Congress announced $400 million of aid to Greece and Turkey. This helped the Greek government defeat the communists. The Americans also installed ballistic missile sites on the Turkish border with the USSR. The Soviets were even more alarmed as they had no nuclear weapons.

The Marshall Plan

The Truman Doctrine, with its policy of 'containment' of communism, is usually seen as the start of the Cold War. The Marshall Plan, which accompanied the Truman Doctrine, aimed at helping Europe recover from the war. The Americans feared that an impoverished post-war Western Europe would turn to communism. To prevent this they needed to help Europe recover economically as quickly as possible. To do this the Americans set up the Marshall Plan to provide economic aid wherever it was needed in Europe, including the East. As a matter of economic self-interest this also made sense for the Americans, as Europe's recovery would once again make it a strong trading partner for the USA.

The Marshall Plan set up a fund of $15 billion for Europe. The idea was that Eastern Europe could also draw on this money. However, Stalin realised this would make Eastern Europe more dependent on the USA than the USSR. He did not want that. Stalin denounced the Marshall Plan as economic imperialism, claiming that the USA was trying to spread its influence by controlling the industry and trade of Europe.

Source **D**

Our policy is directed not against any country or doctrine but against hunger, poverty, desperation and chaos. Any country that is willing to assist in the task of recovery will find full co-operation on the part of the US government.

George C. Marshall, the US Secretary of State, speaking about his plan for aiding Europe, June 1947.

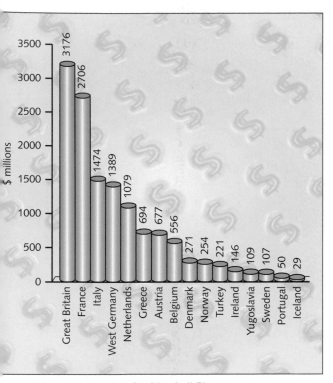

Aid received under the Marshall Plan.

Sixteen nations asked the USA for help. These included wartime allies like Britain and former enemies such as West Germany. The aid often arrived in the form of products, such as machinery and fertilisers. Between 1948 and 1950, industrial production in Western Europe had increased by 25 per cent. By 1952, most West European economies were on their way to recovery. Industrial unrest in France and Italy came to an end and communist influence decreased.

Stalin was unhappy at this development. He had insisted that the Soviet satellites withdraw their applications for Marshall Aid, so he was forced to offer assistance to them himself. The Molotov Plan was introduced, which established the Council for Mutual Economic Assistance. Comecon, as it became known, was intended to offer Soviet aid to the satellite states, but since the Soviet Union lacked the necessary resources, it was never effective. Stalin saw the Marshall Plan as a crude attempt by the USA to dominate Europe. His fear and suspicion intensified the Cold War and further increased the divisions within Europe.

The Cominform

In 1947 communist leaders from all over the world were summoned to a conference in Warsaw, where the Communist Information Bureau (Cominform) was created. This was designed to spread communism and protect communist states from US aggression. In 1948, Stalin ordered Cominform to expel Tito, the communist leader of Yugoslavia, because he would not give in to Stalin's wishes. This shows that Stalin wanted total control of the communist world and would allow no opposition at all. The USA saw Cominform as a serious challenge to the West. Relations between the superpowers deteriorated further.

The post-war division of Germany

After the Second World War, the growth of tension between the superpowers encouraged the Western allies to modify their policy towards Germany. They had initially agreed with the Soviet Union that Germany was a threat and should be kept weak. However, they now saw that the Soviet Union was a greater threat. A weak Germany might be taken over by the communists, but a strong Germany would act as a buffer against communism. In addition, only with a strong German economy could the economic situation in Europe generally improve.

The West now favoured strengthening Germany through industrialisation and reunification. Reparations payments, which were weakening Germany, would be ended and there would be a speedy return to full democracy. A new German currency, the Deutschmark, would be introduced. The Soviet Union saw this as a betrayal of the earlier agreements at Yalta and Potsdam, whereby the Allies would take decisions about Germany jointly. It had not been consulted and became increasingly suspicious of Western motives.

The Berlin Blockade

Berlin, the capital of Germany, was divided into four zones of occupation, just like the rest of the country. As the city was in the Soviet zone, the West depended on the USSR to keep open the routes in and out of the city. But it was decisions by the West which triggered a crisis in the Cold War.

Stalin continued to extract reparations from the Soviet zone of Germany but the other zones in the West, including West Berlin, were beginning to recover because of Marshall Aid. By 1948 Britain, France and America had joined their zones together and were planning to establish a new currency to aid recovery. This was not what Stalin wanted. He saw a prosperous Germany in the West as a threat to the USSR. His response was to close all roads, canals and railways between the West and West Berlin on 24 June 1948. Stalin wanted to force the West to give up West Berlin by starving the two million inhabitants, who only had enough food and fuel to last for six weeks. Truman was faced with giving up West Berlin or going to war. But giving up West Berlin meant giving in to Stalin. To use armed force involved invading the Soviet zone of Germany.

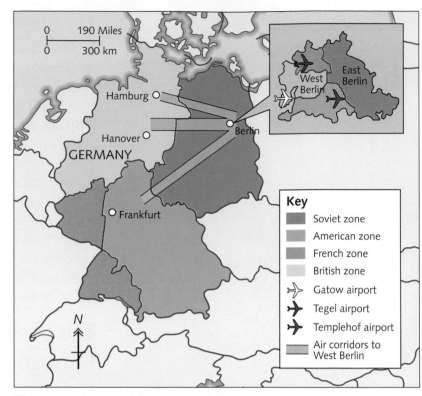

The occupied zones of Germany in 1945.

A less aggressive policy was devised to keep the people of Berlin from starving. The British and Americans flew in supplies.

Source E

When Berlin falls, Western Germany will be next. If we withdraw our position in Berlin, Europe is threatened. Communism will run rampant.

General Clay, the American commander in Berlin, on the dangers of the Blockade.

THINGS TO DO

1. What were the fears of the West and the USSR that helped to create the Cold War? Were these fears real or imaginary?

2. Is **Source C** an accurate view of the Iron Curtain?

3. Which three countries received most from Marshall Aid? Why do you think these three received the most?

4. Why did Stalin not accept Marshall Aid?

5. What does **Source E** mean?

6. (a) Who is the 'bird watcher' in **Source H** and what is he interested in doing?
   (b) What did the 'bird watcher' actually do? Why?

7. How and why do **Sources F** and **G** differ in their view of the Berlin Blockade?

The Berlin Airlift

West Berliners needed over 4,000 tons of fuel, food and other supplies each day if they were to survive the Blockade. The Allies used the three air corridors established in 1945. The airlift began slowly: the first flight was on 26 June, but on average only 600 tons a day were reaching West Berlin. By September aircraft were landing in Berlin every three minutes, day and night, and by the spring of 1949, 8,000 tons a day were being flown in. The Soviets tried to put more pressure on the Berliners by cutting off electricity supplies and offering them extra rations if they moved to East Berlin. Only 2 per cent of the population did this, showing that the people of West Berlin were prepared to undergo hardship to remain part of the West.

Stalin realised the Allies were determined to keep the airlift going. He could only stop it by shooting down the planes. Soviet planes did track supply planes in case they moved out of the permitted air corridor, but dared not shoot them down as this would be an act of war. Stalin called off the Blockade in May 1949. The West had shown how determined it was to resist communism. The Blockade was costly to the Allies and 79 British and American pilots were killed in accidents, but it ended the ill-feeling between the Americans and the defeated Germans in the West.

Any hopes for a united Germany had ended, for the time being. In 1949 the three Western zones, including West Berlin, became known as the Federal Republic of Germany (West Germany), with its own elected government. The USSR responded by turning its zone into the German Democratic Republic (East Germany) which had a communist government. The Allies were now determined to build up West Berlin into a showcase for capitalism.

International History 1900–91

Source **F**

When we refused to be forced out of Berlin, we demonstrated to Europe that we would act when freedom was threatened. This action was a Russian plan to probe the soft spots in the Western Allies' positions.

President Truman speaking in 1949 about the Berlin crisis.

Source **G**

The crisis was planned in Washington, behind a smoke-screen of anti-Soviet propaganda. In 1948 there was the danger of war. The conduct of the Western powers risked bloody incidents. The self-blockade of the Western powers hit the West Berlin population with harshness. The people were freezing and starving. In the spring of 1949 the USA was forced to yield; their war plans came to nothing

A Soviet version of the Berlin crisis.

THE BIRD WATCHER

Source **H** A *Punch* cartoon from July 1948. It shows Stalin watching the Allied 'storks' flying supplies to Berlin during the Blockade.

Exam-style assessment – OPTION V

In the exam, the questions will follow the same pattern in each option. In the examples in the book, this does not always apply in order to show the variety of questions that can be set. In the examination, if you choose Option V, you must answer two of the three questions in the section.

Question 1: The alliances and the outbreak of war in 1914

Study **Sources A** and **B** and then answer the following questions.

Source A: The formation of the Triple Entente 1904–7

In 1904 Britain signed the Entente Cordiale with France. To Britain this was a colonial agreement which solved areas of dispute between Britain and France. The diplomatic support promised to France made Morocco the centre of European disputes in the next few years. The completion of the Triple Entente three years later marked the division of Europe into two rival camps. It was no military alliance but, since France was Russia's ally, most European statesmen believed that Britain had cast her vote on the side of Russia and France against the Triple Alliance.

From *Europe since Napoleon* by David Thomson, a British historian, published in 1957

Source B: An Austrian comment on the assassination at Sarajevo 1914

The assassination at Sarajevo is not the crime of a single fanatic; assassination represents Serbia's declaration of war on Austria-Hungary.

From a speech by Conrad von Hotzendorf, the Chief of Austrian General Staff, made immediately after the assassination

(a) According to **Source A**, what was the importance of the alliances Great Britain made in 1904 and 1907? **(3 marks)**

(b) Describe what happened at Sarajevo on 28 June 1914. **(6 marks)**

(c) How reliable is **Source B** to an historian writing about the importance of the assassination at Sarajevo? Use **Source B** and your own knowledge to answer the question. **(6 marks)**

(d) Was the system of alliances that existed in 1914 the main cause of World War One? Explain your answer. **(10 marks)**

Question 2: Attempts to keep peace after World War One

Study **Source C** and then answer the following questions.

Source C: The Manchurian Crisis 1931–32

For some years past unpleasant incidents have taken place in the region of Manchuria where Japan has special trade interests and treaty rights. The area has been subject to the raids of Chinese bandits and in September a detachment of Chinese troops destroyed the tracks of the South Manchurian Railway near Mukden and murdered Japanese guards. The Japanese army had to act swiftly to restore order.

From an official report of the Japanese Government published in September 1931

(a) According to **Source C**, why did the Japanese invade Manchuria in 1931? **(3 marks)**

(b) Do you think that **Source C** is a reliable account of the causes of the invasion? Use **Source C** and your own knowledge to answer the question. **(6 marks)**

(c) Describe how the League of Nations tried to solve the Manchurian Crisis. **(6 marks)**

(d) Was the Manchurian Crisis the most important reason for the failure of the League of Nations? Explain your answer. **(10 marks)**

Question 3: From World War Two to Cold War

Study **Sources D** and **E** and then answer the following questions.

Source D: The Yalta Agreement February 1945

At Yalta, the USA, the USSR and Great Britain agreed that Germany would be divided up into four zones of Allied occupation, as would Berlin. The three powers agreed that they would assist any European state which had been freed from German control, to form a government which was representative of all democratic elements in the population. They pledged themselves to the establishment through free elections of governments responsible to the will of the people.

From a British historian writing in 2000

Source E: The spread of Communism

This French cartoon was published after World War Two. It shows the Russian leader, Stalin, spreading communism to other countries.

(a) According to **Source D**, what was agreed at Yalta ? **(3 marks)**

(b) Describe the main problems facing the Allied leaders when they met at Potsdam in May 1945 and how they solved them. **(6 marks)**

(c) How reliable is **Source E** to an historian writing about the Soviet expansion in Eastern Europe after World War Two? Use **Source E** and your own knowledge to answer the question. **(6 marks)**

(d) In the period 1945 to 1949, Germany was often at the centre of the Cold War. Explain why this was so. **(10 marks)**

NATO and the Warsaw Pact

The Marshall Plan was a great success and by 1950 the output of West European countries had increased by 25 per cent. The Truman Doctrine and the Marshall Plan were clear signs that the Americans had no intention of returning to the isolationism of 1919. Their action in defeating the Berlin Blockade reinforced this view and led to the formation of a military alliance in the West. In 1949 the North Atlantic Treaty Organisation (NATO) was formed, made up of the USA, Canada, Britain, France, Belgium, the Netherlands, Iceland, Luxembourg, Italy, Norway, Denmark and Portugal. Greece and Turkey joined in 1952 and West Germany in 1955. All members agreed to go to war if any one of them was attacked.

Stalin responded to the Truman Doctrine by strengthening his hold on Eastern Europe. All non-communists were driven from office and Cominform (Communist Information Bureau) helped all European communist parties, including those in France and Italy, to work and plan together. When the Czechs showed an interest in Marshall Aid, Stalin refused to allow them to apply for it, and an election, influenced by the Soviets, confirmed the Communists as the the only political party in Czechoslovakia. After NATO was formed, Stalin set up a trading union of communist countries under the USSR called Comecon (Council for Mutual Economic Aid). When Stalin died in 1953 there was a 'thaw' in the Cold War. However, when West Germany was allowed to join NATO in 1955 Soviet fears of a recovered Germany were revived. With Germany as part of a military alliance again, the Soviets and East Europeans signed the Warsaw Pact to form a defensive alliance controlled by the Soviet Union. This was seen by the West as the USSR's response to NATO.

Source A

A Soviet cartoon expressing the fear that Germany would emerge again to threaten the USSR.

Source B

A British cartoon, dated 2 March 1948, commenting on the spread of communism in Europe.

"WHO'S NEXT TO BE LIBERATED FROM FREEDOM, COMRADE?"

North Atlantic Treaty Organisation			
1949	1952	1955	1982
Belgium	Greece	West Germany	Spain
Britain	Turkey		
Canada			
Denmark			
France			
Iceland			
Italy			
Luxembourg			
Netherlands			
Norway			
Portugal			
USA			

Warsaw Pact
Albania (Expelled 1968)
Bulgaria
Czechoslavakia
East Germany
Hungary
Poland
Romania
USSR

Membership of NATO and the Warsaw Pact.

Soviet and US involvement in Korea

From 1910 to 1945 the Japanese had occupied Korea. Japan was defeated in the Second World War and had to pull out of Korea. Soviet forces in the north and American forces in the south replaced Japanese troops. At this point, both promised to leave once free elections had been held under the control of the United Nations, as had been agreed at the Yalta Conference. However, the Soviets changed their minds and when the UNO tried to organise free elections in the northern part of Korea, they would not allow UNO officials entry.

Instead, a communist satellite was established under Kim Il Sung in the North Korean capital, Pyongyang. Free elections were never held. In South Korea, elections were held and an anti-communist, military government was set up under Syngman Rhee, based in the South Korean capital of Seoul.

Korea is divided

It had proved impossible to unite the country. The setting up of separate governments after the 1948 elections encouraged the USA and Soviet Union to withdraw their troops. So Korea became permanently divided along the 38 °N parallel. It still remains divided today. Each side claimed to be the rightful government of all Korea. Frequent border clashes occurred along the demilitarised zone into 1950.

In 1949, all of China except Taiwan became communist. South Korea felt very isolated because communist North Korea, China and the Soviet Union surrounded it. The Americans were frightened of the spread of communism and the threat to Japan and other non-communist counties in the Far East. They believed in the so-called domino theory that, once one state became communist, others would also fall.

Stalin and the Chinese encouraged Kim Il Sung to attack South Korea. They saw a perfect opportunity to spread communist influence by taking over South Korea. They provided aid and military equipment, but the Soviets never involved themselves directly. In June 1950, North Korea attacked the South and the Korean War began.

The Korean War

North Korea was very successful at first. Most of South Korea fell, except the Pusan Pocket in the south-east. In desperation, South Korea asked the UNO for help. It had the power to support South Korea if all the permanent members of its Security Council – Britain, France, the USA, nationalist China (the West failed to recognise the communist government in mainland China) and the Soviet Union – agreed to do so. Normally the Soviet Union would have vetoed any attempts to send aid, but in 1950 it was boycotting UNO meetings in protest at the refusal to admit communist China. So the Security Council declared North Korea to be the aggressor and promised to send help to the South.

Sixteen nations, headed by the USA, took part immediately and later 32 countries participated. The commander-in-chief was the American war hero, General Douglas MacArthur. He organised a successful seaborne landing at Inchon that surprised the communists and forced them to retreat. North Korean resistance collapsed and UN troops advanced into North Korea and approached China.

Communist China feared for its security and warned UN troops not to approach the Yalu River. MacArthur disobeyed Truman's orders and did so. He wished to invade China and was prepared to use nuclear weapons. Truman dismissed him in April 1951 and appointed General Ridgeway as his replacement. Meanwhile, in November 1950, China sent 200,000 'volunteers' to help North Korea, and UN forces were pushed back to the 38 °N parallel.

The rest of the war was a stalemate in which neither side made gains and many lives were lost. Finally, both sides agreed on a cease-fire at Panmunjom in 1953. Stalin had died and the Soviets now had their own internal problems to deal with. They wanted the war to end as quickly as possible.

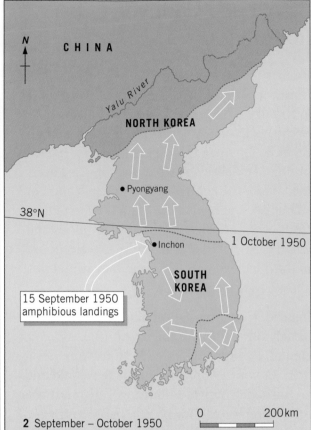

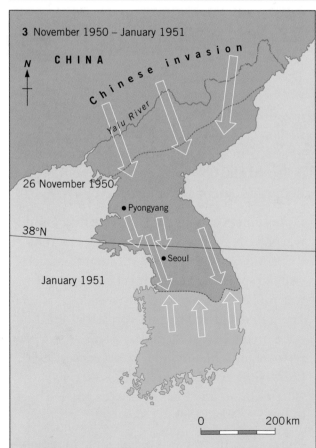

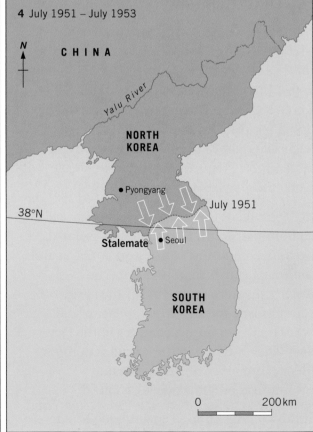

The Korean War, 1950–3.

The impact of the Korean War

During the Korean War, the Cold War had intensified and spread into new areas. It was no longer confined to Europe. Mistrust increased between the USA and the Soviet Union with the foundation of the South East Asian Treaty Organisation (SEATO) in 1954. SEATO was a copy of NATO, designed to contain communism in the Far East. Korea was devastated by the war – one in ten of the population was dead and the country remained divided – but the South had not fallen to communism.

From the point of view of the USA, a bid to break through the Truman Doctrine had been beaten off, and the USA turned its attention to other threatened areas in the Far East, particularly Vietnam. Korea was also a success for the UNO because it had shown itself capable of standing up to aggression and seemed to be much stronger than its predecessor, the League of Nations. However, the war also revealed that China was no longer weak and was prepared to stand up to the West.

Changing attitudes and policies in the 1950s

Khrushchev and co-existence

Stalin was the dictator of the Soviet Union from the late 1920s to 1953. His regime was cruel and repressive. Anyone who opposed him was arrested, and the secret police were active everywhere (see Chapter 4). The Soviet people greeted Stalin's death with relief. In 1955 he was succeeded by Nikita Khrushchev, who started to relax the Stalinist system.

In 1956 Khrushchev made a secret speech to the Communist Party at its 20th Party Congress. He used this to denounce Stalin as part of his bid for power. Stalin's statues came down, cities were renamed, the secret police became less active, Stalin's body was removed

from the Kremlin, and more consumer goods were produced. This whole process was called destalinisation. It proved to be very popular in the Soviet Union, and since the people of the Soviet Union seemed to be gaining more freedom, the policy was popular in the West too. The capitalist states particularly liked Khrushchev's change of policy towards the West. He wanted to replace the old policy of confrontation with a new policy of peaceful co-existence, recognising the Western powers' right to exist. This led to a reduction in Cold War tensions that became known as the 'thaw'.

Raised expectations in Eastern Europe

The satellite states of Eastern Europe also expected changes. Destalinisation within the Soviet Union encouraged them to demand concessions and to try to weaken Soviet influence. But they, like the West, had misunderstood Khrushchev's motives. Khrushchev could not grant widespread concessions in the satellite states because he feared that they could result in the end of communism in Eastern Europe and the destruction of the buffer against the West. He was not prepared to compromise the security of the Soviet Union. So when revolts against Soviet control took place in East Germany in 1953 and Poland and Hungary in 1956, they were ruthlessly suppressed by the Soviet Union. This led to a renewed deterioration in Cold War relationships and the end of the 'thaw'.

THINGS TO DO

1 Why did the UNO become involved in Korea?

2 What were the consequences of the Korean War?

Challenging the West

It soon became clear to the capitalist states that, despite co-existence, Khrushchev was determined to show that communism could compete with, and beat, the West. This was demonstrated in a number of differing areas:

- The Soviet Union set out to challenge the domination of the USA in sport. The Olympic games became particularly important.

- Khrushchev undertook high-profile visits across the globe to meet foreign leaders and offered aid to newly independent Third World states. In this way, he deliberately raised the political profile of the Soviet Union.

- The Soviet Union challenged the West's lead in nuclear weapons. It exploded its first atomic bomb in 1949, four years behind the Americans. It exploded its first hydrogen bomb less than a year after the Americans had done so. The nuclear race that developed clearly increased tensions and aggravated the Cold War situation.

- Khrushchev engaged in a space race with the USA in order to demonstrate technological superiority. The Soviets launched the first satellite, Sputnik, in 1957. In the same year they put a dog into space, and in 1961 they put the first man into orbit. They took an early lead in the space race (see page 61).

The Hungarian Rising, 1956

The Hungarians were inspired by the death of Stalin and by the emergence of Khrushchev. They believed that destalinisation and the 'thaw' had created a new atmosphere in which the country could undergo reform. The revolt in Poland in June 1956 had resulted in the Soviet Union granting concessions to the Poles, and this seemed to be confirmation that changes could be achieved. The Hungarians wanted an end to Soviet control in Hungary. This would lead to more political freedom and economic improvement through greater contact with the West. Some even hoped for the withdrawal of Soviet troops from Hungary.

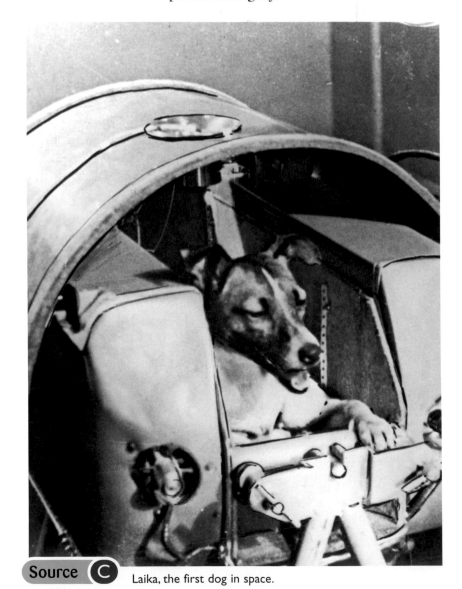

Source C

Laika, the first dog in space.

A photograph taken in Budapest in November 1956.

Reform in Hungary

Demonstrations and protests in the capital of Hungary, Budapest, led to the election of Imre Nagy as Prime Minister in October 1956. He had been Prime Minister from 1953 to 1955 and was known to be a moderniser. In the demonstrations, the Soviet Union was caught off guard by the strength of opposition, and retreated. However, its retreat was not a defeat but a tactical move to regroup and strengthen its forces. Khrushchev also hoped that the withdrawal would calm down a difficult situation.

The new Hungarian leadership began to implement a programme of reform. Government control of the press and radio was ended. Non-communists were allowed to participate in government and Nagy demanded the right for Hungary to leave the Warsaw Pact and to become neutral and independent. He also promised free democratic elections.

The Rising is crushed

These developments were completely unacceptable to Khrushchev. On 4 November 1956, the Soviets returned in strength and crushed the revolt. In the bitter fighting that followed, 30,000 Hungarians were killed and 200,000 fled to the West.

Nagy took refuge in the Yugoslavian embassy. He emerged later when promised safe passage, but was arrested and later executed. Protesters were imprisoned and the reform programme was reversed. A hard-line communist government was re-established in Hungary under János Kádár.

Source **E**

There is no stopping the wild onslaught of communism. Your turn will come, once we perish. Save our souls! Save our souls! We implore you to help us in the name of justice and freedom.

A broadcast to the West from Hungarian fighters on 4 November 1956.

The nuclear arms race, 1945-63

For four years after the war, the Americans were the only nuclear power and therefore 'contained' the USSR with little fear of response. But when the Soviets successfully tested an atom bomb in 1949 this changed. Nuclear weapons were far more destructive than any weapons ever known to man. Both East and West feared for the future. The Americans and Soviets embarked on developing better nuclear weapons and better ways of delivering them to their targets. The Americans tested the first hydrogen bomb (H-bomb) in 1952. This could destroy a city the size of Moscow. The following year the USSR tested its own H-bomb which could destroy any American city.

Until 1957 nuclear bombs would have been dropped from long-range aircraft. This changed when the USSR launched a satellite, Sputnik 1, into space using a rocket in 1957. These rockets could be fitted with nuclear warheads and launched at targets thousands of kilometres away. The Americans responded by developing their own rockets. Both countries were now engaged in a 'space race', which led to the development of Inter-Continental Ballistic Missiles (ICBMs). These were land-based strategic missiles stored in concrete silos in underground bases from which they could be launched.

The race moved on in 1960 when the Americans fired a new Polaris missile from a submarine. It was now possible to fire missiles with a range of over 1,600 kilometres (1,000 miles) from anywhere under the sea. The Soviets soon followed with their own nuclear submarines.

Both sides tried to locate ICBMs in friendly countries close to their enemy. The Americans based missiles in Turk on the border with the USSR, which explains why the USSR tried to install similar missiles in Cuba pointing at the USA. This created confrontation between the superpowers, with the world on the edge of nuclear war. Fortunately it ended in compromise, an improvement in relations between the USA and the USSR, and the signing of a Test Ban Treaty in 1963 (see page 69).

Nuclear deterrent

In the early 1960s the Americans were still ahead in the nuclear race. Even so the Soviets had enough nuclear weapons to inflict massive destruction on the USA, even if the Americans got the first strike in. This realisation made it unlikely the superpowers would use such weapons in war against one another. This in fact has been the argument in favour of keeping nuclear weapons. It is known as the nuclear deterrent.

THINGS TO DO

1 Why was the Hungarian Rising so easily put down in November 1956?

2 Why were 1949 and 1957 important years in the nuclear arms race?

NATO and the Warsaw Pact.

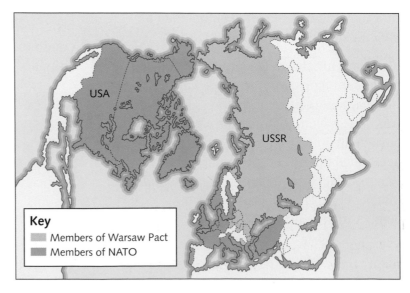

Key
Members of Warsaw Pact
Members of NATO

USA

USSR

Disarmament

Nuclear weapons made it hard for countries to disarm. From 1946 to 1962 over 800 international disarmament meetings failed to reach any agreement. In the 1950s the emphasis was on 'arms control', not complete disarmament. While the superpowers distrusted one another, there could be no agreement. The Soviets actually stopped nuclear testing in 1958. But the Berlin crisis of 1961 and renewed testing by the USSR made it more urgent to find an agreement on nuclear weapons and led to a meeting between President Kennedy and Khrushchev. They agreed a set of principles and the Geneva Disarmament Conference opened in March 1962. In October 1962 the Cuban missile crisis began (see page 66).

Date	Country	Event
4 October 1957	Soviet Union	Sputnik 1 first artificial Earth-orbiting satellite
3 November 1957	Soviet Union	Sputnik 2 first animal in space, a dog called Laika
31 January 1958	USA	First US satellite in space
12 September 1959	Soviet Union	Luna 2 hits the surface of the Moon
4 October 1959	Soviet Union	Luna 3 takes pictures of the far side of the Moon
12 April 1961	Soviet Union	First man, Yuri Gagarin, put into orbit in Vostock 1
5 May 1961	USA	Alan Shepherd becomes first American in space
20 February 1962	USA	Colonel John Glenn becomes the first American to orbit the Earth
16 June 1963	Soviet Union	Valentina Tereshkova becomes the first woman in space

Key events in the space race, 1957–63.

The beginnings of the space race, 1957–62

The launch of the satellite Sputnik in 1957 upset US pride and was the start of a race that was to continue well into the 1980s. The rocket that blasted Sputnik into space was a more immediate threat. A rocket powerful enough to do this could also carry a nuclear weapon to its target. Advances in space technology therefore encouraged the development of nuclear missiles, particularly inter-continental ballistic missiles (ICBMs), by both sides. By 1960, each had enough nuclear missiles to destroy the Earth. This balance of terror stabilised the Cold War because both superpowers realised that a nuclear war would be mutually destructive. The policy of peaceful co-existence came to be increasingly important in the politics of the Cold War.

At the end of the 1950s, Khrushchev could argue that the Soviet lead in space proved that communism could outdo capitalism. However, the vast amount of money spent on the space race would later lead to superpower scientific co-operation in space. Money spent on both the space race and the arms race would also help to put so much strain on the Soviet economy that the country faced bankruptcy in the 1980s.

Source F

The Sputniks prove that communism has won the competition between the communist and the capitalist countries. The economy, science, culture and the creative genius of people in all spheres of life develop better and faster under communism.

Khrushchev comments on the successes of communism.

THINGS TO DO

1 Why did the Soviet Union take part in the space race against the USA?

2 'Source F is of no use because it is just exaggerated opinion.' Do you agree?

Crises in the early 1960s and their causes and results

The U2 crisis

Although the West had hoped that the succession of Khrushchev to power in the Soviet Union might lead to better relations with the West, events in Hungary in 1956 had shown that the Cold War was still very much in operation. In 1960 that Cold War intensified.

The year had begun with great hope. A summit meeting of the 'Big Four', Eisenhower of the USA, Khrushchev of the Soviet Union, De Gaulle of France and Macmillan of Britain, had been arranged for Paris in May. Perhaps the time had come for East and West to patch up their differences and begin a new period of friendly relations. Yet before the leaders even arrived in Paris, those hopes had been dashed.

The 'Spy in the Sky'

By the 1950s the Americans had developed a lightweight spy plane that could fly at 75,000 feet. This meant that even if it was picked up on Soviet radar it was too high for Soviet planes to intercept. Hi-tech cameras meant that even at that height it could take pictures of military sites in the Soviet Union.

On 1 May 1960, just two days before the summit conference, a U2 plane, piloted by Gary Powers, took off from a US base in Peshawar, Pakistan. The flight went well and Powers was able to take photographs deep inside the Soviet Union. Then came disaster. As Powers crossed the Ural mountains near the Soviet town of Sverdlovsk, his plane was hit by a Soviet SAM-2 missile. Powers ejected from the plane and parachuted to the ground, where he was captured by the Soviet forces. The U2 crashed near Sverdlovsk and was recovered by Soviet scientists for study.

Source **G** — A Soviet cartoon, called 'The Art of Camouflage', comments on the USA's attitude to peace.

Source **H**

Instructions to Mr Powers and other pilots on similar missions is to feel free to tell the full truth about their mission. We think this is a firmly American way of behaviour – we can leave the bald-faced lying to the Soviets. We have to do this work, but we can be manly about it.

An extract from the **Washington** Daily News *after Gary Powers' release from the Soviet Union.*

The intended route of Powers' U2.

The end of hopes for peace

Khrushchev accused the USA of being 'unable to call a halt to their war effort', but offered to attend the summit meeting as long as the Americans apologised. Eisenhower refused to apologise and said that it was the responsibility of the USA to protect itself from the possibility of a surprise attack. The U2 flights were an important part of US defence strategy. Not surprisingly, Khrushchev was not satisfied with this answer and stormed out of the summit meeting. He then cancelled an invitation for Eisenhower to visit the Soviet Union. The Cold War had just got colder.

Postscript: Gary Powers

Powers was tried in Moscow on charges of spying. He was found guilty and sentenced to ten years imprisonment. After serving seventeen months of his sentence he was sent back to the USA in return for the release of a top Soviet spy from a US prison.

The American response

As soon as the Americans discovered that the spy plane had been shot down, they began an elaborate campaign to cover up what had happened. If they admitted to spying on the Soviet Union, the summit talks would be ruined. At first the Americans announced that a U2 research plane studying weather conditions at high altitude had disappeared somewhere over Turkey.

What the Americans did not know was that the Soviet Union had captured Powers alive and that he had admitted to spying. They also had the remains of the U2 with thousands of photographs. The Americans had been caught spying and there seemed no way it could be denied. On 7 May Khrushchev announced that he had both Powers and the U2. He demanded a full apology from the USA.

Source ❶ A cartoon from a British newspaper in 1960.

The Berlin Wall

Although Khrushchev declared his policy to be 'peaceful co-existence' with the West, it did not stop him challenging the Western presence in Berlin. Berlin was a huge embarrassment to the USSR. American economic aid helped transform the city into a showpiece of capitalism. While people in the west of the city enjoyed the benefits of recovery, such as being able to buy luxury goods, those in East Berlin worked long hours and suffered from food shortages. Eventually they rebelled in 1953, but were suppressed by the army.

Even more embarrassing for the Soviets was the defection of so many East Berliners to West Berlin. Over two million did so up to 1961. It was easy to escape as there was no barbed wire, minefields and watch towers between the different parts of the city, as there was on the border between East and West Germany. In 1961 the Soviets again declared that the West should give up Berlin. President Kennedy refused. This time Khrushchev decided to make it far more difficult for East Berliners to travel to and from West Berlin to work and shop.

On 13 August 1961 the East Germans erected a border of machine guns and barbed wire between East and West Berlin. President Kennedy protested, but was unwilling to risk war over Berlin. Three days later work started on building a 45-kilometre concrete wall to replace the barbed wire. The gap in the frontier between East and West was now filled.

Source **J** The Berlin Wall.

The Soviets made it clear that anyone trying to cross the Wall would be shot. Even so, many were desperate enough to try. In the first year of the Wall 41 East Berliners were shot trying to cross. The Wall separated families and friends. East Berliners also saw it as a sign of their inferiority. But it did achieve one thing: it cut down the number of defectors from East to West Berlin.

Propaganda

Relations between the superpowers, already strained by the U2 spying incident, got much worse. The Americans used the Berlin Wall for propaganda purposes, asking why, if communism was such an ideal system, it was necessary to build a barrier to cage people in. In 1963, President Kennedy visited West Berlin. The people turned out to hear him and applauded him warmly when, in his speech to them, he said, 'Ich bin ein Berliner' (I am a Berliner). He was using the opportunity to show the USA's commitment to the people of West Berlin by suggesting that the USA would never desert the city. This angered the communists, who saw the visit as a deliberate attempt to cause trouble.

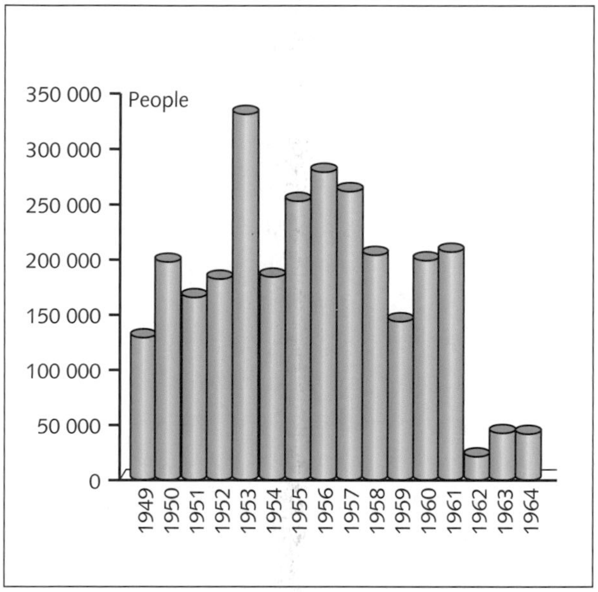

This graph shows the number of people who escaped from East Germany to West Germany, 1949-64.

Source K

In no part of the world are so many spies of foreign states to be found as in West Berlin. Nowhere else can they act with such freedom. These spies are smuggling agents into East Germany, causing sabotage and riot.

The view of the East German government, 1961.

Source L

Democracy may not be perfect but we never had to put up walls to keep our people in.

The view of J. F. Kennedy in 1962.

THINGS TO DO

1 Why do you think the Americans sent U2 planes across Soviet air space?

2 Why did the Americans feel the need to pretend that Powers' plane was lost whilst researching weather conditions?

3 What do you think the cartoonists were trying to say in **Sources G** and **I**?

4 What does **Source H** tell us about attitudes in the USA towards the Cold War in the 1960s?

5 Why was the Berlin Wall built?

6 Was it successful?

7 Why did J. F. Kennedy say 'I am a Berliner' in his speech of 1963 when in fact he was American?

1.9 How close to war did the world come over Cuba in 1962?

Communist rule in Cuba

The dictator Batista ruled Cuba from 1933. Cuba was a poor country largely controlled by American big business. Its main crop, sugar cane, was bought by the Americans. Batista's cruel rule was threatened in the 1950s by guerrillas led by Fidel Castro. In spite of the support he received from the USA, Batista was defeated in 1959 and Castro became ruler of Cuba. The Americans did not like Castro as they believed he was a Marxist, so they refused to trade with Cuba. Castro took over the possession of all land from the Americans and made an alliance with the USSR who promised to buy Cuba's sugar. The USA now had a neighbour allied to her greatest rival.

The Bay of Pigs, 1961

When John F. Kennedy became President in January 1961 he was convinced by the Central Intelligence Agency (CIA), the American secret service, that Castro could be overthrown in an attack by supporters of Batista. The rebels, with American support, landed at the Bay of Pigs in Cuba in April 1961. The attack was a total disaster. The rebels received no support when they landed and were defeated in a few days. Kennedy was severely embarrassed, realising he had been wrongly advised. Castro was now convinced that the USA was an enemy and looked even more to the USSR for support. In December 1961 Castro publicly declared himself a Marxist, convincing the Americans that Cuba had become a Soviet satellite.

Cuba now had to depend on the Soviet Union for protection. In June 1962 huge shipments of Soviet arms were received by Castro. The first of these were classified as defensive weapons, as they were aircraft, patrol boats and ground-to-air missiles. In September however medium-range offensive nuclear missiles and bombers had arrived in Cuba. The Americans were aware of these, but the Soviets insisted they were defensive. On 14 October 1962 U2 spy planes photographed Soviet missiles in place on launch pads in Cuba. This proved the Russians had lied. The missiles had a range of around 4000 kilometres (2500 miles). This put most large American cities within their range of attack in minutes. More ships carrying missiles were reported to be on the way from the USSR to Cuba. What was the American President to do?

The Cuban missile crisis

Kennedy had suffered two failures in his dealings with the Soviets. He gave the go-ahead for the Bay of Pigs invasion disaster and was helpless to stop the Soviets building the Berlin Wall. Some historians think Khrushchev saw this as a sign of weakness and was trying to establish Soviet supremacy over the Americans. Placing missiles in Cuba was a test of how strong Kennedy was and how far he was prepared to go. Certainly Cuba was an ideal base for the USSR and would counteract the

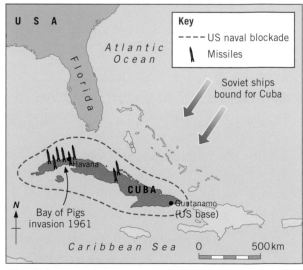

The Cuban missile crisis.

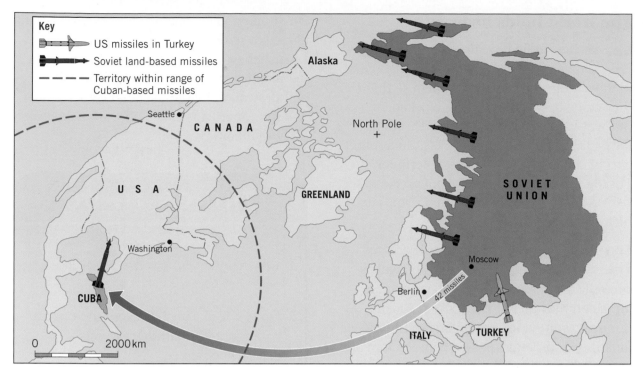

The threat from nuclear missiles based on Cuba.

American bases in NATO countries, especially Turkey, which was on the southern border of the Soviet Union. This caused the Soviets great anxiety in 1962 as they had not yet developed missiles that could be fired from submarines. Another argument is that Khrushchev was simply helping Cuba defend itself from a possible attack from the USA.

Kennedy gathered around him a group of advisers who were in almost constant touch during the 13 days the crisis lasted. They proposed seven alternative policies to the President for dealing with the crisis. These were:

1 To do nothing and allow the USSR to keep its bases on Cuba.

2 Make a diplomatic protest to the Soviets.

3 To discuss the missiles directly with Castro.

4 To place a naval blockade around Cuba.

5 To launch an airstrike on Cuba with non-nuclear weapons.

6 To invade Cuba and seize the bases.

7 To launch a nuclear attack on Cuba.

The first two were ruled out because it would appear as if the USA was prepared to back down whenever Khrushchev threatened. As for the third, Castro was unlikely to negotiate with the Americans after the Bay of Pigs. The last three would cost too many lives and risk nuclear war. This left option 4. On 22 October Kennedy announced on television that he was placing a 500 mile naval blockade around Cuba to prevent Soviet missiles reaching the island. This would be enforced by the US navy. He also planned to carry out options 5 and 6 if needed, but hoped the blockade would succeed. On 24 October the first Soviet ships carrying missiles encountered American ships blockading Cuba. How would Khrushchev respond?

Source A

Even when people were enjoying themselves having a drink in the student bar, the conversation turned to Cuba. What would happen? Would it mean the end of the world? Everyone felt so helpless. There was nothing you could do to prevent destruction except pray. Special prayers were said in churches. The end of the crisis was greeted with a tremendous feeling of relief.

Memories of a 19-year-old British university student in 1962.

The world holds its breath

Khrushchev could have done several things. He could have ordered his ships to sail on and send warships to accompany them so that they could defy the American blockade. But war would have broken out. He could have taken action against the USA in another part of the world, such as West Berlin or Turkey. But Khrushchev was not prepared to risk nuclear war, so he ordered his ships to turn back.

This did not end the Cuban missile crisis. There were still missile sites in Cuba which could be made ready quickly to launch an attack on the cities of the USA. President Kennedy wanted to keep talking to the Soviets and a series of letters passed between him and Khrushchev during this part of the crisis. The Americans insisted that the Soviets dismantle the missile sites in Cuba. Khrushchev sent two letters to Kennedy which he received on 26 and 27 October. In the first Russia offered to remove missile sites if Kennedy called off the blockade and promised not to invade Cuba. The second letter took things further: Khrushchev would remove the missiles from Cuba only if the Americans withdrew their missiles from Turkey, on the border of Russia.

Kennedy was determined not to give in on this issue. He was not prepared to do a deal with Khrushchev on the basis of the missiles in Turkey. While this was going on, several incidents occurred which could have sparked off a war: an American U2 plane was shot down over Cuba and a Soviet ship was boarded and inspected by the US navy – it was found to be carrying nuclear bomb parts. Some of Kennedy's advisers recommended an attack on Cuba, but the President held firm against it. He ignored Khrushchev's second letter and replied to the first, telling the Soviet leader that he accepted the terms in the letter of 26 October and giving him until 29 October to reply. If Khrushchev did not accept, American forces would invade Cuba.

On Sunday 28 October the Soviet government agreed to remove its missiles from Cuba. Khrushchev made no mention of American missiles in Turkey. The crisis was over. The withdrawal of missiles began on 3 November and the Americans called off the blockade on 20 November.

THINGS TO DO

1 Why did the USA oppose Soviet missiles on Cuba?

2 Do you think Kennedy chose the correct option of the seven alternatives? Explain your answer.

3 What does **Source A** tell us about feelings in Britain about the Cuban crisis?

4 Why did Kennedy ignore Khrushchev's second letter (**Source B**)?

5 Who was victorious in the Cuban crisis? Give reasons for your answer.

6 Why does **Source C** ignore the letter of 27 October? Is **Source C** reliable as evidence about the Cuban crisis?

7 Is **Source D** an accurate interpretation of the Cuban crisis? Explain your answer.

Source B

You are worried about Cuba because it is 90 miles from America, but Turkey is next to us. We agree to remove from Cuba those means which you find offensive. The United States will for its part remove its missiles from Turkey.

Extract from Khrushchev's letter of 27 October 1962.

Results of the crisis

The Cuban missile crisis was the nearest that the world had ever been to nuclear war. The two leaders realised that the responsibility for the future of the world lay with them. Steps had to be taken to improve relations between East and West.

In August 1963 a Test Ban Treaty was signed in Moscow. This banned the testing of nuclear weapons in the air or under water. A few months before, in June, a 'hot line' direct phone link between Washington and Moscow had been set up. This would enable the two leaders to discuss matters quickly and avoid the build-up of crises. On 17 October, a UN resolution banned the placing of nuclear weapons in outer space. All these points had been discussed at the Disarmament Conference which had begun in Geneva in March 1962. The conference ended with the first agreements on the control of nuclear weapons in the spirit of greater co-operation which developed after Cuba.

Both Kennedy and Khrushchev claimed to have won a victory over Cuba. Kennedy had stood up to the Soviet Union and forced them to back down. His prestige in the USA and the West increased enormously. Khrushchev posed as the peacemaker. The Secretary General of the United Nations, U Thant, had appealed to both leaders to do all they could to avoid nuclear war.

Khrushchev claimed that his action in withdrawing from Cuba was in response to U Thant's appeal. His action had secured peace for the world. He could also claim a victory in that the USA had promised not to invade Cuba, which remained a useful friend for the Soviets because of its proximity to the USA. But it was also true that Khrushchev's demand for the withdrawal of American missiles in Turkey had been unsuccessful.

Source C

We agreed to remove our missiles and bombers on condition that the President promised that there would be no invasion of Cuba by the forces of the United States or anybody else. Finally Kennedy gave in and agreed to give us such an assurance. It was a great victory for us, a spectacular success without having to fire a single shot.

*From **Khrushchev Remembers** published in 1971.*

Source D

British cartoon showing Kennedy and Khrushchev struggling over the Cuban crisis with nuclear war only the press of a button away.

SUMMARY

1945	USA uses the atom bomb.
1949	USSR tests the atom bomb.
1950	Korean War begins.
1952	USA tests the H-Bomb.
1953	USSR tests the H-Bomb. Death of Stalin.
1955	Geneva Summit.
1956	Hungarian Rising.
1957	USSR launches Sputnik I.
1960	U2 Incident – failure of Paris Summit.
1961	Berlin Wall. Bay of Pigs.
1962	Cuban crisis.
1963	Test Ban Treaty.

Exam-style assessment – OPTION W

In the examination, if you choose Option W, you must answer two of the three questions in the section.

Question 1: The Treaty of Versailles

Study **Sources A** and **B** and then answer the following questions.

Source A: Comment on the Treaty of Versailles

Severe as the Treaty seemed to many Germans, it should be remembered that Germany might easily have fared much worse. If Clemenceau had had his way, the Rhineland would have become an independent state, the Saar would have been annexed to France and Danzig would have become a part of Poland.

From *A History of Germany* by W Carr, a British historian, published in 1972

Source B: Peace and Future Cannon Fodder

The Tiger: *"Curious! I seem to hear a child weeping!"*

A cartoon published in Britain in 1920.

(a) According to **Source A**, why should Germany have been satisfied with the Treaty of Versailles? **(3 marks)**

(b) The cartoon in **Source B** shows Clemenceau, Lloyd George and Woodrow Wilson, who all attended the Paris Peace Conference in 1919. What were their aims at that conference? **(6 marks)**

(c) How accurate is the view of events shown in the cartoon in **Source B**? Use **Source B** and your own knowledge to answer the question. **(6 marks)**

(d) Why did many people in Germany hate the Treaty of Versailles? **(10 marks)**

Question 2: The policy of appeasement

Study **Sources C** and **D** and then answer the following questions.

Source C: Chamberlain and appeasement

Neville Chamberlain followed a policy of appeasement because he believed that Hitler would be satisfied if all German-speaking people were governed by Germany. He considered that the best way to avoid war was to settle Hitler's legitimate demands. The memory of the death of seven million young men in World War One greatly influenced Chamberlain who commented that in war 'there are no winners, but all are losers'. Britain was afraid of the growth of the communist USSR and saw a strong Germany as a useful buffer against this danger. In any case, Chamberlain's military advisers urged him to play for time as rearmament had only just begun.

From a British historian writing in 1996

Source D: Sudeten Germans greet German troops

A private photograph taken in the Sudetenland in October 1938.

(a) According to **Source C**, why did Britain try to appease Hitler?　　　**(3 marks)**

(b) Describe how Hitler took over the Sudetenland in Czechoslovakia in 1938.　　　**(6 marks)**

(c) How useful is **Source D** to an historian writing about the German entry into the Sudetenland in October 1938? Use **Source D** and your own knowledge to answer the question.　　　**(6 marks)**

(d) Was the policy of appeasement the most important reason for the outbreak of the Second World War? Explain your answer.　　　**(10 marks)**

Question 3: The Cold War 1950–62

Study **Sources E** and **F** and then answer the following questions.

Source E: The effect of Khrushchev's speech in 1956

In 1956 the new Soviet Premier, Khrushchev, attacked Stalin's leadership of the USSR. This speech gave people in the satellite states of the USSR new hope. They wanted a higher standard of living, less direction from Soviet Russia in economic life and more political freedom from the Soviets. Each satellite state wanted to develop a new communist state of its own.

From *The Great Power Conflict after 1945* by P Fisher,
a British textbook published in 1985

Source F: Khrushchev's views on Soviet communism and the West in 1958

The launching of the Soviet sputniks first of all shows that a serious change has occurred in the balance of forces between communist and capitalist countries, in favour of the communist nations.

Extract from a speech by Khrushchev made in 1958

(a) According to **Source E**, what were the aims of Soviet Russia's satellite states after 1956?　　　**(3 marks)**

(b) Describe how Hungary tried to achieve these aims in 1956.　　　**(6 marks)**

(c) How accurate is Khrushchev's view of the balance of power between the USSR and USA stated in **Source F**? Use **Source F** and your own knowledge to answer the question.　　　**(6 marks)**

(d) Why did the USA oppose the USSR in Korea in 1950 and in Cuba in 1962?　　　**(10 marks)**

In the later 1960s there were hints of a thaw in the Cold War. The Cuban missile crisis had frightened all nations. However, events in Czechoslovakia in 1968 suggested that the Cold War was just as intense in the late 1960s as it had been in 1962.

Czechoslovakia, 1968

Czechoslovakia had been a Soviet satellite since 1948, with its government taking orders from Moscow. However, the Czech people felt bitter about the loss of their political and economic independence. They remembered that Czechoslovakia had been a democracy in the period before the Second World War. They resented the fact that Czech industry produced very few consumer goods and seemed to be run entirely for the benefit of the Soviet Union.

Source **A**   Alexander Dubcek.

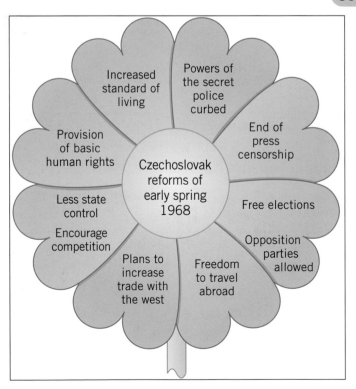

Czechoslovak reforms of early spring 1968

- Increased standard of living
- Powers of the secret police curbed
- End of press censorship
- Free elections
- Opposition parties allowed
- Freedom to travel abroad
- Plans to increase trade with the west
- Encourage competition
- Less state control
- Provision of basic human rights

The Prague Spring.

Dubcek and the Prague Spring

Protests began to grow in the 1960s and the demand for changes brought someone new to power. In January 1968, Alexander Dubcek took over as the new Czech leader. Although he led the Communist Party, he saw a need for some limited democratic reforms and began to introduce changes. These changes were known as the 'Prague Spring' because they seemed to reveal a thawing of the old harsh system of communism. Dubcek promised the people 'socialism with a human face'. He hoped to increase people's standard of living and make the political system more democratic. He allowed competition between different factories. This was unheard of in the communist world. He wanted to increase trade with the West and to borrow funds from the USA to restructure and rebuild Czech industry. He proposed to abolish censorship and allow free travel abroad. He did, however, try to reassure Brezhnev, the Soviet leader, that his changes would not threaten the security of the Soviet Union, and he promised that Czechoslovakia would not leave the Warsaw Pact.

The Soviet response

Brezhnev remained unconvinced by Dubcek's reassurance. To allow reform in Czechoslovakia would weaken communism and encourage the growth of capitalism and increased contact with the West. He felt that if these changes continued they would also be demanded elsewhere in Eastern Europe. The Iron Curtain might well disappear and the Warsaw Pact might collapse. The very existence of the Soviet Bloc would be threatened and, if Soviet influence were removed from eastern Europe, the security of the Soviet Union would be undermined.

Dubcek's reform programme was highly popular in Czechoslovakia because it offered the possibility of free, democratic government, human rights and an improved standard of living. However, the other Warsaw Pact countries disapproved and asked Dubcek to stop. They were concerned that the dominant position of the Communist Party was being weakened, and this could undermine Soviet-style socialism in Eastern Europe and turn Czechoslovakia against its communist neighbours. The whole system of 'people's democracies' could be threatened.

Dubcek reacted by promising even more changes, particularly the setting up of opposition parties and the holding of free elections. Faced by what they saw as defiance, the neighbouring Soviet satellites and the Soviet Union decided to use force. On 20 August 1968, 500,000 troops from the Warsaw Pact countries invaded Czechoslovakia.

Source **B**

The effects of the change in leadership in January were felt almost within days. Books that had been held up for months or years were suddenly freed for publication. Banned films that had been gathering dust were distributed.

The Times, *23 February 1968.*

Source **C**   A drawing on a wall in a Prague street in 1968.

In Hungary in 1956, the Soviet Union had sent in troops to prevent a similar move away from communism, and the people had actively resisted this intervention with considerable loss of life (see pages 58–9). As a result the Czechs did not resist in the same way. They wanted to avoid the bloodshed of Budapest. At the same time they were clearly outnumbered by the military might of the invading forces, and the Czech army could not act independently because many Soviet officers occupied important positions within it. Yet although there was no armed resistance, there was passive resistance from the population. This was largely non-violent in nature and took the form of demonstrations, sit-ins and peaceful protest.

Organised violent protest against the Soviet troops was discouraged. However, violent acts did occur. Soviet tanks were attacked with home-made petrol bombs called molotov cocktails, and one student, Jan Palach, set himself alight in Prague in January 1969 as a protest against the Soviet occupation of his country. Secret radio and TV stations kept the outside world informed of events until they were discovered and silenced.

Modern World History for AQA

Source D

Youths with flaming rags and newspapers set fire to Russian tanks encircling the Prague radio building. Others threw wooden crates, rubbish bins and mattresses at the occupying forces who had moved swiftly into the city. Snipers kept up fire much of the day. Scores of people were injured and several killed when the Russians answered back and when munitions lorries exploded.
 I saw four young Czechs killed, minutes after a machine gun from a Russian tank had opened fire upon their vehicle.

The Times, *22 August 1968.*

Source E   Czech youths attacking a Soviet tank on the streets of Prague in August 1968.

The Brezhnev Doctrine

Eventually, the Soviets forces crushed all resistance in Czechoslovakia. Many supporters of Dubcek were imprisoned. He was taken to Moscow and made to abandon his reform programme. At first, he was sent abroad as ambassador to Turkey. Later he was forced to resign this post and was expelled from the Communist Party.

The new leader who replaced Dubcek, Gustav Husak, returned to the old ways. The reforms of the Prague Spring were reversed. The Soviet grip on Czechoslovakia was once again secure. Brezhnev set out Soviet policy in what became known as the Brezhnev Doctrine. He stressed that a threat to one socialist country was a threat to all. He indicated that force would be used whenever necessary to keep the satellite states firmly under Soviet influence. He was determined that there would be no repeat performance of the Prague Spring.

Source F

> Go to your places of work. Carry out passive resistance. Do not resist. We are incapable of defending these frontiers.
>
> ***Radio Prague, 21 August 1968.***

Source G

> When forces that are hostile to socialism try to turn the development of some socialist country towards capitalism, the suppression of these counter-revolutionary forces becomes not only a problem of the country concerned, but a common problem and concern of all socialist countries.
>
> ***The Brezhnev Doctrine, August 1968***

East–West relations

The invasion of Czechoslovakia did nothing to help improve East–West relations. Western states had welcomed Dubcek's relaxation of communism in Czechoslovakia. The Soviet invasion of Czechoslovakia showed the West that the Soviet Union would not allow reform, or permit any opposition of which it disapproved. East–West relations remained very frosty. The West had watched the invasion with horror, but it was not prepared to intervene and so risk the outbreak of a war. In September 1938, Western countries had left Czechoslovakia to its fate to avoid war. They did so again in August 1968.

For 20 years, Alexander Dubcek worked in a lowly position in the Forestry Department, but during the anti-communist revolutions of late 1989 (see pages 88–9), he was able to appear in public once more. He spoke of the need for reform and received warm and enthusiastic praise from the Czechoslovak people. He was able to see many of his policies of 1968 come to fruition at last.

THINGS TO DO

1 Explain the meaning of the following terms:
   (a) Prague Spring
   (b) molotov cocktail
   (c) passive resistance.

2 Why did the Warsaw Pact disapprove of Alexander Dubcek's reforms?

3 What point was the person who drew **Source C** trying to make?

4 'The new leaders of Czechoslovakia returned to the old ways after 1968.' What does this mean?

Détente

In the late 1960s and through most of the 1970s, the word 'détente' was used to mean a relaxing of tension between East and West. The USA and the Soviet Union became less hostile towards each other. People talked of a thaw in the Cold War. It was really an extension of Khrushchev's policy of peaceful co-existence (see page 57).

Source

In the Cold War, everything moved on the level of a cheap western. You have an enemy who is the source of all evil. The policy of détente is more difficult to grasp. You have to be able to see the possibility and desirability of co-existence and co-operation between nations that are vastly different in their social systems and political values. You have to realise that despite all differences and difficulties, they still might have overwhelming mutual interests.

Georgi Arbatov, a member of the Soviet Central Committee, looking back in 1983 at the period of détente.

Reasons for Détente

The Cuban missile crisis of 1962 (pages 66–9) had shown how dangerous the Cold War was. Attempts to improve relations between the superpowers had started in the 1960s. But relations had remained difficult because of continuing fears and suspicions, both generally and over specific issues. For example, during the 1960s the USA had become increasingly involved in Vietnam.

Then events in Czechoslovakia in 1968 had seemed to put an end to all hope of better relations. However, both the USA and the Soviet Union had come to accept each other's areas of influence in the world, and both felt the need to improve relations with their 'enemies' for a variety of reasons.

Economic problems for the USA and the USSR over inflation

By the early 1970s there was rising inflation in the USA. This, together with huge expenditure on the war in Vietnam, was crippling the US economy. The Soviet Union had low living standards and poor industrial efficiency, and needed to trade more with the West.

Weapons

Both sides were spending vast sums of money on defence. In the case of the Soviet Union it was 20 per cent of total spending by the government. Both sides had stockpiles of weapons with a capacity to destroy the earth many times over.

Oil

Both the USA and the Soviet Union were worried about conflict over the Middle East. Oil supplies from that area were vital for both countries, and the Suez Canal was important for sea routes. Communist and non-communist countries had become involved in the conflict between Arabs and Israelis.

Contacts with China

Both the USA and the Soviet Union were worried about the growing power of China. Although China and the Soviet Union were co-operating over Vietnam, they were quarrelling over other issues. The USA, on the other hand, was afraid of the possibility of the two communist giants, China and the Soviet Union, reaching agreements that threatened the USA.

Initiatives of President Nixon

In the USA, President Nixon and his Secretary of State, Henry Kissinger, were keen to establish better working relations with Moscow (and also Peking (Beijing)). In the Soviet Union, President Brezhnev was keen to extend Khrushchev's policy of peaceful co-existence. He wanted to persuade the West to accept Soviet control in Eastern Europe. He also wanted to increase the Soviet Union's trade with the West in order to improve Soviet living standards.

Therefore, throughout the late 1960s and 1970s, US and Soviet leaders tried hard to reduce tension.

Consequences of Vietnam War

North Vietnam was Communist, and Americans feared the spread of Communism to South Vietnam. Although South Vietnam had a corrupt and harsh government, the USA backed it because it was anti-Communist. Firstly, American advisers were sent in to help the South Vietnam armed forces. Before many Americans were aware of what was developing substantial numbers of US troops were stationed in Vietnam.

After the death of President Kennedy in 1963, America's involvement in Vietnam greatly increased, so that by the end of 1965, 180,000 US soldiers were fighting in Vietnam. By 1969 the figure was half a million. Communist countries such as the USSR and China were obviously greatly suspicious of American motives. Even so, from the American point of view the war was becoming increasingly disastrous. Many of the South Vietnamese supported Communism and hated the American invaders, who had brought death and destruction to their land.

Many Americans wanted the USA to withdraw from Vietnam. Students held anti-war demonstrations at universities. One of the worst incidents took place at Kent State University in Ohio in May 1970. A peaceful student demonstration turned into violence when the National Guard was sent in to disperse the students. Four students were killed and others injured. Such incidents demonstrated the depth of feeling against the war, and showed the deep divisions that had been created within American society.

America's reputation in the world was effectively weakened.

Source **I** A US anti-war poster from the Vietnam War.

Source **J** This cartoon was published in a British newspaper in 1976. It shows Kissinger of the USA on the left and Brezhnev of the Soviet Union on the right.

détente is... ...the exchange of sweet nothings

détente is... ... covering up his treaty violations.

détente is... ...knowing when to give something for nothing

During the 1960s, there had already been agreements between the Soviet Union, the USA and Britain over nuclear weapons. For example, the Test Ban Treaty of 1963 had banned nuclear tests in the atmosphere, in outer space and under water. Then, in 1968, the same countries had signed the Nuclear Non-Proliferation Treaty with the aim of stopping the spread of nuclear weapons. When Richard Nixon became US President in 1969, both he and President Brezhnev of the Soviet Union began talking about ways in which to slow down the arms race.

SALT 1 (1972)

The Strategic Arms Limitation Talks (SALT) started in 1969 and led to the SALT 1 agreement in 1972. This agreement, which ran for five years, limited the number of inter-continental ballistic missiles (ICBMs) and anti-ballistic missiles (ABMs) on both sides. Each side was allowed to use spy satellites to check that the other was not breaking the agreed limits. The signing of the agreement in Moscow was seen as a huge achievement at the time. However, it did not reduce existing stocks of weapons.

Helsinki Agreement (1975)

In August 1975, at Helsinki in Finland, 35 countries, including the USA and the Soviet Union, signed the Helsinki Agreement. This marked the high point of détente.

- The West recognised the frontiers of Eastern Europe and Soviet influence in that area.

- West Germany officially recognised East Germany.

- The Soviets agreed to buy US grain and to export oil to the West.

- All countries agreed to improve human rights – freedom of speech, of religion and of movement.

Source **A** A cartoon about the reasons for the SALT talks. It was published in the USA in 1970.

Presidents Nixon and Brezhnev meeting in 1974.

the Soviet Union since F. D. Roosevelt went to the wartime conference at Yalta. In return, Brezhnev visited Washington in 1974.

Relations between the USA and the Soviet Union were helped by events in Germany. The Chancellor of West Germany, Willy Brandt, worked hard to form closer ties with communist East Germany, in spite of the Berlin Wall. In 1972 agreements were signed between East and West Germany recognising each other's frontiers and developing trade links. This removed one of the areas of tension for the leaders of the superpowers. It also helped the USA and the Soviet Union to develop trade links. For example, the USA sold its surplus wheat cheaply to the Soviet Union.

All this pleased the Soviet Union. It had gained definite statements from the West about Soviet boundaries and spheres of influence. In return the Soviet Union had made promises about human rights issues.

In fact, abuses of human rights continued in the Soviet Union, and President Carter of the USA complained about this in a follow-up conference at Belgrade in 1977. Within the Soviet Union itself, leading opponents of the communist government criticised travel restrictions and prison conditions. These dissidents (those who disagreed with the government) included the scientist Andrei Sakharov, who wanted a worldwide ban on nuclear weapons, an end to the Cold War and the introduction of democracy in the Soviet Union. He was eventually put under house arrest by the Soviet government.

Other contacts between the superpowers in the 1970s

In the 1970s there were many aspects to détente – political, cultural, sporting, economic and scientific. The leaders of the USA and the Soviet Union began to meet each other. For example, in 1972 President Nixon visited Moscow, the first US President to go to

At the same time, relations between the USA and communist China improved. In 1971 the USA agreed that communist China should be allowed to join the United Nations. (Previously the USA had insisted that the Chinese people of the island of Taiwan should have the Chinese seat in the United Nations, to avoid another large communist country being there.) The US table tennis team visited and played matches in Peking (now Beijing). This 'ping pong diplomacy' went on side by side with meetings between government officials. In 1972 President Nixon visited Peking and met the elderly Chinese leader, Mao Zedong. Meanwhile, relations between the Soviet Union and China remained poor, mostly because of border conflicts and suspicion of each other, and this helped the USA during the period of détente.

Stars and Stripes Flies Over the Kremlin

Mr Nixon began his visit to the Soviet Union today, becoming the first American President to visit Moscow.

The Times, 23 March 1972.

There was also co-operation in space. In July 1975 three US astronauts and two Soviet cosmonauts docked their Apollo and Soyuz spacecraft together in orbit round the world. It was a very visible sign of détente.

The failings of Détente in the later 1970s

The mid-1970s marked the high point of détente. The USA was pleased that the Soviet Union and China were still quarrelling; yet communism triumphed in Vietnam, and support for communism was growing in parts of Africa.

The West was becoming frustrated by the low priority given by the Soviet Union to improving human rights. There were also suspicions about whether the Soviet Union was keeping to the terms of the SALT 1 agreement. In fact, both the Soviet Union and the USA were positioning more missiles against each other.

The SALT 1 agreement had been due to last for five years, so it ended in 1977. The new US President, Jimmy Carter, attempted to achieve more arms reductions through the SALT 2 talks. However, he annoyed Brezhnev by trying to link cuts in weapons to discussions on human rights in communist countries. The talks went on and on, until an agreement was finally reached in 1979. But before the agreement came into effect, an event happened in the last days of 1979 that shattered any hopes of détente continuing in its present form. The Soviet Union invaded Afghanistan.

THINGS TO DO

1 What was détente?

2 Why did it come about?

3 What were its most important consequences:
   (a) for the USA
   (b) for the Soviet Union?

Source D

The badge worn by the American crew who took part in the Apollo–Soyuz space link-up.

Soviet involvement in Afghanistan

Background

Although Afghanistan was poor and mostly barren, it occupied an important position in East–West land routes. It also provided the Soviet Union with a land route to the oil-rich Middle East. The two superpowers had been competing for influence in Afghanistan for some time. Ever since Afghanistan had become a fully independent state in 1921, it had held strong ties with the Soviet Union. These were strengthened in 1955 when Khrushchev visited the capital, Kabul, and promised the Afghanistan government aid and armaments. The USA was increasingly worried about Soviet influence there and tried to compete by also offering aid, but it never gave more than one-third of the Soviet total.

Meanwhile to the west of Afghanistan in neighbouring Iran, the Shah (King) was overthrown in a Muslim revolution in January 1979. As the USA had supported the Shah, the revolution was very anti-American. In November 1979, 53 US hostages were seized at the US Embassy in Tehran and were held for over a year. The USA and its leader, President Carter, felt humiliated. To the east of Afghanistan, the Chinese government was worried about its borders and was seeking to extend its influence in neighbouring countries such as Pakistan.

Afghanistan itself had an unstable government. In 1979 Hafizullah Amin seized power as president. He was a communist, but was not friendly with the Soviet Union, and large Muslim groups in the country also opposed him. The Soviet Union feared that these Muslim groups were planning to take control of the country and set up a Muslim state in the style of Iran. The Soviet Union was also aware that it, too, had a large Muslim population in its areas near the Afghanistan border. This Muslim population might try to break away from the Soviet Union and support the Afghans.

Soviet invasion

On 25 December 1979, Soviet troops invaded Afghanistan. The airport at Kabul was quickly captured and in the next few days 350 Russian aircraft landed there with troops and equipment. Within a week about 50,000 Soviet troops were in Afghanistan. The president's palace at Kabul was captured and President Amin was killed. On New Year's Day 1980 a new government was set up in Kabul, led by Babrak Karmal. He was a previous Afghan leader who had been in exile in the Soviet Union and had been specially flown back to take over the government.

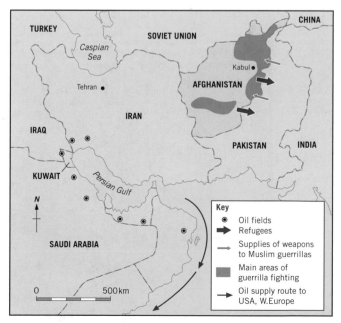

A map showing the strategic importance of Afghanistan.

Reactions from the other world powers

President Brezhnev announced to the world that the airlift of Soviet troops and equipment was justified to restore order. He told the US President, Jimmy Carter, that Soviet troops had been invited in by the Afghan government to protect it, and that troops would be withdrawn from Afghanistan as soon as the situation stabilised. However, the Americans were furious. Carter described the Soviet invasion as a threat to world peace. China also reacted angrily – it promised to support the Mujaheddin, who were Islamic Afghan fighters carrying out guerrilla warfare against the Soviet troops to seize back control of their country.

Source A

In the next few days the leaders of the world must make it clear to the Soviets that they cannot upset world peace without paying severe consequences.

President Carter's response to the Soviet invasion of Afghanistan.

Source C

Russia's actions are a stepping-stone for a southward thrust towards Pakistan and the Indian sub-continent. There will be no peace in southern Asia with Soviet soldiers in Afghanistan.

**Peking People's Daily,
1 January 1980.**

The Soviet Union retaliated by accusing the USA and China of interference. But President Carter had decided to take steps to show the USA's disapproval of what had happened in Afghanistan. In late January 1980, he pulled the USA out of the forthcoming Moscow Olympic Games. He also advised the US Senate not to ratify (agree to) the SALT 2 treaty. He sent a US Navy Task Force of 1,800 marines to the Arabian Sea to protect oil routes. To damage the Soviets economically, he cut trade between the USA and the Soviet Union. For example, he stopped the export of 17 million tons of grain and the sale of technological goods such as computers and oil-drilling equipment to the Soviet Union.

Source B

In this cartoon from *The Guardian* in 1980, President Carter views the Soviet invasion of Afghanistan.

The war continues

After the first few months of 1980, Soviet troops controlled the towns where they were based, but the Afghan rebels, the Mujaheddin, controlled the countryside. The Mujaheddin were not just fighting to get rid of Soviet troops. They were fighting to turn Afghanistan into a Muslim country. They were well equipped because both China and the USA gave them weapons.

The war was similar to the Vietnam War in that a superpower had difficulty defeating a less powerful enemy – but this time it was the Soviets rather than the Americans who were on the receiving end. The Mujaheddin attacked Soviet supply routes and shot at Soviet planes. The Soviets suffered increasing casualties, but succeeded only in propping up the unpopular communist government in Kabul. Although there were 125,000 Soviet troops in Afghanistan by the early 1980s, they found it impossible to defeat the Afghan rebels. In 1982 a massive attack against the Mujaheddin in the Panjahir Valley failed.

The Soviet Union faced hostility from Muslim nations such as Pakistan. Indeed, the Soviet Union increasingly became worried that some of the 30 million Muslims within the Soviet Union might revolt in support of the Mujaheddin.

In 1985 a new Soviet leader, Mikhail Gorbachev, realised that the war could never be won. He started talks in 1987 with the USA and agreement was reached at Geneva in 1988 between himself and the US President, Ronald Reagan. The last Soviet troops left Afghanistan in February 1989.

The consequences of the war were disastrous for Afghanistan. Over 3 million refugees fled to Pakistan or Iran. About a million people died – and the fighting continued between rival Afghan groups after the Soviet departure. Afghans who remained suffered from food shortages because the war had destroyed so much farmland.

The Soviet Union had lost about 20,000 soldiers in the war against the Mujaheddin. The war also caused great damage to the Soviet economy, costing several billion dollars a year.

THINGS TO DO

1 Why did the Soviet Union invade Afghanistan in December 1979?

2 Why could the Soviet Union, a superpower, not defeat the rebel forces of Afghanistan?

3 What were the consequences of the Soviet invasion of Afghanistan?

Source **D** Some boys who fought for the Mujaheddin against the Soviet Union.

International History 1900–91

The renewed Cold War under Reagan and Brezhnev

By early 1980, just as the Afghanistan conflict was beginning, relations between the USA and the Soviet Union were very bad. Brezhnev denounced the USA as 'an absolutely unreliable partner, whose leadership is capable – at any moment – of cancelling treaties and agreements' (January 1980).

In late January 1980 President Carter withdrew America from the Moscow Olympics. He described the Soviet Union as an 'unsuitable site for a festival meant to celebrate peace and goodwill'. Détente had totally collapsed.

Ronald Reagan became US President in January 1981 when criticism over Soviet involvement in Afghanistan was at its height. Reagan's tough anti-communist stance helped his election; he referred to the Soviet Union as 'that evil Empire'.

Development of new weapons

Reagan increased the USA's defence spending from $178 billion in 1981 to $367 billion in 1986. New weapons were developed, such as the Cruise missile, and NATO agreed that 464 US Cruise missiles should be positioned in Western Europe. In 1981, Reagan announced that the USA had developed a new type of bomb – the neutron bomb. This could kill many people without destroying much property. The Americans were also developing the MX missile. This powerful missile could be transported underground and be launched from different underground launch sites.

The Soviet Union was afraid that these developments would upset the existing 'balance of terror'. This balance was based on the idea of mutually assured destruction (MAD), which meant that, as each side had the ability to destroy the other side totally many times over, neither side would be prepared to risk nuclear war.

The Strategic Defense Initiative (SDI)

In 1983, US scientists began work on the Strategic Defense Initiative. This came to be known as the 'Star Wars' project, after a popular film. It was a satellite anti-missile system that would orbit the earth. The aim was to make it impossible for Soviet missiles to reach US targets by creating a huge laser shield in space.

Arms talks between the USA and the Soviet Union nevertheless resumed in 1982 at Geneva in Switzerland. They were called START (Strategic Arms Reduction Talks) and their main aim was to limit nuclear weapons, initially in Europe. Reagan knew that the USA was vastly superior to the Soviet Union in its nuclear capacity, but the USA had huge debts and could not afford to continue spending at its current level.

Source **E** A cartoon from the *Sunday Times*, 29 November 1981.

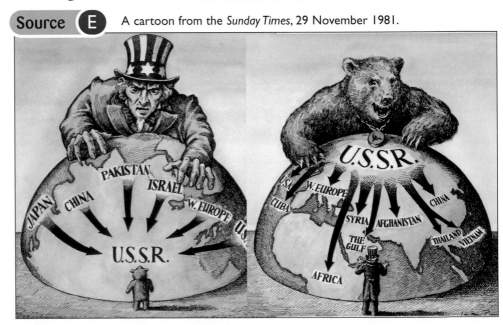

Solidarity in Poland

Meanwhile the Soviet Union had its own problems. In 1980 there were protest movements in Poland, caused by high prices and food and fuel shortages. The shipyard workers in Gdansk went on strike. They were led by an electrician, Lech Walesa, who created Solidarity, the first free trade union in the entire Soviet system. Most Poles were Catholics (which was not approved of by their Communist leaders) and were encouraged to speak out about their discontent by Pope John Paul II who was himself a Pole.

The unrest grew into nationwide strikes. Solidarity soon had a membership of 9 million. The Polish government was losing its grip, and many Poles feared a Soviet invasion (as had happened in Hungary in 1956 and Czechoslovakia in 1968). This did not happen – partly because the Soviet Union had just invaded Afghanistan.

However, the Soviet Union was alarmed at the prospect of the breakdown of government in one of the key members of the Warsaw Pact. The Soviet Army was ordered to carry out 'training manoeuvres' near the Polish border. Soviet invasion was a real threat.

Then in 1981 the Polish Communist government under its new military leader, General Jaruzelski, imposed rule by the army – martial law. Political opponents to the Communist government were either arrested (10,000 of them, including Walesa) or forced to hide. Solidarity itself was declared an illegal organisation.

Jaruzelski's attempts to destroy Solidarity did not work. Walesa was imprisoned, but that seemed to make him even more of a hero. The movement survived underground, and the USA provided secret support for those in the banned Solidarity movement.

In November 1982 Walesa was released from prison, and in 1983 he was awarded a Nobel Peace Prize.

Leadership of the Soviet Union

The Soviet Union's leadership was weak in the early 1980s. Brezhnev was ill for some time before he died in 1982. He was followed as leader by Yuri Andropov and then by Konstantin Chernenko. These men both suffered from ill health, and they died in 1984 and 1985 respectively.

There were a lot of petty squabbles at this time between the Soviet Union and the USA. In 1984, along with other communist countries, the Soviet Union boycotted the Los Angeles Olympics.

Mikhail Gorbachev became President of the Soviet Union in 1985. This allowed Reagan to complete his eight years as US President with some positive achievements.

Meanwhile tensions remained high in Poland, but the political situation began to change when Mikhail Gorbachev became President of the Soviet Union in 1985. He called for greater freedom in the Soviet Union, and this encouraged Walesa and the still-banned Solidarity to organise more strikes and demonstrations. By the end of the 1980s the Polish Communist government commanded little support or respect, and Jaruzelski was forced to legalise Solidarity and allow free elections. (see pages 88–9).

Source **F** Lech Walesa.

Changing Soviet and US attitudes

Mikhail Gorbachev

Mikhail Gorbachev became a member of the Politburo, the most powerful group within the Communist Party, in 1980. When Chernenko died in 1985, Gorbachev was chosen as the leader. At the age of 54, he was the youngest man to hold supreme power in the Soviet Union since Joseph Stalin. He appeared to be open to new ideas and was keen to see progress, both within the Soviet Union and in world relations.

Gorbachev saw that the economy of the Soviet Union was on the edge of disaster. Too much money was being spent on the arms race and on the war in Afghanistan. Industry was being run in the same way as it had been under Stalin, but without the climate of fear that had kept workers trying to meet production targets. These factors, combined with growing corruption within the Communist Party and an increasing problem with alcoholism, meant that both industrial output and the quality of goods produced was falling. Many people believed that the system could not be changed. But Gorbachev knew that there had to be changes, even though introducing reforms would anger some members of the Communist Party.

New Soviet policies

Gorbachev introduced new policies. The two most famous were perestroika and glasnost:

- *Perestroika* means restructuring – that is, changing some economic policies to allow more competition and more incentives to produce goods. He believed that the Soviet Union could survive only if it changed from the command economy that had existed since the era of Stalin.

- *Glasnost* means openness – in this case, restoring faith in government and ending corruption. Gorbachev believed that people should not be punished for simply disagreeing with government policies. There should be a more open debate. This feeling of openness applied both within the Soviet Union and in its relations with the West.

Source **A**

Ronald Reagan and Mikhail Gorbachev in 1987.

In addition, Gorbachev believed that the Soviet Union would have to cut back on its world commitments and abandon the Brezhnev Doctrine by loosening control over its satellite states. This would mean cuts in arms expenditure and pulling out of Afghanistan.

US attitudes

President Reagan was naturally pleased to learn of Gorbachev's changing policies for the Soviet Union. The government of the USA had also come to realise that cuts in expenditure were essential. As the Soviet Union planned to cut its defence expenditure, Reagan felt that it was safe for the USA to do the same.

Arms reduction

Reagan and Gorbachev met several times in the 1980s. In Geneva in November 1985, they agreed in principle to cut offensive weapons by 50 per cent. A summit meeting in Iceland in 1986 was only partially successful as the USA refused to give up its SDI. However, the Soviet Union confirmed that its troops would be withdrawn from Afghanistan, and promised that the Soviet Union would not test any more nuclear weapons unless the USA did so.

In December 1987 the two leaders agreed to get rid of all medium- and short-range nuclear weapons. This was called the Intermediate Range Nuclear Forces Treaty (INF). This was an amazing turn-around for both countries, which had been building them up just a few years before. The dismantling of these weapons began at once.

Reforms in the Soviet Union

Gorbachev also introduced reforms in the Soviet Union. Many people who had been imprisoned for disagreeing with communist policies were released. Others, such as the physicist and human rights campaigner Andrei Sakharov, were allowed to return from exile. In 1987 changes in economic policy meant that people were allowed to buy and sell at a profit for the first time since Stalin had come to power over 60 years before.

However, hard-line communists were horrified at what Gorbachev was doing. They said that he was stirring up trouble and raising the expectations of the Soviet people too much. In some respects, they were right. For instance, once freedom of speech was allowed, Gorbachev could not control the media. Many people wanted to get rid of communism altogether. This was especially true in Eastern Europe.

The end of Soviet control of Eastern Europe

In 1989, Mikhail Gorbachev's popularity in the world was at its height. In October he was awarded the Nobel Peace Prize. Then, in December 1989, he and the new US President, George Bush, met to announce the end of the Cold War. Yet at the same time, Soviet control of Eastern Europe was rapidly collapsing. Indeed, the speed of that collapse stunned the world.

The communist countries of Eastern Europe had become more and more discontented with control from Moscow during the 1980s. In Poland, the trade union Solidarity campaigned against the government and received considerable support (see page 85). In Hungary in 1986, there were widespread demonstrations using the banned Hungarian flag. The police beat up the demonstrators. In particular, the economic problems of Eastern Europe were becoming more severe than ever.

In March 1989, Gorbachev told the communist leaders of Eastern Europe that the Red Army would no longer be able to defend them. It became clear to the people of those countries that Soviet tanks would not be used to put down demonstrations. Indeed, when there were troubles in Hungary in early 1989 and it was agreed that other political parties could be formed, Gorbachev began the withdrawal of Soviet troops.

Poland

In June 1989 free elections were held in Poland for the first time since the Second World War. Solidarity won nearly all the seats that it contested, and Lech Walesa became the first non-communist leader in Eastern Europe since 1945. Gradually the Soviet Bloc began to disintegrate.

East Germany

By the autumn of 1989 thousands of people were fleeing East Germany through Austria. Massive demonstrations took place in East German cities when Gorbachev visited the country. Gorbachev told the unpopular East German leader, Erich Honecker, to allow reforms. He responded by telling his troops to fire on the demonstrators, but they refused. Honecker was forced to resign. On 10 November 1989 thousands of East Germans marched to the Berlin Wall, and the guards even joined the demonstrators in pulling it down. The symbolic barrier between East and West had disappeared nearly 30 years after it had been built.

Czechoslovakia

Thousands of people demonstrated in Prague, the capital city of Czechoslovakia, on 24 November 1989. The police tried to stop the demonstrations. However, Alexander Dubcek, the deposed communist leader, and the playwright Vaclav Havel appeared in public to encourage the demonstrators to continue. In December, the communist leader resigned and was replaced by Havel. Free elections were held in 1990.

Hungary

The communist government under Imre Pozsgay accepted the need for change and led the moves for reform in Hungary. Other political parties were allowed, and in November 1989 the Communist Party renamed itself as the Socialist Party, promising free elections in 1990.

Source B

Citizens of united city overcome their disbelief

Yesterday Berlin ceased to be a divided city. Tens of thousands of East Berliners streamed to the West, unhindered for the first time since the Wall was put up 28 years ago. Most crossed just for the experience of freedom they had been denied so long.

Huge crowds built up on the Western side of the Wall as West Berliners witnessed the historic developments, some even crossing over into the East for a walk. In front of the Brandenburg Gate and elsewhere, they perched precariously on top of the Wall, clapping and calling for it to go.

East Berliners have been offered free tickets for a football match today in West Berlin as well as to a number of concerts and the opera. It was unclear last night how many East Berliners planned to stay in the West. Although the West German cities of Bremen and Hanover said they could take no more refugees, Berlin was still offering a warm welcome.

'After all we are not just one people, we are also one city,' said one West Berliner, who described the last 24 hours as 'simply unbelievable'.

From* The Guardian, *11 November 1989.

Romania

In December 1989 there was a short and very bloody revolution in Romania. The hated communist dictator, Nicolae Ceausescu, and his wife, Elena, were executed.

Bulgaria

In November 1989 the communist leader resigned, and free elections were held the next year.

The Baltic States

In 1990 Latvia, Lithuania and Estonia declared themselves independent of the Soviet Union.

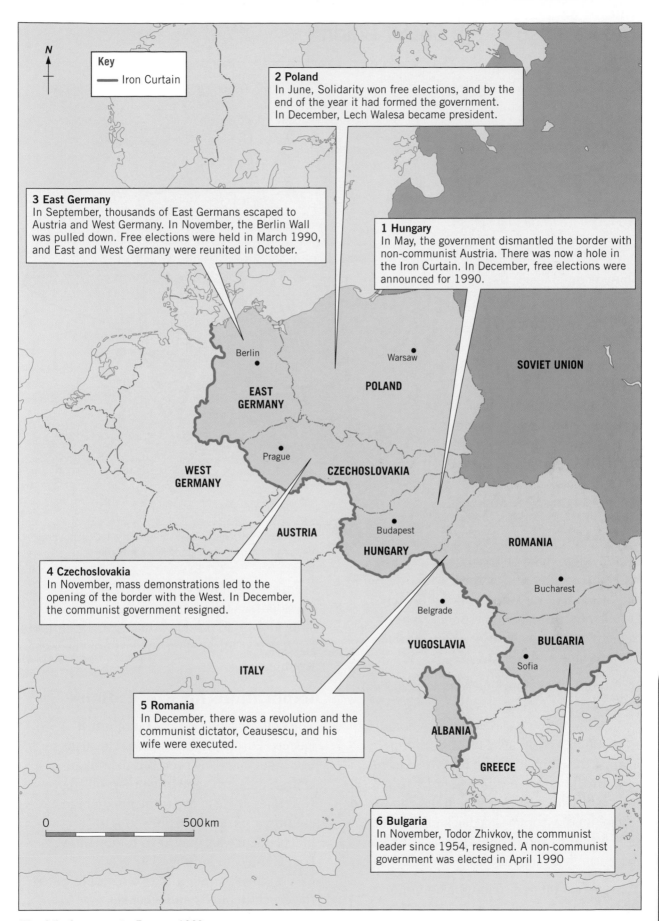

Key
— Iron Curtain

2 Poland
In June, Solidarity won free elections, and by the end of the year it had formed the government. In December, Lech Walesa became president.

3 East Germany
In September, thousands of East Germans escaped to Austria and West Germany. In November, the Berlin Wall was pulled down. Free elections were held in March 1990, and East and West Germany were reunited in October.

1 Hungary
In May, the government dismantled the border with non-communist Austria. There was now a hole in the Iron Curtain. In December, free elections were announced for 1990.

4 Czechoslovakia
In November, mass demonstrations led to the opening of the border with the West. In December, the communist government resigned.

5 Romania
In December, there was a revolution and the communist dictator, Ceausescu, and his wife were executed.

6 Bulgaria
In November, Todor Zhivkov, the communist leader since 1954, resigned. A non-communist government was elected in April 1990

SOVIET UNION

Berlin

Warsaw

EAST GERMANY

POLAND

WEST GERMANY

Prague

CZECHOSLOVAKIA

AUSTRIA

Budapest

HUNGARY

ROMANIA

Bucharest

Belgrade

YUGOSLAVIA

BULGARIA

Sofia

ITALY

ALBANIA

GREECE

0   500km

The fall of communist Europe, 1989.

The collapse of the Soviet Union

To many people, it seemed that Gorbachev had done very little to prevent the fall of communism in Eastern Europe. Many Soviets saw this as weakness. They were also aware that economic reforms in the Soviet Union had produced no immediate effect. They still suffered from food shortages and rising prices. Many wanted to see the collapse of the communist system, not just reforms within communism.

In February 1990, 250,000 people demonstrated in Moscow against communism. In the annual May Day parade in Moscow's Red Square, Gorbachev was booed. Although he was immensely popular in the West, among the Soviet people Gorbachev was increasingly criticised – both by those who believed he had gone too far, and by those who believed that more reforms were needed. The new President of the Russian republic, Boris Yeltsin, encouraged the break-up of the Soviet Union.

In August 1991, hardline communists led a coup against Gorbachev, who was made a prisoner in his own *dacha* (country home) in the Crimea. Yeltsin led a demonstration against the coup, insisting that the reform movement had to continue in order to save Russia. Yeltsin was seen as a hero, who would rescue Russia from a slide back into the days of communist repression. He was also seen increasingly as the man with the power.

Yeltsin went on to disband the Communist Party in Russia, and formally ended the Soviet Union in December 1991. Later in the same

Source **C**   A cartoon from *The Guardian* in January 1990, showing the communist hammer and sickle in tears.

month, Gorbachev resigned as Soviet President, as there was no longer a Soviet state for him to preside over. The communist red flag was lowered for the last time over the Kremlin.

Implications for world affairs

The Cold War had ended. Communist Eastern Europe had collapsed. The arms race was at an end. However, this did not, of course, mean the end of world problems. New ones arose in the former Soviet Bloc countries, as ethnic groups sought independence for their own nationalities. For example, in January 1993, Czechoslovakia split into two separate states, the Czech Republic and Slovakia.

The worst troubles were in the former

Yugoslavia, as a number of areas tried to win independence after the collapse of communist control in 1990. The Serbs refused to accept a Croat as leader, and both Slovenia and Croatia declared independence in 1991. The resulting civil war, with all its horrors of so-called ethnic cleansing, continued on and off for years, as long-held national attitudes fuelled people's hatred for each other.

East and West Berlin were reunited in 1991, and East and West Germany became a single country. Since then, eastern Germany has undergone many reforms and received considerable aid from western Germany to reduce the gap in living standards between the two parts of Germany.

Although the the Cold War caused much bitterness and cast a large shadow over the late-twentieth century, it could be argued that it had achieved something positive. Compared with the first half of the twentieth century, there had been no world war. It was an open question whether, in the absence of a Cold War, this relative peace could be continued into the next millennium.

THINGS TO DO

1 Why did Gorbachev need to carry out reforms in the Soviet Union?

2 Why did the reforms lead to the collapse of the Soviet Union and the loss of its control of Eastern Europe?

3 Read **Source D** carefully.
According to the article, why did the USA become so powerful in the twentieth century?
Using your own knowledge, what other reasons would you add?

Source D

America's unique blend of confidence and self-doubt should guarantee another era of dominance

When the phrase 'the American century' was coined in 1941, it was used at a time when America was being told off for not fulfilling its duty as 'the elder brother of nations'. America then dominated the Second World War and the post-war world.

In the year 2000 America is more dominant in the world than ever before – its economy booming, its military power unmatched, its technology thriving, and its culture over all the globe. In science, art, war and business America has played the leading role in framing the modern world.

Yet only ten years ago in 1990 the USA appeared to have overstretched itself. Japan's economy was roaring, China was a rising power and a united Europe was coming to life. Meanwhile spiralling US debt, economic problems and government indecision seemed to be attacking America from inside.

However, at the end of the 1990s it is clear that the last decade of the twentieth century has been more America's than any decade before it. Japan is still struggling out of economic problems, the euro cannot compete over the world with the dollar, and the Cold War has been won. Next month, the US economy will be able to declare the longest period of sustained growth in its history. The astonishing success of the 1990s has been typical of American success in the twentieth century.

The Times, *3 January 2000*.

Exam-style assessment – OPTION X

The three questions provided here are on the period 1970-1991. In the real examination for Option X, the questions will cover the whole period of 1945-1991. A question covering the earlier part of this option can be found on the overlapping Option W's questions on pages 70-71.

Question 1: Détente in the 1970s

Study **Source A** and then answer the following questions.

SOURCE A

America cannot live in isolation if it expects to live in peace. We have no intention of withdrawing from the world. The only issue before us is how we can be most effective in meeting our responsibilities, protecting our interests, and thereby building peace.

From a speech by President Nixon to Congress
and the American people, February 1970

(a) What was Nixon saying in **Source A** about US involvement in world affairs? **(3 marks)**

(b) How reliable is **Source A** to an historian studying US foreign policy in 1970? **(6 marks)**

(c) Describe attempts at arms control and improving human rights under détente in the 1970s. **(6 marks)**

(d) Détente broke down because of the Soviet Union's invasion of Afghanistan in 1979. Is this true? Explain your answer. **(10 marks)**

Question 2: The renewed Cold War in the early 1980s

Study **Sources B** and **C**, and then answer the following questions.

SOURCE B: Why the USSR invaded Afghanistan

The USSR has been invited in by the Afghan Government to come and protect it from threats by other nations. The USSR will remove its forces from Afghanistan as soon as the situation has stabilised.

Brezhnev using the hot-line to President Carter of the USA, 28 December 1979

SOURCE C: The invasion of Afghanistan

The Soviet Union made a massive airlift into Kabul over Christmas on December 25/26 and now have concentrated five divisions along the border.

From a British newspaper, The Times, 27 December 1979

(a) According to **Source B**, will Soviet troops stay in Afghanistan for long? **(3 marks)**

(b) Which **Source**, **B** or **C**, is more reliable for studying the invasion of Afghanistan in December 1979? Explain your answer. **(6 marks)**

(c) Describe how the Solidarity movement in Poland in the 1980s gradually succeeded. **(6 marks)**

(d) Why did the Cold War become worse in the early 1980s? **(10 marks)**

Question 3: The end of the Cold War

Study **Sources D** and **E** and then answer the questions which follow.

SOURCE D: Gorbachev's wish for world peace

Force or the threat of force neither can nor should be how foreign policy is carried out. The principle of the freedom of choice is essential. Refusal to recognise this principle will have serious consequences for world peace.

From a speech to the United Nations by Gorbachev, 7 December 1988

SOURCE E: Gorbachev explains the problems within the USSR

I knew that an immense task awaited me. The USSR was at the end of its strength. Production figures were slumping. The people's standard of living was clearly declining. Corruption was gaining ground. We wanted to reform by launching a democratic process. It was similar to earlier reform attempts.

Gorbachev writing in 1992, after he had lost power

(a) What was Gorbachev saying in **Source D** about the USSR's relations with other countries? **(3 marks)**

(b) How reliable is **Source E** for studying why Communism collapsed in the USSR? **(6 marks)**

(c) Describe how Communist rule ended in ONE East European country in 1989. **(6 marks)**

(d) Explain the immediate consequences for the world of the collapse of Communism in Eastern Europe and the end of the USSR, 1989–91. **(10 marks)**

INTRODUCTION

Britain joined the First World War when the Germans invaded neutral Belgium in August 1914. Immediately the British Expeditionary Force was sent to France to try to defend Belgium. The German Schlieffen Plan was meant to end the war in six weeks and it succeeded in taking control of most of Belgium, but the resistance of the Belgians, the BEF and the French stopped the German army and ended the war of movement. The failure of the Germans to achieve a quick victory led to trench warfare and stalemate on the Western Front for the next three and a half years. New weapons such as gas and tanks were introduced but the breakthroughs gained were not consolidated until 1918.

As the war continued, the British army, enlarged by troops from the Empire, began to play an increasing part in the battles on the Western Front. The battles of the Somme in 1916 and Passchendaele in 1917 were largely British offensives and formed part of the Allied Strategy of attrition. The USA entered the war in 1917. The Germans launched their last attack in 1918 but this was defeated and an Allied counter-attack, aided by American troops, led to the surrender of Germany.

The war at sea consisted of blockade and counter-blockade. The British Navy protected Britain and also attempted to prevent goods from reaching Germany. The Germans countered this by using their U-boats in the Atlantic to attack ships that were bringing supplies to Britain. Britain was nearly starved to defeat, the hardship caused to Germany led to increased disease and weakness. Fortunately for Britain, the measures of the Government against the U-boats began to succeed in 1918. There was only one major sea battle in the war at Jutland in 1916, which did not change the balance of the two navies.

The First World War had a lasting effect on life in Britain. The government took greater control over the lives of its citizens. When voluntary recruitment failed to keep pace with the number of deaths on the Western Front, men were forced to join the armed forces and women took their place in industry. Censorship and propaganda were used to keep up morale. Food shortages eventually resulted in rationing. Air and sea attacks by the Germans made the people of Britain realise that modern warfare was no longer restricted to soldiers on the battlefield.

1914	BEF sent to France
	DORA introduced in Britain
	Battle of the Marne
	Failure of Schlieffen Plan
	Battle of Ypres
	German ships shell east Britain
	Battle of the Falkland Islands
1915	Zeppelin attacks on Britain
	Gas used on the Western Front
	Sinking of *Lusitania* by German U Boat
1916	Introduction of conscription in Britain
	Verdun
	Jutland
	The Somme
	First use of tank
1917	German aircraft bomb south Britain
	Unrestricted submarine warfare introduced
	USA enters war
	Battle of Passchendaele
1918	Britain introduces convoys
	Rationing of food in Britain
	Mutiny of German fleet
	Defeat of German army

2.1 What was the part played by Britain in the defeat of Germany in the First World War?

The BEF

When the Germans attacked Belgium in August 1914, Britain joined the First World War and was determined to defend Belgium and stop the German Schlieffen Plan. The British Expeditionary Force (BEF), arrived in France on 21 August and was in action the following day. It was a small force of 100,000 men under the command of Sir John French, but it was well trained and equipped and had the advantage over the other armies as they had experienced field fire in the Boer War. The BEF advanced to Mons and delayed the German advance for a full day on 23 August. The Germans suffered heavy casualties, but the BEF was forced to retreat because of lack of support. The British showed they were not defeated and made a stand at Le Cateau on 26 August where their rifle fire was so rapid that the Germans believed they had 28 machine-guns per battalion when in fact they only had two.

The German Schlieffen Plan depended on speed for its success. The BEF's action in Belgium and Northern France delayed the German advance and gave the French army time to change their own plan and launch a counter-attack on the Germans in the battle of the Marne. The BEF contributed to the battle of the Marne which force the Germans to retreat to the river Aisne where they dug trenches and set up barbed wire and machine-guns to defend them. The Schlieffen Plan had failed and its failure ensured that Germany had to fight a war on two fronts, in the West against Britain and France and in the East against Russia.

There followed one final battle in the war of movement, the battle for the Channel Ports. This, the first battle of Ypres, took place between 12 October and 11 November 1914. The BEF resisted the German attack at a cost of 50,000 men, though the Germans lost at least twice as many. The BEF saved the Channel Ports for the Allies. This was very important as it meant that Britain was able to continue to transport troops and supplies to France through these ports.

Source **A** German troops 'digging in' at the end of 1914.

The long slog

The war of movement was over and all hopes of a short war were ended. The Germans had lost many of their best men, the French had suffered over a million casualties and most of the BEF had been killed at Ypres. Both sides now concentrated on defence and dug trenches. The war now developed into a long slog. The stalemate had begun: the Western Front did not move more than ten miles either way for the next four years.

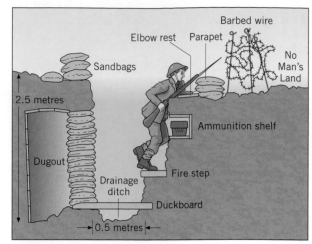

A cross-section of a trench.

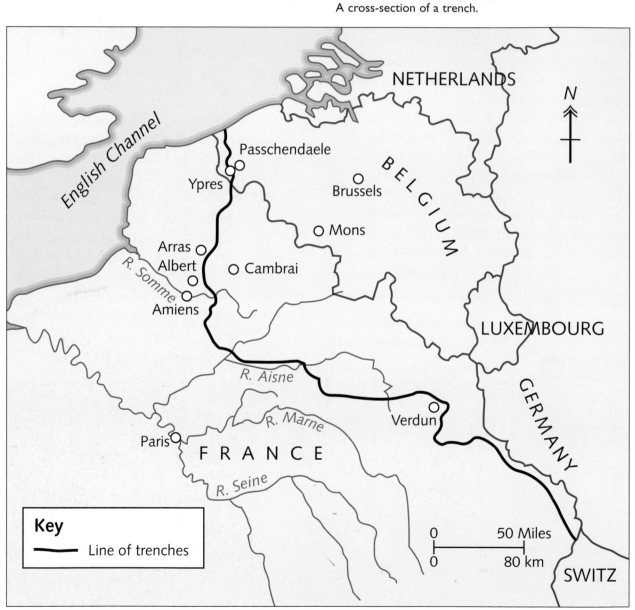

The Western Front, 1914–18.

Trenches, weapons and strategy

Up until the First World War most military leaders believed that battles and wars were won mainly by cavalry charges, with the infantry (foot soldiers) following behind the cavalry. The use of trenches and new weapons soon made them realise that this was no longer possible. Horses were easy targets for the rapid fire of machine-guns, especially when trying to gallop across the mud of a battlefield.

Technology had made it possible to produce heavy artillery more powerful than anything seen before. Large guns, such as the howitzer, could fire shells at enemy targets hundreds of yards away. Smaller versions of field guns were also used in artillery attacks and hand-held trench mortars were used by the men in the trenches.

The machine-gun was the main weapon used on the Western Front. But it was underestimated by the British generals who believed that a battalion needed only two machine-guns. The Germans were much quicker to recognise its value and set up machine-gun posts, enclosed in concrete, to protect their trenches. The rapid fire of the guns made it very difficult to capture trenches. The only defence against them was to 'dig in' by building trenches. These new weapons and the trenches led to a stalemate, with neither side being able to make any significant advances. Both sides were forced to make greater efforts to develop new weapons to break the stalemate. Until they did there seemed little prospect of either side winning the war.

THINGS TO DO

1 What was the importance of the failure of the Schlieffen Plan?

2 What part did the BEF play in preventing a German victory in 1914?

3 Why was the first battle of Ypres so important?

4 Why did both sides dig trenches at the end of 1914?

Source British soldiers defending their trench with a Vickers machine-gun.

The nature of trench warfare

The generals believed that the only way to win the war on the Western Front was to take over the enemy's trenches and drive their forces back until they surrendered. For four years the army generals followed the same tactics in their attempts to create a break-through. Each attack would begin with a heavy artillery bombardment from behind the front line which was intended to break up the barbed wire defences, destroy the machine-gun posts and many of the front trenches. This bombardment would often continue for days before the next stage in the attack.

When the bombardment finished, the men in the trenches were ordered to go 'over the top'. This meant that they climbed out of the trenches and advanced across 'No Man's Land' towards the enemy trenches. On their backs the men carried their personal kit, including clothing, and weapons which weighed at least 28 kilograms. They advanced over ground which had been churned up by previous attacks and artillery bombardment. When they reached the enemy trenches, they had to weave their way through the barbed wire and capture them.

As early as March 1915, a British attack at Neuve Chapelle broke through the German front line, but poor communications and lack of ammunition led to a delay which gave the Germans time to recover and build a second line of defence using bicycle-mounted sharp-shooters. But this success convinced the British generals that with better support a breakthrough could be achieved by these methods.

The use of gas, 1915

When the Germans broke through the Allies' front line at Ypres in April 1915 their success was due to a new weapon – poison gas (chlorine). The gas attack took the Allies by surprise and caused panic in the trenches. The Germans were then able to make the initial advance, but the wind changed direction and blew the gas towards the German lines, causing more German casualties than Allies. Soon both sides were using gas.

The chlorine gas irritated the lungs and many of those affected died of suffocation. The Germans later used phosgene which was more powerful and in 1917 used mustard gas which had no smell. This gas temporarily blinded its victims, burned their skin and poisoned their lungs. In the worst cases death was slow and painful, taking up to four weeks. Others who survived the war died later of lung disease.

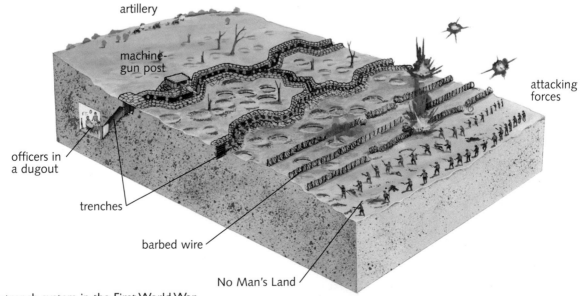

The trench system in the First World War.

But gas became largely ineffective when gas masks were introduced to protect soldiers against it. The main effect was psychological: soldiers lived in fear of the next gas attack.

Verdun, 1916

The military leaders decided that the only way to win the war was to wear down the enemy by attrition. This involved shelling the enemy's defences and launching attacks that used up the enemy's supplies of men and equipment.

The British and French strategy for 1916 was to launch a joint offensive on the German line at the River Somme in the summer. However, the Germans made the first move and launched an attack on the French fortress of Verdun in February. Falkenhayn, the successor to Moltke, felt that he could defeat the whole of the French army at Verdun because they would defend it to the last man. The Germans succeeded in taking some of the outer forts, but the main fortress held firm under the leadership of General Pétain, who announced, 'Ils ne passeront pas' ('They shall not pass'). The French suffered greatly at Verdun and urged the British to launch their offensive on the Somme as early as possible in order to lift the siege of Verdun.

Source

Kitchener is firmly convinced that we waste ammunition here. I told him quite plainly that neither he nor his advisers had any idea of what modern war was really like. The enemy's trenches must be broken down, his wire torn up, and the machine-gun resistance reduced by artillery fire and an unlimited supply of ammunition.

From the diary of Sir John French, commander of the BEF until December 1915.

Source A British field gun used in the First World War.

Source

We have heaps of gassed cases. I wish those who call this a holy war could see the poor things burnt and blistered all over with great mustard-coloured blisters, with blind eyes all sticky and glued together; always fighting for breath with voices a mere whisper saying their throats are closing and they will choke.

An eyewitness account of the effects of gas on the Western Front.

THINGS TO DO

1 Why was it difficult to take enemy trenches in the First World War?

2 Explain what Sir John French meant in **Source C**.

3 How effective was gas as a weapon?

The Somme 1916: a battle of attrition

Verdun changed the offensive on the Somme. Instead of being a joint offensive it became largely a British attack – the French were able to contribute only half the men they had promised at the beginning of the year. The offensive was rushed forward to the end of June and the main aim of the Somme now became to relieve Verdun, or as Rawlinson, one of the commanders of the 4th army, put it, 'to kill as many Germans as possible'. The British commander in chief, General Haig, was still intent on achieving a breakthrough, but this was not now the main priority.

The battle began with a five-day bombardment of the enemy trenches. On 1 July Haig ordered the advance to begin. He told his troops that they should walk across 'No Man's Land' because there would not be 'even a rat' alive in the German trenches. While the bombardment was taking place, the Germans had withdrawn into especially prepared deep dugouts. Once it had stopped, they prepared for the advancing British soldiers.

The Germans had only one order to give, 'Fire!' The British suffered 60,000 casualties, including 20,000 deaths, on the first day of the attack alone. But not even this scale of loss convinced the generals to change their minds about the methods of warfare they employed.

Source F

Our men at once clambered up the steep shafts leading from the dug-outs and ran for the nearest shell craters. The machine guns were hurriedly placed into position. A series of extended lines of British infantry was seen moving forward from the British trenches. The first line appeared to continue without end to right and left. It was quickly followed by a second line, then a third and fourth. They came on at a steady, easy pace as if expecting to find nothing alive in our front trenches.

A German soldier describing what he saw when the bombardment stopped. The German machine-guns cut down thousands of British soldiers as they walked across 'No Man's Land'.

Source G

British troops going 'over the top' at the Somme, a scene from the British government's film, *The Battle of the Somme*, released in August 1916.

Haig realised that a major breakthrough was unlikely and settled for a long-drawn-out war of attrition. His aim was 'to maintain a steady pressure on the Somme battle.'

The last chance of a breakthrough came on 15 September when the British used tanks for the first time. They were intended to lead the infantry, protecting them against German gun-fire and crushing their barbed wire and trench system. The German troops were taken by surprise and retreated. But again the British were too slow to take advantage and the Germans were given time to build up their defences. By the end of the day all of the tanks had broken down, were stuck or had been eliminated by the Germans. Haig has been criticised for using tanks before the design was fully developed. But the failure in 1916 does not appear to have affected the surprise value of tanks which were used to great effect at Cambrai in 1917.

Source

When the German troops crept out of their dug-outs in the mist of the morning and stretched their necks to look for the English, their blood chilled. Mysterious monsters were crawling towards them over the craters. Nothing stopped them. Someone in the trenches said, 'The devil is coming', and word was passed along the line. Tongues of flame leapt from the sides of the iron caterpillars. The English infantry came in behind.

A German war correspondent describing the effect the sight of British tanks had on German soldiers at the Somme.

Tanks could get up to speeds of 6 kilometres an hour on solid ground, but were much slower in the mud of battle.

They were armed with two high-powered naval guns and three machine-guns, protected with armoured steel. Eight men were needed to crew a tank. Inside, the tank was noisy and extremely hot, with temperatures rising to 38°C. A crew could die if they stayed in the tank for more than three hours.

A major effect of the tank in battle was psychological. They frightened the enemy, and the morale of those at home watching newsreels, and those on the battlefield

Source I

British tanks and infantry advancing at Cambrai in 1917. The tanks carried fascines which they dropped into trenches to allow them to pass over.

watching from the trenches was raised by the sight of these 'metal monsters' lumbering towards the enemy. As technology improved they came to play a greater part in trench warfare.

Britain in the First World War

Effects of the Somme

At the end of September the rain fell and the Somme battlefield turned to mud. No side could advance in these conditions. The battle of the Somme ended in November 1916. Very little ground was won or lost. But the loss of life was massive. The British lost 420,000 men, the French 200,000 and the Germans 500,000.

The Somme offensive failed to achieve the breakthrough Haig had hoped for. Advances had been slow and when the enemy front line was broken the support was too slow in reaching the advancing soldiers. Artillery bombardments failed to destroy the enemy's defences, and they warned the Germans that a major attack was about to be launched, which gave them time to prepare for it.

However, for the Allies there were some positive results. Verdun had been saved partly by the attack on the Somme, though a Russian attack in the east, launched on 4 June 1916, probably had a greater effect as the Germans had to withdraw men from Verdun to resist the Russians. The French and British had co-operated and tanks and aerial photography had been used for the first time to support an advancing army. The British army had shown it could maintain a lengthy attack and German losses had a long-term effect on their military strength.

Source J

As a result of the Somme fighting we were completely exhausted on the Western Front. If the war lasted like this our defeat seemed inevitable. I cannot see as I look back how Germany could have mastered the situation if the Allies had continued their blows as they did in 1916.

An extract from the memoirs of General Ludendorff.

Losses in the major battles of 1916.

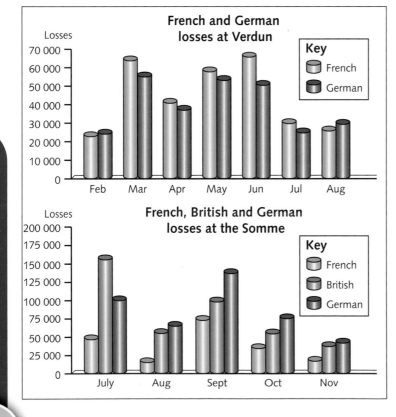

THINGS TO DO

1 Why did the British launch an attack along the River Somme?

2 Does Ludendorff's statement (**Source J**) justify Haig's tactics at the Somme?

3 Would you say that the introduction of tanks on the Western Front was a success? Explain your answer.

4 How far can paintings and photographs of the Western Front help us to understand what it was like?

The war at sea

The main role of the British navy in the war was to guard the shores of Britain against any attacks from German ships. In addition, the Royal Navy convoyed troops across the Channel to enable them to fight on the Western Front and protected British commerce and shipping. A more offensive role was their attempt to blockade the German coast and starve Germany into defeat. The British Channel Fleet tried to control the exits from the North Sea while the Grand Fleet, based at Scapa Flow in the Orkneys, patrolled the North Sea and was ready for action if the German fleet was to emerge from port.

In the early years of the war there were two sea battles. The Germans lost three light cruisers at Heligoland in August 1914, and the cruiser *Blücher* at Dogger Bank in January 1915. These losses appeared to alarm them and they withdrew to their home waters. The German East Asia Squadron, under Vice Admiral Graf Maximilian von Spee, was out of port when war broke out in 1914 and defeated a small British fleet at Coronel off the coast of Chile on 1 November. A British defeat at sea was a concern to the people of Britain and Admiral Fisher was determined to defeat von Spee. This was achieved at the battle of the Falkland Islands on 8 December 1914.

By July 1915, Allied seapower controlled the oceans. The object of the British blockade was to gain the maximum blockade possible without offending the USA. The British Navy intercepted ships which had goods bound for Germany. This included ships using neutral ports in Holland. The ships were searched and any forbidden goods were seized by the British. This policy caused objections from neutral countries, including the USA, who regarded it as theft, but fortunately for Britain it was seen as preferable to the German policy of unrestricted submarine warfare which resulted in deaths. By the end of 1916 Germany was suffering from the effects of the blockade. The lack of imported fertilisers resulted in poor harvests in 1915-16 and the outlook for 1917 was grim. Malnutrition lowered the resistance of the Germans to disease and led to an increase in the death rate within Germany in 1917 and 1918. The blockade was one of the reasons for the German surrender in 1918.

THINGS TO DO

1 Why was the battle of Coronel a cause for British concern?

2 Explain how the British blockade of Germany worked?

3 How did this blockade weaken Germany?

4 How did the British blockade of Germany differ from the German blockade of Britain?

Source *Blücher* sinking at the Dogger Bank

Submarine warfare

The Germans launched their own blockade of Britain using the U-boat (German name for a submarine) to try to stop supplies coming to Britain from abroad.

In February 1915 the Germans declared the seas around the British Isles a 'war zone' and reserved the right to sink all ships, including neutrals, in these waters. This policy was called 'unrestricted submarine warfare'. The problem for the Germans was that U-boats had never been used before in a war and there were no rules governing their use. It was normal to warn a ship before it was fired upon so that the people on board could be rescued. This was not possible with a submarine because of the surprise nature of the attack. This policy resulted in the sinking of the British liner the *Lusitania* in 1915. A German submarine fired a single torpedo at the liner without warning and it sank in 18 minutes, killing over 1,000 passengers, including 128

Americans. The Germans, who believed the liner was carrying weapons, saw it as a great victory, but it offended many neutral countries, especially the Americans who protested against the German action. Britain made the most of the event in the propaganda war, portraying the Germans as murderers of innocent people. Although the British propaganda failed to bring the USA into the war, it managed to cover up other awkward questions being asked, such as whether the *Lusitania* was carrying explosives. American protests also caused the Germans to withdraw unrestricted submarine warfare and this reduced the effectiveness of their submarines.

Source L

The sinking of the giant English steamship is a success. With joyful pride we contemplate this latest deed of our Navy. It will not be the last.

A report of the sinking of the *Lusitania* in a German newspaper.

Source M

An artist's impression of the sinking of the *Lusitania*, 1915.

The Battle of Jutland

This was the only major sea battle of the war and took place in the North Sea on 31 May and 1 June 1916. The British fleet under Admiral Jellicoe trapped the German fleet under Admiral Scheer, but the British were let down by faulty shells which broke up when they hit the German ships. The Germans escaped at night and retreated to their home waters where they remained in port for the remainder of the war and mutinied when they were ordered out to sea in 1918.

In the battle of Jutland, the Germans claimed a victory because the British lost 14 ships and 6,000 men whereas they lost only 11 ships and 2,500 men. The Germans proved to have better armoured ships and more reliable weapons. The British also claimed a victory because the Germans did not dare to risk another battle and remained in port. They argued that the inactivity of the German fleet led to the mutinies in 1917 and 1918. The real result was that the battle was indecisive. Jellicoe had played safe and taken no risks

because if the British Navy had been defeated, the war would have been lost. The problem for Britain was that the continued existence of the German fleet meant that the British Grand Fleet had to remain on guard in the North Sea and could not be used in the struggle against the U-boats.

Source **N** Jellicoe's flagship at Jutland.

Source **O** Beatty's flagship firing the first shots in the battle.

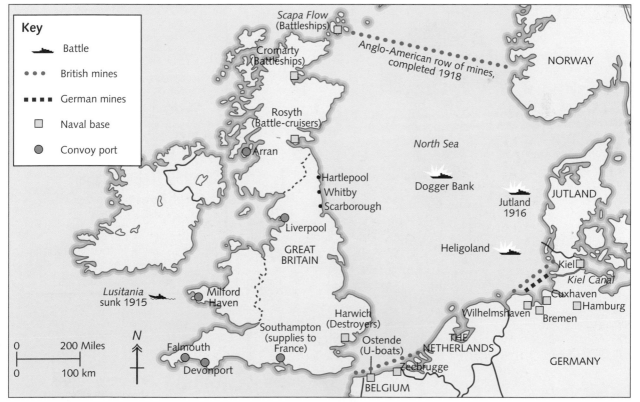

The British Blockade.

Renewal of unrestricted submarine warfare, 1917

The Germans called off unrestricted submarine warfare in 1915 because of protests from neutral countries.

The Germans now had far more U-boats available and they were certain that they could starve Britain into defeat. They were nearly successful. In April 1917, Admiral Jellicoe claimed that there was only six weeks' food supply left in Britain. In January 1917, Allied losses at sea amounted to 386,000 tons. After the German decision to resume unrestricted submarine warfare, this rose to 881,000 tons in April. If losses had continued at this rate, it would have brought the Germans victory. Measures had to be taken to maintain essential food supplies that Britain needed to avoid starvation.

THINGS TO DO

1 How did the British Navy help to win the war?

2 How successful was the German U-boat campaign against Britain?

3 List the methods used by Britain against the U-boat.

4 'The German U-boat campaign was very successful and nearly won the war.'
'The German U-boat campaign was a mistake which helped lose the war.'
Explain which of these two interpretations you think is more accurate.

5 Who won the Battle of Jutland? Explain your answer.

THINGS TO DO

1 What does 'splendid isolation' mean?

2 Which figure represents Britain in the cartoon? Why?

3 What shape are the U-boats in the cartoon? Why?

4 How useful is the cartoon as evidence?

Source A German cartoon showing Britain in its 'splendid isolation'.

Defeat of the U-boats

The most effective action taken by the British government against the U-boats was the introduction of armed convoys in April 1917. This meant that merchant ships travelled in groups across the Atlantic and were guarded by warships which had depth charges. This made it far more difficult for the U-boats to attack and put the U-boats in greater danger. Other ships, called Q ships, were camouflaged and disguised to confuse the U-boats. The mining and placing of submarine nets and floodlights in the Dover Straits prevented the U-boats from using the Channel and forced them to waste fuel by going around the coast of Scotland. There were also attempts to mine other waters around Britain to make things more difficult for the submarines.

These methods were successful. Convoys ensured that far more supply ships were reaching Britain and more U-boats were being destroyed. The most effective weapon against the U-boat in 1917 was the mine, which was responsible for the destruction of 20 U-boats. Surface patrols destroyed 16 U-boats and Q ships 6. In 1918 convoy escorts and surface ships destroyed 34 U-boats and mines destroyed 18. In 1917 and 1918, 132 U-boats were destroyed, and although construction just about kept up with the losses, unrestricted submarine warfare was failing. The British were now building more merchant ships than they were losing and, though rationing was introduced in 1918 (see page 114), food supplies were never again as low as at the beginning of 1917. Germany's unrestricted submarine warfare damaged much of America's shipping and led directly to the USA entering the war on 6 April 1917. The extra help given by the Americans in providing escort ships for convoys and soldiers for the Western Front contributed to the Allied victory in 1918.

Source Q   A German cartoon showing a couple nursing their 'baby' U-boat.

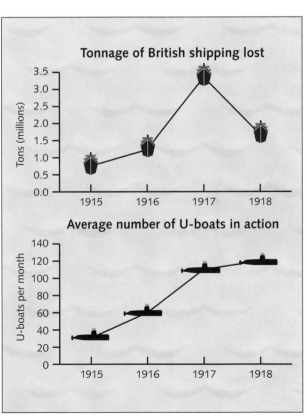

British losses and U-boats in action.

The Battle of Passchendaele, 1917 – attrition continues

In 1917 the British launched a further offensive at Ypres. The attack began with a two-week bombardment on 31 July and made steady progress at first. Heavy rain then affected the battlefield and when the fighting centred on the village of Passchendaele the rain had turned the ground into a 'porridge of mud' and the attack ground to a halt in November.

The Battle of Passchendaele won very little land for the Allies. But it did weaken German morale because of the loss of life. However, it also affected British morale for the same reason. The British lost 250,000 and the Germans 200,000. Following the Somme no one wanted a repeat of this destruction of human life for such little gain. In 1917, both sides had hopes for the future: the Germans because the Russian Revolution led to Russia leaving the war, the Allies because the USA had entered the war on their side because of action by the German U-boats in the Atlantic. Germany was desperate to move its troops (around 400,000) from the Eastern Front to the Western Front to make a breakthrough before thousands of fresh American troops arrived.

The defeat of Germany, 1918

In 1918, the German General Ludendorff realised that Germany must win the war before the Amercan forces entered Europe. He had to force a victory in the West. Ludendorff launched the first part of his last offensive (code-named Operation Michael) in March 1918 at St Quentin. Early breakthroughs were aided by fog, but the attack ran out of steam. The Germans won 1200 square miles of land but had gained an extra 80 kilometres of front which had to be defended. Ludendorff tried two further attacks, the first in the north, code-named Georgette, in April, and the second (Blücher) in May in the Champagne region of France. Both had early successes, but were eventually stopped with the help of the newly arrived American soldiers, and the Allies began a counter-offensive.

Under the new commander-in-chief of the Allied army, General Foch, the Allies began to advance. The lessons of Passchendaele appear to have been learned as the attacks were carried out on methodical lines: as soon as an attack lost its initial impetus, it was broken off and another one launched close enough to profit from the success. German morale appeared to have finally broken, with cases of whole companies surrendering to single tanks.

The attacks continued until Germany was forced to accept defeat. The Armistice (ceasefire) was signed on 11 November 1918.

Source **R** The town of Ypres after the Passchendaele campaign.

Life in the trenches and its effects

Men spent long spells in the trenches during the war. During battle they might have spent several weeks in the front trench, though normally it was only about four days at a time in the front trench and a similar time in the supporting trenches. During lulls in the fighting, life was boring. Sleeping was difficult.

Sentries on daytime duty feared being shot by enemy snipers if they moved about too much. Despite the dangers trenches had to be repaired and food had to be distributed. At night the barbed wire had to be repaired and No Man's Land was patrolled to spot enemy activity and to recover the wounded.

There was a shortage of food and the menu was usually the same every day – beef, a biscuit and jam. There were few washing facilities and many men were infested with body lice. The crude sewage systems and rotting dead bodies created a foul stench, particularly in summer. Rats fed on the dead bodies. There was little protection from the cold and wet of winter. Men had to stand in pools of water, their toes swelling into the condition known as trench foot. Over 75,000 British soldiers suffered trench foot during the war. Washing and drying feet daily was one attempt to prevent it, but often toes had to be amputated. Disease and illness were common under these conditions.

And there was worse. There was the fear of death. Men lived in constant fear of attack from shells, gas and snipers. They knew that if they went 'over the top', the chance of returning was slim. Living in such constant fear caused some men to suffer shell shock, in which their whole body would shake uncontrollably and they would often stammer. Another fear was of falling into a shell hole of mud and drowning.

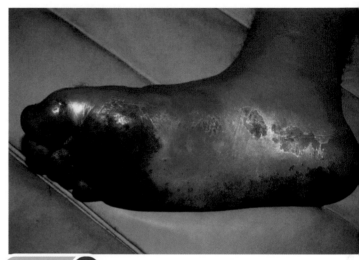

Source **S** Trench foot.

Source **T** British soldiers in a trench during the Battle of the Somme, 1916.

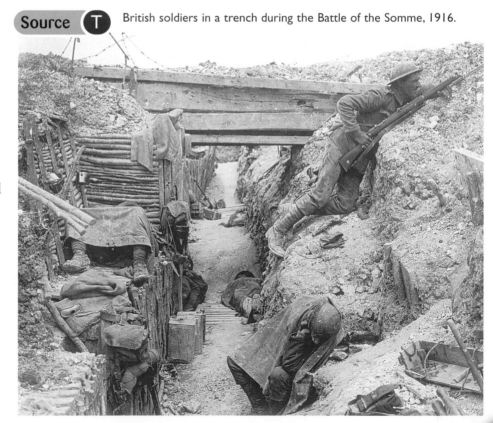

Views of the Front

Having to live in these conditions and suffering the loss of comrades in attacks and the absence from loved ones at home changed the soldiers' attitudes to the war. Soldiers wrote home, but their letters were censored, so their families had no idea what conditions were like. Officials fed them stories of Allied victories. Newspapers were also censored and official photographers and war artists appointed by the government were the only ones allowed to depict scenes in the trenches. And they were allowed to photograph or represent only certain parts of the trenches – artists, for example, were not allowed to include dead bodies in their paintings.

Modern World History for AQA

Source U

Forward Joe Soap's Army, marching without fear

With our own commander, safely in the rear.

He boasts and strikes from morn till night and thinks he's very brave,

But the men who really did the job are dead and in their grave.

An extract from a popular song sung by soldiers in the trenches.

Source V

The battlefield is fearful. One is overcome by a peculiar sour, heavy and penetrating smell of corpses. Men that were killed last October lie half in swamp and half in beet-fields. The legs of an Englishman stick out into the trench, the corpse being built into the parapet: a soldier hangs his rifle on them.

Extract from a letter written by a German soldier, 27 April 1915.

Source W

The Harvest of Battle, a painting by a war artist of the aftermath of battle on the Western Front, completed in 1921. The artist will have made sketches of the battle and used his sketches to complete the painting later.

Source A painting showing men blinded by gas, queuing for treatment.

The contribution of Empire troops to the war

Britain's Dominions and dependencies gave full support to the war effort from its beginning. The only area where there was opposition in favour of Germany was in South Africa but the rebellion was quickly defeated by the Dominion troops. The troops of the Dominions, India and the smaller colonies and dependencies of Britain provided over a quarter of the whole British contribution to the Allied cause. Most of the contribution was made in Europe as can be seen from the many war graves, though there was some in other areas of fighting.

New Zealand provided a higher proportion of its population than any other Dominion, sending 100,000 men overseas to aid the war effort, 58,000 of whom became casualties. In Australia by the end of the war, 332,000 had served overseas with 318,000 casualties. Canada had 365,000 volunteers serving in Europe by March 1918 when service became compulsory. Many French Canadians did not regard the war as being their struggle and only 16,000 of them had volunteered by that date. The Canadian efforts on the Western Front particularly at Vimy Ridge in 1915 have lived on in the folklore of the country. The other major contributor was India who provided 1,000,000 volunteers by the end of the war. Considering that the standing army of India was less than 160,000 at the outbreak of war, this represents a remarkable achievement. Not only were these men provided by the Dominions and colonies, they were also trained and equipped, fighting as national armies though conforming to the British military system.

THINGS TO DO

1 List the discomforts, the fears and the diseases of the men in the trenches.

2 Why were newspapers not allowed to tell the story of the war?

3 What attitude towards the generals is shown in **Source U**? Why did the soldiers feel like this?

4 How reliable are **Sources U** and **V** to an historian writing about the First World War?

5 'Sources W and X are artists' impressions of the war, so they are no use to historians.' Do you agree with this statement? Explain your answer.

6 How important was the contribution of Britain's Dominions and dependencies to the war effort?

2.2 How did the war change life in Britain?

Recruitment

People in all countries greeted the war with enthusiasm in 1914. Lord Kitchener was placed in charge of the war effort in Britain and, as Britain only had a small force of trained soldiers, he realised the need to recruit men quickly. Kitchener launched an appeal for volunteers. Posters were displayed in all main towns. They appealed to people's patriotism, their family responsibilities and their fear and disgust of the Germans. Any able-bodied men who did not volunteer to fight were branded cowards. The feeling towards these men was publicly expressed by those women who handed out white feathers, the mark of cowardice, to any such man they saw in the street. At first there was a huge response to the appeal: half a million men signed up in one month. Many rushed to volunteer, afraid that the war would be over before they could take part, some believing it would be over by Christmas. They reported to their local recruitment office, took the oath to fight 'For King and country' and signed on 'for the king's shilling'.

Source

We said we would serve. We offered ourselves. Call it patriotism.

I was quite empty-headed and bored to tears with shop life. The chaps round about started to go, so I said 'I'm going'.

Well it was gonna be a change. Most volunteers went to get away from their environment.

The views of some recruits on why they joined up to fight in the war in 1914.

Source
Recruitment poster using women to persuade men to enlist for the war.

Source

Oh we don't want to lose you,

But we think you ought to go,

For your King and your country

Both need you so.

We shall want you and miss you,

But with all our might and main,

We shall cheer you, thank you, kiss you,

When you come back again.

A recruitment song from 1914.

FOR HONOUR

"A SCRAP OF PAPER"

Source D Propaganda postcard showing the British attitude to Germany invading Belgium.

By 1916 over two million men had been recruited to the armed forces.

As the war continued, volunteers became fewer: in December 1915 only 55,000 volunteered compared to 436,000 in September 1914. People at home became weary of the war, sickened by news of casualties on the Front, suffering shortages at home and worried by attacks on Britain by air and sea. The enormous casualties on the Western Front meant that Britain needed more fighting men. So in January 1916 the government introduced conscription. All able-bodied men between the ages of 18 and 41 could be enlisted to fight in the forces. Some saw conscription as limiting their freedom, particularly those who refused to join up because they were against war. They were known as conscientious objectors. Some were brought to trial and imprisoned or sent to the Front to act as stretcher-bearers.

Before conscription many of those who volunteered were skilled workers in essential industries, such as mining, which left those industries short of skilled workers. Many of these workers had to be sent back home. So when conscription was introduced skilled workers in industries such as mining and farming were exempt; and up until March 1916 all able-bodied married men were also exempt.

Propaganda

Throughout the war the government used propaganda to encourage the people to continue making sacrifices and help the war effort. From the beginning, posters and postcards were published, stressing the justice of the war and the evil action of the Germans.

This was necessary to convince British people to make the sacrifices necessary to win the war.

THINGS TO DO

1 Why did people volunteer for the armed forces in 1914?

2 Why was conscription introduced in 1916?

3 Explain the techniques used in **Source D** to turn the British people against the Germans.

DORA

The Defence of the Realm Act (DORA) was introduced by the British government in August 1914. This law gave the government far more power than it previously had so that it could protect the country from invasion and do everything possible to win the war. Censorship was introduced, not only on news and letters coming from the Western Front, but on all matters concerned with the war. Newspapers were censored and it was forbidden to even discuss the war in a public place in an attempt to stop the spread of rumours. The only news of the Western Front that the public was allowed to hear through the media were stories of British heroism and German brutality. Official photographers took pictures of mock raids to give people at home an idea of the war. Even films had a patriotic theme.

DORA gave the government the power to take over factories and land for war production. Production of weapons and ammunition was increased by allowing women to work in the munitions industry, lengthening the hours of work and gaining more control over the use of skilled labour. British summer-time was introduced to allow more daylight for working, while beer was watered down and pubs were allowed to open only at certain times to reduce drunkenness which caused absence from work.

Source **F** A British government poster encouraging people not to waste food.

Shortage of food caused by the German U-boat blockade (see page 106) was also addressed by additional laws through DORA. Public parks were taken over for the growing of vegetables, the Women's Land Army was set up and posters were produced to encourage people to support the country by reducing the amount of food they had at meal times (Source F). Even feeding bread to pigeons was forbidden by law to prevent waste.

Despite these restrictions the government, in 1918, was forced to introduce rationing of foods such as sugar, butter and beef. People received ration books with coupons in them. The coupons had to be given in, along with the money, when food was bought, so this limited the amount of certain goods that people could buy each week and ensured that everyone was entitled to the same. But there wasn't enough time to extend rationing to everything during the war. Even so, the fact it was introduced showed how much more the government was involved in the lives of its citizens.

Source **E**

I am not allowed to tell you where I am, because the General is afraid you might tell someone at school, and he might tell the German master, and the German master might telegraph the Kaiser and tell him. And then of course the Kaiser would send an aeroplane to drop bombs on us.

A soldier's letter written to his family in 1914.

Women and the war

Before the First World War, women were often not treated as equals by men. The suffragettes had been campaigning for women to get the vote, but called off their campaign when war started. Women were to play a vital role in the war.

At the beginning of the war women were used to encourage men to join the forces, but later they began to take on the jobs left by men. This meant that women began to do jobs which they had never done before. They delivered the post, drove buses, worked as mechanics, window cleaners, firefighters and did much heavier work in shipbuilding and steelmaking. They proved that they could do the jobs as well as, and in some cases better than, men but they still received lower pay.

Over 100,000 women also responded to the government's appeal to work on the land by joining the 'Women's Land Army'. These 'Land Girls' replaced the farm labourers who had joined the forces and kept the country supplied with food. Other women wanted to play a more direct role in the war. About 23,000 women served as nurses close to the fighting and a further 15,000 volunteered for Voluntary Aid Detachments (VADs) run partly by the Red Cross. They served behind the lines, tending to the casualties on the Western Front. The work was hard and often unpleasant. The Women's Army Auxiliary Corps (WAACs) was formed in 1917 to take over the office jobs in the army, freeing the men to fight.

Edith Cavell

Edith Cavell was an English nurse in charge of a nursing school in Belgium when that country was occupied by the German army. The school was converted into a Red Cross hospital, with Edith as matron, to nurse the thousands of wounded Allied soldiers who had been captured by the Germans.

But Edith Cavell did more than nurse the soldiers, she also helped hundreds of them to escape. In 1915 she was arrested as a spy by the Germans and sentenced to death. Countries around the world pleaded for her to be spared. But the Germans executed her by firing squad.

Edith became a national heroine in Britain. Her death was used in the propaganda war against Germany and in recruitment campaigns to show how evil the Germans were. It also raised the image of women in Britain, showing them to be capable of great courage.

Women and munitions work

During the war many women began to work making shells in munitions factories. The work of these 'munitionettes' was vital for the war effort. The working day was lengthened because of the needs of the war and some women worked 12-hour shifts. Much of the work was dangerous as the women worked with toxic chemicals, and explosions and fires were common. In 1917 a fire in the Silvertown munitions works in East London caused an explosion which killed 69 people and injured 400. Those who worked regularly with TNT found that their skin became yellow and they became known as 'canary girls'. This was a condition known as 'toxic jaundice' and could be fatal. By the end of the war over 900,000 women worked in the munitions industries, representing 60 per cent of the workforce.

Women welcomed the independence they gained during the war, when they could do the work of men and earn their own wages. They were proud to have played their part in the victory and men had recognised their ability and willingness to contribute to the war effort. It was partly because of the role they played in the war that women over the age of 30 were given the vote in 1918. In other ways the war changed little: when men came back from the war they replaced the women in the heavy jobs and women's employment returned largely to the pattern that it was before the war. Women had, however, gained a more positive image of themselves and attitudes were changing slowly.

Source G

Mabel Lethbridge volunteered for service in the danger zone where high explosives were poured and packed into shells. She worked a machine that forced amatol and TNT down into the eighteen pounder shell case. Four girls hauled on a rope to raise a massive weight then at a signal let it drop on the mixture until it was packed tight.

Description of a woman's job in a munitions factory.

Source H   Women in a munitions factory in 1916.

Danger of invasion

People on the east coast of Britain received a shock in December 1914 when German ships shelled Hartlepool, Scarborough and Whitby. There were over 500 civilian casualties in these raids, which created the fear of a German invasion. But the raids also helped to unite the British people and build up hatred towards the Germans. The government made full use of this in its recruiting campaign.

The danger of invasion also came from the air. The Germans had developed Zeppelin airships. The first attack by air on Britain was in January 1915 when two Zeppelins bombed Great Yarmouth and King's Lynn, killing two people and damaging houses. Further Zeppelin attacks in 1915 and 1916 concentrated on London, but they stopped in 1917 because of the British defences. The British used barrage balloons to defend themselves against the Zeppelins and sent fighter planes to intercept them. They also illuminated the sky with searchlights so the Zeppelins could be easily spotted and fired at. If a Zeppelin was hit it burst into flames, because it was filled with hydrogen. The crew had little chance of surviving.

THINGS TO DO

1 Give examples of how DORA changed life in Britain.

2 What do **Sources E** and **F** tell us about people's fears in 1914? Do you think they were realistic?

3 What new jobs did women do in the First World War? Why were they needed? What new dangers did they face?

4 How did the war affect the position of women in society?

Source A Zeppelin.

Aeroplane warfare

This was not the end of the air attacks. Aeroplanes had been used for reconnaissance since 1914 to photograph the enemy positions and aid an offensive. This led to dogfights between aircraft in the sky. The early planes were crude machines made of wood and canvas, held together by piano wire. The pilots sat in the open cockpits with only goggles, leather helmets and thick coats to protect them from the cold. They had no radio, no parachutes and few navigational instruments. Even the engines were unreliable and it needed a lot of courage to fly them, let alone fight in them. In 1917 the average fighting life of a front line pilot was two weeks.

Each side had their own 'air aces' such as Britain's Albert Ball and Mick Mannock, whose daring exploits were told at home, raising the morale of the people. The German hero was the 'Red Baron', Baron Manfred von Richthofen, who destroyed 80 Allied aircraft before he was shot down in 1918.

The first weapons used were handguns, though these were soon replaced by machine-guns. But the machine-guns were mounted on the cockpit and a pilot couldn't fire straight ahead without shooting off his propellor. When the synchronised propellor was invented, the problem was solved. The machine-gun was now mounted on the propellor and bullets were fired between the propellor blades as they spun round.

Towards the end of the war faster and more manoeuvrable aeroplanes, such as the German Albatross and the British Sopwith Camel, were developed. Then planes, such as the German Gotha IV and the British Vickers Vimy, were developed to carry bombs. German bombers began raiding towns on the south coast from 1917 onwards. Over 1,000 people were killed in these attacks and many houses and shops were damaged.

The effect of these attacks on the war effort was not great. More important was the psychological effect they had on people. Britain was an island and had always been safe from invasion. This was no longer the case. For the first time British civilians realised that they were vulnerable. The government had to take measures to defend its citizens from future attacks. The British fleet guarded the east coast against further attacks and defences were introduced against air attacks. Improvements were made to British aircraft so they could launch attacks on German towns, and in 1918 the Royal Air Force was formed.

Source J

The whole street seemed to explode. There was smoke and flames all over, but the worst of all were the screams of the wounded and dying and mothers looking frantically for their kids.

Description of an air raid on Folkestone in May 1917.

Source K

Air raid damage in London during the First World War.

Exam-style assessment

This question follows the pattern of questions to be set by AQA for Paper 1, **Section B**, of its new Modern World History specification.

Study **Sources A, B, C** and **D** and then answer all parts of the Question which follows.

Source A: Problems with food supplies

By 1917 food supply in Britain had become quite desperate. In April German U-boats were sinking one in every four British merchant ships. In April 1917 Britain had only six weeks' supply of wheat left. As food supplies ran short, so prices rose.

From *Modern World History* (1996) by BEN WALSH

Source B: Eat less bread!

A government poster of 1917.

Source C: A cross-section of a trench

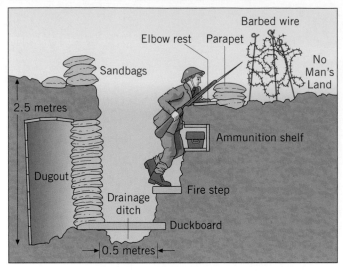

From *Modern World History* (2000) by
D. FERRIBY, D. HANSOM and S. WAUGH

Source D: Civilian attitudes in Britain to the war

At the beginning of the war, cheering crowds had gathered in the streets of London, and young men had eagerly enlisted 'to fight for King and Country'. But the mood of the people quickly changed from cheerful optimism to grim acceptance of the horrors of trench warfare.

From *Britain Since 1700* (1968) by R. J. Cootes

Questions

(a) What can you learn from **Source A** about food supplies in Britain in 1917? **(3 marks)**

(b) How useful is **Source B** for studying about food shortages in Britain in the First World War? Use **Source B** and your own knowledge to explain your answer. **(8 marks)**

(c) Use **Source C** and your own knowledge to explain what conditions were like for soldiers in the trenches during the First World War. **(6 marks)**

(d) Is **Source D** a fair interpretation of how attitudes towards the war changed in Britain in the years 1914–18? Explain your answer by using **Source D** and your own knowledge. **(8 marks)**

3 Britain in the Second World War

INTRODUCTION

Technological improvements made the Second World War a very different war from the First. The development of aircraft and motorised transport meant that attacks could be quicker. Britain declared war when the Germans invaded Poland in September 1939. A British Expeditionary Force was sent to France, but Poland was too far away and was quickly overcome by Hitler. The defeat of Poland was followed by a period of calm called the Phoney War until Hitler launched his successful attack on Norway in April 1940. This was followed by the overrunning of the Netherlands, Belgium and France in May. Many of the BEF escaped from France through the port of Dunkirk.

Hitler had used Blitzkrieg tactics against Poland and the West. This involved the use of aircraft and tanks in attacks which relied on speed and surprise. In order to use these tactics against Britain, Germany needed to control the air so that troops could be moved safely across the Channel. This led to the Battle of Britain. RAF pilots resisted German attacks and forced Hitler to change his tactics. Intensive bombing attacks on British towns marked the beginning of the Blitz as Hitler tried to force Churchill to make peace. Britain refused to surrender and, with the support of American aircraft, increased its own bomber attacks on Germany, resulting in the destruction of many German cities.

The use of aircraft and bombing attacks meant that civilians were more at risk in the Second World War and this led to the British government taking control of many aspects of the lives of its people. Children were evacuated from towns and cities to the country while air raid shelters and gas masks were delivered to the people. Conscription was introduced, Civil Defence Forces were formed and blackouts enforced to protect the population of cities from air attacks. Armed convoys were used to guard ships entering Britain with much needed supplies from attack by the German U-boats. The shortage of food caused by the U-boat blockade resulted in the government introducing rationing, and propaganda was used to urge people to support the 'Grow your Own' campaign. Women helped on the land, were conscripted to replace men in vital industrial work, while others joined the women's military forces.

The final defeat of Germany began with the D-Day landings in Normandy in 1944. The American and British armies freed the West, while the Soviet armies attacked Germany from the East. The leadership of Churchill had maintained British morale and the will to resist the Germans throughout the war. The economic and military support of the USA and Soviet Russia ensured that the Germans were defeated in 1945.

1939	Conscription
	Evacuation
	Poland attacked
	Convoys introduced
	BEF sent to France
	Poland defeated
	Phoney War
1940	Rationing in Britain
	Blitzkrieg in West
	Defeat of Norway
	Defeat of Netherlands, Belgium and France
	Dunkirk
	Home Guard formed
	Battle of Britain
	Blitz
	Bombing of Germany
1941	USA entered war
1942	Bombing of Germany intensified
1943	Turning point in battle of the Atlantic
1944	Britain and USA gain control of air over Germany
	D-Day – advance into Germany
1945	Bombing of Dresden
	Defeat of Germany

Britain in the Second World War

3.1 How did Britain resist and contribute to the defeat of Germany in the Second World War?

The Phoney War, 1939–40

The German attack on Poland from the west and the Soviet attack from the east on 17 September 1939 were successful. By the end of September, Poland had been defeated and ceased to exist as a state. Britain and France had been unable to help the Poles. From the end of September to April the following year little progress was made in the war in the west. This became known as the Phoney War (pretend war) in Britain and as the Sitzkrieg (sitting war) in Germany.

The Phoney War appears to have been an attempt by Hitler to push Britain and other West European powers into backing down over Poland, as they had backed down at Munich in 1938. Hitler's strategy for fighting a war was based on a series of quick campaigns. Germany did not have the depth of resources for a long, drawn-out war.

Britain and France prepared for war during this period and a British force was sent to France to support the French. But the military preparations were half-hearted. The French felt safe from attack by the Germans because of the Maginot Line, a line of fortifications they had built in the 1930s, all along the border with Germany, stretching from Belgium to Switzerland. The French believed it was impossible for any invading army to break through this series of forts, which were linked by underground tunnels.

Source **A** German tanks rest during the invasion of France.

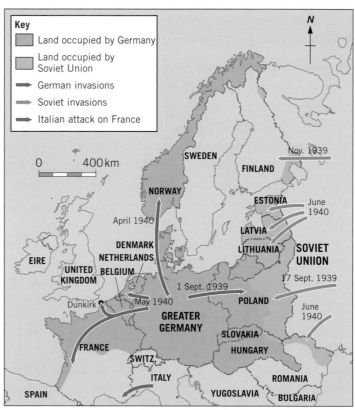

German and Soviet conquests, 1939–40.

Modern World History for AQA

The German invasion of Norway, April 1940

The Phoney War ended in April 1940 when Germany attacked Norway. The Germans relied on Norway and neighbouring Sweden for over half of their iron ore imports. The British Prime Minister, Neville Chamberlain, had considered occupying Norway to cut off Germany's vital supplies, but feared that world opinion would be against Britain as Norway was a neutral country. He lost his chance. Hitler ordered a Blitzkrieg attack by sea, and seized points along the Norwegian coast as far north as Narvik. German paratroops were dropped to capture places inland, such as bridges and airfields. The British and French were unable to provide sufficient help to prevent Norway being defeated.

However, perhaps the most important result of the British failure to help Norway was the resignation on 10 May 1940 of the Prime Minister, Neville Chamberlain.

Winston Churchill was chosen to lead a coalition government for the duration of the war. He took office just as Hitler began the invasion of France.

THINGS TO DO

1 What is meant by the 'Phoney War'?

2 What differences do you think the Phoney War made to Hitler's chances of winning?

3 What message was given to the British public by **Sources B** and **C**?

Source B

I have nothing to offer but blood, toil, tears and sweat. You ask, what is our policy? I will say: It is to wage war, by sea, land and air, with all our might. You ask, what is our aim? I can answer in one word: Victory – victory at all costs, victory, however long and hard the road may be.

Winston Churchill speaking in the House of Commons, 13 May 1940.

Source C A British poster from May 1940.

"LET US GO FORWARD TOGETHER"

The defeat of France, 1940

The nature of Blitzkrieg warfare

Blitzkrieg is German for 'lightning war', and it was the key to the rapid German successes in the early part of the Second World War. The Germans wanted surprise and speed, using tanks and planes. Their importance had been seen at the end of the First World War.

Attacks were carried out by firstly bombing key targets, such as enemy headquarters and centres of communication. At the same time, parachutists were dropped behind enemy lines. Then tanks and trucks containing infantry (foot soldiers) carried out the main attack. The tanks and infantry would start by attacking all the enemy's weak points, so that the enemy's strongholds could be encircled while more troops were arriving. Meanwhile, the tanks and infantry would advance further.

Using this tactic meant that the Germans concentrated their tanks in large groups in a few places, to very great effect. On the other hand, the British and French were still using tanks to back up each infantry division and not using tanks as a spearhead.

When they attacked France on 10 May 1940, the Germans by-passed the Maginot Line by attacking through the forests of the Ardennes in Southern Belgium, which the French thought was impossible to do. The German forces bombed the Dutch port of Rotterdam. Resistance in Belgium lasted until

THINGS TO DO

1 What is meant by Blitzkrieg?

2 Why was Germany able to defeat Norway, the Netherlands, Belgium and France so easily in 1940?

3 Why was the Maginot Line useless?

4 How did the Nazi–Soviet Pact help the Germans 1939–40?

5 What happened to France after the defeat of Germany?

28 May. The Germans swept into France through the heavily forested Ardennes, by-passing the Maginot Line and taking the French by surprise. Soon British and French forces were in retreat.

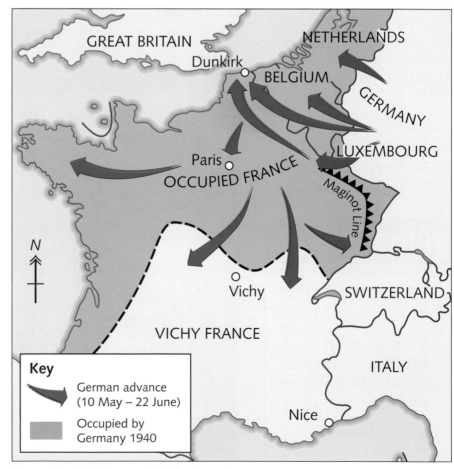

Key

➤ German advance (10 May – 22 June)

▨ Occupied by Germany 1940

The path of the German Blitzkrieg in 1940.

The evacuation from Dunkirk

A contemporary painting by Charles Cundall showing British troops being rescued from the beaches of Dunkirk.

In May 1940, the British Expeditionary Force (BEF) under the command of Lord Gort consisted of ten divisions which had been placed under the overall control of the French Commander. When the French were being defeated by the German Blitzkrieg, the BEF was in danger of being cut off from the coast. On 27 May 1940, Gort was instructed to abandon any co-operation with the French and to evacuate France. This task appeared almost impossible as Calais had been taken and Belgian forces surrendered to the Germans on 28 May. Operation Dynamo, the evacuation from Dunkirk, began on 27 May, though on that day only 7000 men were moved.

Operation Dynamo was a greater success than the British could have hoped for. Most of the men were brought home by destroyers which were helped by every sort of privately owned vessel: pleasure boats, river ferries, fishing boats. Around 860 ships took part and between 27 May and 4 June, 338,000 men were brought to England from the beaches at Dunkirk. Of these, 139,000 were French. The 'miracle' of Dunkirk was made easier by the fine weather and the decision of the Germans to halt their armed forces. Why Hitler did not press on is uncertain. Perhaps he thought that Britain was already defeated or would make peace after the defeat of France. Certainly Goering, the German commander of the Luftwaffe, had boasted that the British forces at Dunkirk could be destroyed by the airforce without help from the army. The men on the beaches at Dunkirk were under constant fire from the Luftwaffe but they still escaped under the defence of the RAF.

The evacuation from Dunkirk was hailed as a great victory by the British. The BEF casualties totalled 68,000 so most of them had been saved and these men would form the core of the new army. Yet the men had to abandon their equipment on the beaches. Hitler claimed that his armies had captured 1200 British field guns, 1250 anti-aircraft guns, 11,000 machine-guns and 75,000 vehicles. Nearly all the guns and tanks had been abandoned by the BEF and many of the men had also lost their rifles. In addition, the RAF lost 474 aeroplanes defending the beaches.

Churchill used the the evacuation from Dunkirk for propaganda purposes. British morale was boosted by reference to 'Dunkirk Spirit' and the evacuated soldiers were available to fight again. In other ways, Dunkirk was a defeat for the allies. The British army had been forced out of continental Europe and lost so many arms and equipment that it was impossible for Britain to defend France. Within a month of the Dunkirk evacuation, Paris had been captured and France had surrendered to Germany. The Germans occupied Northern France and gained control of submarine bases on the Atlantic coast, which were to be a great help to them in the U-boat campaign against Britain. Instead of occupying the whole of France, Germany allowed southern France to set up a government at Vichy run by General Pétain. This Vichy government was really controlled by the Germans.

Source **E** Dunkirk, 1940.

THINGS TO DO

1 Was Dunkirk a victory or a defeat for Britain?

2 'Source D is an artist's impression of Dunkirk so it is of no use to an historian.' Do you agree with this statement? Explain your answer.

3 Is Source E more use to an historian than Source D? Explain your answer.

4 How did Hitler's mistakes help Britain at Dunkirk, in the Battle of Britain and in the Blitz?

5 How could Source F be used to help the war effort in Britain?

Battle of Britain and the Blitz

After defeating France, Hitler planned to invade Britain. The plan was known as Operation Sealion. To do this the German airforce (Luftwaffe) needed to control the skies above Britain. In the summer of 1940 the Luftwaffe attacked British airfields, ports and radar stations in an attempt to gain superiority in the air. Britain was defended tenaciously by its airforce, the RAF, but came very close to defeat. In the first week of September, the British lost 185 aircraft and 300 airmen. New planes had to be built rapidly, but it took longer to train new airmen. This was the Battle of Britain. It was a change of tactics by the Germans that saved the country from defeat in the air. Hitler decided to bomb some of Britain's most vital cities. On 7 September 1940 the first German bombing attack on Britain was launched at night against London. This marked the end of the Battle of Britain and the beginning of the Blitz, the bombing of British cities.

Hitler's change of tactics was partly in response to British bombing raids on Berlin, but the main purpose was to try to break the morale of the British people and force Churchill to sue for peace. Though the Luftwaffe had failed to defeat the RAF and Operation Sealion was called off, the bombing attacks on major cities continued throughout the winter causing much damage. Over a period of 77 days London was bombed every night except one. Other cities to be bombed included Bristol, Liverpool, Plymouth, Southampton, Manchester Birmingham, Coventry and Glasgow – all of them ports or industrial centres.

The bombing of Coventry in November 1940 destroyed industrial targets, such as motor-works and aero-engine factories. It also destroyed the city's Cathedral, the destruction of which became a symbol of German ruthlessness and was used by the British in the propaganda war. The raid lasted 10 hours, a third of the city was destroyed and 4,000 people were killed. The most remarkable effect of the raid was that industrial production in Coventry rose following the attack.

By the time the Blitz ended in the summer of 1941 about 43,000 people had been killed and 2 million were homeless. Hitler apparently believed that Britain had been defeated because in June 1941 he began to carry out his long-planned search for *Lebensraum* (space) by breaking the Nazi–Soviet Pact of 1939 and attacking the USSR.

Source F

The ruins of Coventry Cathedral after the German bombing of the city in 1940.

The Battle of the Atlantic

In the First World War the Germans had almost defeated the British by using U-boats to destroy merchant shipping carrying supplies to Britain. Within a few hours of the Second World War breaking out, a British passenger liner *Athenia* was sunk by a U-boat. The Germans believed that the U-boats would have more success in 1939 than they had in 1917. The aim was to cut off Britain's supplies of food, oil and raw materials from overseas. The British countered this by organising merchant ships into convoys and using warships to defend them. But after the Germans occupied France they were free to use French Atlantic ports as bases from which their submarines attacked British ships. Britain simply did not have enough warships to protect all its merchant ships from attack. The development of sonic techniques, which could detect U-boats under water, was an advantage to the British, but the German tactic of hunting convoys in groups of up to 40 U-boats, known as 'wolf packs', was successful in the first years of the war. The 'wolf packs' attacked on the surface and at night so they could not be detected by ASDIC.

When America entered the war in December 1941 the fight against the U-boats changed. The USA provided warship escorts for convoys, and radar, which was invented in 1935, was used to detect submarines on the surface. By 1943 Britain had more warships and was able to give support to every convoy of its merchant ships. When U-boats were detected, some of the escort warships broke away from the convoy to hunt them. Aircraft were used more to spot U-boats and destroy them using depth charges. By 1943 aircraft using radar could detect enemy submarines, even in the worst weather. In 1943 the Allies for the first time were building more new ships than were being destroyed by the U-boats.

THINGS TO DO

1 Which period of the Battle of the Atlantic do you think the Germans called the 'happy time'?

2 When was the turning point in the Battle of the Atlantic? Explain your answer.

Source G

Britain's ability to maintain her supply lines is the decisive factor for the outcome of the war.

Admiral Raeder, Chief of German Naval Staff, speaking in 1940.

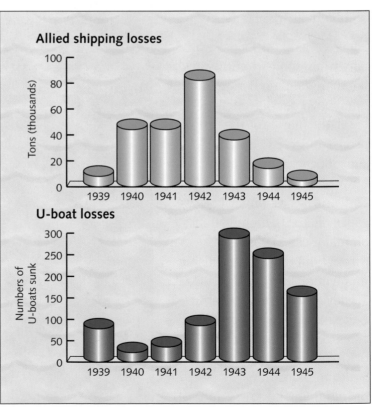

These charts show the amount of allied shipping losses and corresponding losses of U-boats in 1939–45.

Modern World History for AQA

The bombing of Germany

The first British bombing attacks on Germany took place in 1940 when Britain stood alone against Germany, her army defeated, and with no other way to strike at the Germans. The attacks began by targeting strategic areas, but by 1942 British aircraft were bombing entire cities in an attempt to break Germany's military power and its people's morale. The first 'Thousand Bomber' raid on Cologne in May 1942 killed about 400 Germans. British Bomber Command, led by Air Chief Marshal Sir Arthur 'Bomber' Harris, continued the bombing offensive in 1943, with 43 raids on the industrial Ruhr Basin, 33 on Hamburg and 16 on Berlin.

Because the bombing raids were at night it was impossible to hit the targets accurately and many civilian areas were damaged by mistake. The Germans used this in the propaganda war. Worse for Bomber Command was the number of planes being lost in the attacks. The attacks were seen as important in helping Britain's new ally, the USSR, and raising people's morale in Britain. German industry and transport were severely damaged by the bombings: war production did rise until July 1944, but how much greater would it have been without the bombings?

"HOW HARD FOR US POOR PEOPLE OF DUSSELDORF—"

"—AND OF WARSAW, ROTTERDAM, BELGRADE, COVENTRY...... "

BEGINNINGS OF FELLOW-FEELING

Source H A British cartoon published after the bombing of German cities in 1943.

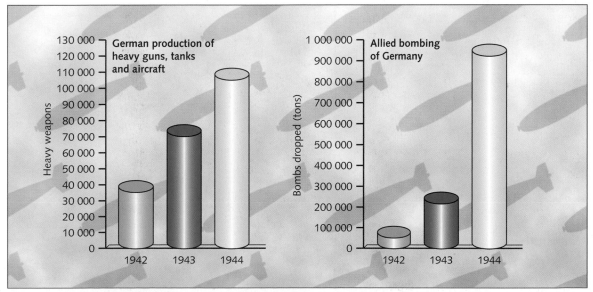

A comparison of Germany's production of weapons with the amount of bombs dropped on Germany.

Victory in the air

American bombing raids on Germany began in August 1942. Unlike the British, the Americans bombed during the day, which made the attacks more accurate, but raised the number of aircraft and crew lost. The breakthrough in the bombing raids came with the development of heavy precision bombing techniques in 1944. By late 1944 Britain and the USA controlled the air above Germany and made devastating attacks on roads, railways and industry, which contributed to the final defeat of Germany.

In February 1945, three months before the end of the war, British aircraft destroyed the city of Dresden with incendiary bombs, killing 25,000 civilians. Were these attacks on civilians justified? Even Churchill described the attacks on Dresden as 'mere acts of terror and wanton destruction'. By the end of the war about 600,000 German civilians had been killed in air raids. However, German morale did not break until the final collapse of Germany in 1945, so what part did the bombing attacks play in the final victory?

Percentage of German cities destroyed by Allied air attacks.

Bonn	83%
Bochum (Ruhr)	83%
Bremerhaven	79%
Hamburg	75%
Kiel	69%
Kassell	69%
Hagen (Ruhr)	67%
Munster	65%
Dusseldorf	64%
Mainz	61%
Cologne	61%
Hanover	60%
Bremen	60%
Dresden	59%
Aachen	59%
Koblenz	58%
Emden	56%
Dortmund	54%
Munich	54%
Stettin	53%
Frankfurt	52%
Nuremberg	51%
Essen	50%

THINGS TO DO

1 Explain the meaning of the cartoon in **Source H**.

2 Compare the damage in **Source F** with that in **Source I**.

3 What does the graph on page 129 tell us about industrial production in Germany during the bombing raids?

4 Does this mean the bombing raids were pointless?

5 What are the arguments for and against the bombing of civilians?

Source I

Dresden after being bombed by the British, February 1945.

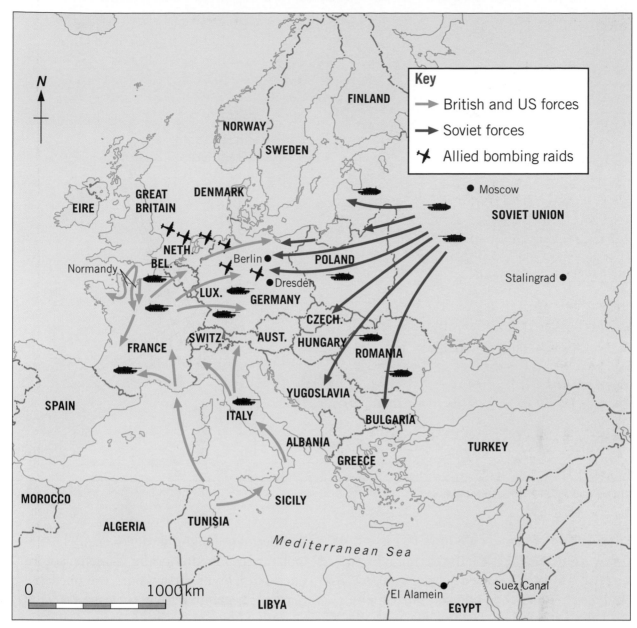

The defeat of Germany 1944–5.

D-Day, June 1944

Ever since the German invasion of the Soviet Union in 1941, Stalin had been asking Britain and the USA to launch an invasion by sea of German-occupied Western Europe. This would force the Germans to transfer some of their 3 million troops from the Soviet Union to the west. Churchill agreed in principle, but decided to concentrate first on north Africa. Stalin believed that this was done so that the communist Soviet Union was weakened first, before it received much help from the Western Allies.

However, in 1944 preparations for landings in France were made on a huge scale. Dwight D. Eisenhower, the US general, was in overall command of 'Operation Overlord'. He led the Germans to believe that the landings would take place near Calais – the shortest Channel crossing-point. The Allies repeatedly bombed the city of Calais. Dummy military camps were built in Kent, complete with wooden tanks. Only a few Germans believed that the invasion would happen in Normandy.

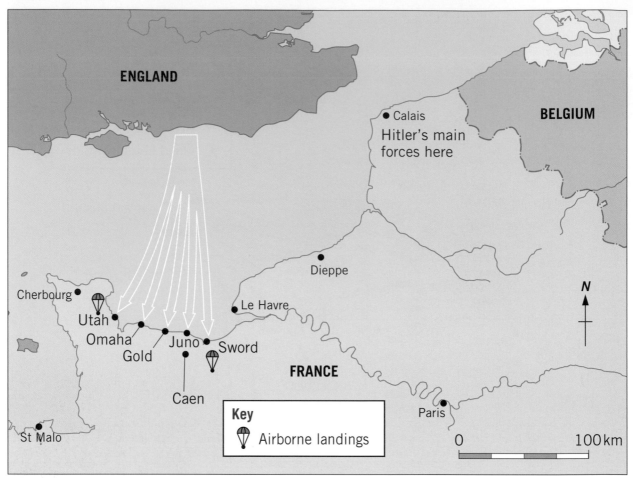

D-Day landings in France, June 1944.

The invasion occurred on 6 June 1944 – D-Day – and its scale took the Germans by surprise. The plan involved five separate landings, in areas code-named Utah, Omaha, Gold, Juno and Sword. The first two were the responsibility of the Americans; the other three, the British and the Canadians. Even when he had realised the full extent of the invasion in Normandy, Hitler refused to move tanks and troops from the Calais area, fearing that another major attack was planned there.

Landing on the Normandy beaches was grim on the first day. About 3600 British and Canadian soldiers were killed or wounded. The Americans lost 6000 men. However, over 150,000 Allied soldiers had landed. In the next few days, they established their positions on the five beaches, and began to move inland to liberate France. By 12 June 325,000 Allied troops were in France.

The Germans fought hard. For example, it took nearly a month for the Allies to capture Cherbourg, an important port. But once the Germans began to retreat, the pace of liberation quickened. On 25 August 1944, Paris was freed and its new leader was Charles de Gaulle, who had been in exile in Britain.

The advance into Germany

In September 1944 the Allies reached the important river crossing, the Rhine, and began capturing bridges held by the Germans. Although most of France had now been liberated, the Allies had problems progressing into Germany. In December 1944 the Germans launched a counter-attack in the Ardennes. At first it achieved remarkable success, but by the end of January 1945 the Germans were once again in retreat.

While German troops were retreating out of Western Europe, the Soviets were moving in from the east. The Germans were also retreating out of Italy. Allied bombing raids on German cities were stepped up (see pages 129–30).

(see pages 129–30)

THINGS TO DO

Why do you think the D-Day landings were successful?

Source Troops going ashore on D-Day.

Recruitment

The government had announced the introduction of conscription after Hitler's invasion of Czechoslovakia in March 1939. It was put into effect when Britain declared war on 3 September. All men between the age of 18 and 40 were conscripted for military service, beginning with those in their early twenties. Certain occupations, such as coalminers, firemen and doctors, were exempt. In May 1940 the Emergency Powers Act gave the government complete control over 'person and property', allowing them to direct adults to work in any part of the country.

When war broke out the government expected the country to be attacked from the air and took precautions to protect its people. Air-raid wardens were appointed, some full-time, but most part-time volunteers, whose job it was to make sure the blackout was followed and to prepare people for air raids. They checked that everyone carried a gas mask to protect them against gas attacks from the air. During the Blitz wardens directed the movement of people into air-raid shelters and organised the clearing up of damage.

In May 1940 the Local Defence Volunteers, later known as the Home Guard, was formed. This was part-time, unpaid volunteer work to help protect the country against invaders. It called for men aged 17 to 65 to volunteer and on the first day of recruitment 250,000 did so.

They met most evenings after work and were taught how to handle weapons and what action to take if the enemy landed in Britain. They were trained in unarmed combat and anti-tank warfare, even though to begin with they had hardly any weapons or equipment. They acted as lookouts – for example, on the coast to spot an invading fleet and in the sky for German parachutists or bombs being dropped. They also removed local signposts that might help invading forces, guarded important buildings and manned road blocks. Lack of weapons was the Home Guard's main problem.

Source A A wartime poster calling on men to volunteer for the job of air-raid warden.

Source B

Such a force is of the highest value and importance. A country where every street and every village bristles with resolute, armed men is a country against which the tactics which destroyed the Dutch resistance would not succeed.

Winston Churchill speaking in Parliament about the Home Guard, November 1940.

Women and the war

Women were far more affected by the Second World War than they had been by the First World War. They were in much greater danger from bombing raids. Women were also affected by the evacuation of themselves and their children and by rationing. Many of them did civil defence jobs, joined the armed forces and helped to reduce food shortages by joining the Women's Land Army to work on the land.

Conscription deprived industry of many of its workers. As in the First World War, women volunteered to do the work of the men who had gone to fight. But by 1941 industry was so short of workers that unmarried women were conscripted to fill the shortage. By 1943, 57 per cent of workers were female. Many of the conscripts had little choice where they worked. New munitions factories were sometimes located in the country for security reasons, and conscripted women had to move to these areas, where they were housed in local hostels. Propaganda posters glamorised the work to make it more appealing (Source D). Actually the work was often repetitive and boring, though far more skills were required in some jobs than in the First World War. Some worked at welding, forging and building aircraft and ships, as well as many other skilled jobs previously thought impossible for women.

Source **E**

> This work the women are performing in munitions factories has to be seen to be believed. Precision engineering jobs which a few years ago would have made a skilled turner's hair stand on end are performed with deadly accuracy by girls who had no industrial experience.
>
> *Clement Attlee, the Deputy Prime Minister, writing about the work women did during the war.*

Source A poster encouraging men to volunteer for the Home Guard.

Source A poster advertising for women to help the war effort by working in factories.

Women in service

Each of the armed forces developed its own auxiliary force for women in the Second World War: the ATS (Auxiliary Territorial Service), the WAAF (Women's Auxiliary Air Force) and the WRNS (Women's Royal Naval Service). These forces helped the men by doing backroom jobs rather than fighting. They worked alongside men and faced the same dangers, but they did not fire the guns. They operated searchlights, filled sandbags or acted as radar controllers. The WAAF repaired the planes and helped on the airfield. Women pilots were allowed to ferry planes from the factories to the airfields, but they were not allowed to fight. Women did important work supporting the men in the front line as nurses, in the intelligence service, and others did dangerous work as spies behind enemy lines.

The Women's Land Army

The food shortages caused by the German U-boat attacks on British shipping in the Atlantic (see page 128) inspired the government to launch a 'Dig for Victory' campaign. The Women's Land Army, which was formed for farm work in the First World War, was re-formed in 1939 and grew to 80,000 strong by 1944. Many travelled the country doing everyday farming jobs, such as haymaking, ploughing, harvesting and looking after the animals. By 1943 production in Britain had almost doubled.

The 'Grow your Own' campaign

Women at home also played their part in the 'Grow your Own' campaign. Farms provided staple foods, such as grain, potatoes, milk and meat, with allotments providing most of the vegetables. The campaign, encouraged by poster advertisements using the cartoon characters Potato Pete and

Dr Carrot, was very successful. Window-boxes and lawns, public parks and golf courses were used to grow vegetables to keep the nation fed and healthy; even the moat of the Tower of London was turned into an area for allotments.

A less patriotic way of gaining food supplies was to buy them on the 'black market'. These arrived in Britain as 'extras' that by-passed customs officials, and were sold at high prices either by traders or 'under the counter' by shopkeepers.

Source **F**   A poster calling for women to join the Women's Land Army.

Rationing

To make sure everyone got a fair share of food, the government introduced rationing in January 1940. Each person had a ration book filled with coupons which they used to buy the amount of food they were entitled to each week. A points system was introduced later to give people greater choice in what they could buy. The Board of Trade also issued recipes showing people how to make healthy meals using food that was available.

People were encouraged to use alternatives to rationed goods. Some goods came from abroad, such as powdered milk and Spam (Supply Pressed American Meat) from the USA. People tried new recipes, such as carrot marmalade.

At first only butter, bacon and sugar were rationed, later this was extended to include meat, tea and most basic food-stuffs, though vegetables were never rationed. Clothes were rationed from June 1941 which led to shorter hemlines and fewer

Source **G** Mending your own clothes to save on materials needed for the war was encouraged by government posters like this one.

buttons on clothing to save on materials. The government also encouraged people to save by mending their own clothes and to use cheaper, more basic clothes and furniture. These were identified with a utility mark so that people buying them would know they were helping the war effort.

Fuel was rationed and many people gave up using their cars so that as much fuel as possible was available for the war effort. The government also encouraged people to use less hot water so that the coal that otherwise would be used for heating the water could be used for the war.

Source **H** These cartoon characters were part of the campaign to encourage people to eat healthy food.

How were civilians protected by the government?

Evacuation

The government expected from the beginning of the war that the Germans would attack Britain from the air. So it took precautions to protect its civilians from bombings and gas attacks. Children were protected by being moved (evacuated) from the likeliest targets, the cities, to the countryside where they would be safe. The first evacuation was announced on 31 August 1939, the day before Hitler invaded Poland. Many parents were reluctant to be separated from their children, but accepted they would be safer. Parents were told what the children needed to take with them and where they were to assemble for the evacuation. The evacuation began on 1 September. Many city schools were closed and many teachers accompanied the children to the countryside to carry on teaching them.

At their destinations the evacuees gathered in village or school halls where they were chosen

Source

Everything was so clean in the room. We were given face flannels and tooth brushes. We'd never cleaned our teeth until then. And hot water came from the tap. And there was a lavatory upstairs. And carpets. And clean sheets. This was all very odd. I didn't like it. It was scary.

The memories of a Second World War evacuee.

by the foster family they were to live with. The children had mixed experiences. Some were very happy, helping on farms and eating better than they had ever done.

Others had a miserable time. Some were resented as a burden by their foster families. They also missed their own families, far away in the cities. Many country families, unaware of how city slum people lived, were in for a shock. They had to deal with children who wet their beds and children who had no experience of using a knife and fork to eat with.

Source Evacuee children on their way from the city to the countryside to escape the danger of German air raids.

Homesickness and the realisation that the war had not begun saw many children drift back to their homes in the cities towards the end of 1939. The government tried to prevent this by running a campaign to encourage children and parents to stay where they were, but had little success. When German bombers started blitzing Britain's cities in 1940 a second evacuation from the cities took place, though not on the scale of the one in 1939.

We left feeling sad for our parents and afraid that they would be killed by the bombs. We were anxious because we had no idea where we were going or whom we would live with, but at least we had been told by our parents that we would be safe. When we arrived in Sandbach, we were chosen for a variety of reasons: for the extra income they received for us, to help on the farm or with the housework. A few were very lucky because they lived with families who cared for them; for those, life was like a holiday and they did not want to leave. I was upset because I was separated from my sister.

School was a joke: we shared it with the locals so there was only half a day attendance and not enough teachers. The children whose school it was resented us being there and threatened us and made fun of us in the playground. There were many fights between the two groups. I was glad when I returned home in time for Christmas, but the following September I was evacuated with my school to Blackpool.

Ted Cummings, who was evacuated from Manchester to Sandbach in September 1939, writing about his feelings.

DON'T do it, mother —

LEAVE THE CHILDREN WHERE THEY ARE

ISSUED BY THE MINISTRY OF HEALTH

Source A government poster trying to persuade parents not to take their children back from the countryside.

Source

Clarence and I used to sleep together and poor Clarence used to wet the bed because he was a very nervous kid. She (the foster mother) could never tell who'd done it so she used to bash the daylights out of the both of us. So, of course, the more Clarence got hit the more he wet the bed. It was then we started to get locked in the cupboard.

The film actor, Michael Caine, remembers his evacuation with his brother.

Britain in the Second World War

The Blitz

The government supplied its citizens with air raid shelters as part of its campaign to protect them from German air raids. The first shelters were delivered in February 1939. These were Anderson shelters, which were sunk into the ground in the back garden. They had enough room for a family and were safer than staying in the house. Every citizen also received a gas mask to protect them against gas attacks. Over 38 million of these were supplied. Public information leaflets (Source O) were sent to every household in July, telling people what to do if there was an air raid. The blackout came into force on 1 September. Every house had to hang thick black curtains or stick brown paper over the windows to stop the house lights being seen from outside by enemy bombers. Street lamps, traffic lights and car headlamps were also blacked out.

Most local authorities drew up civil defence plans before the war started. This was required by the Air Raid Precaution Act of 1937. The civil defence forces involved were air-raid wardens, Auxiliary Fire Service, Auxiliary Police Corps, Red Cross, St John's Ambulance Brigade and the Women's Voluntary Service. They helped the main emergency services deal with the damage caused by the air attacks.

The government encouraged people to use purpose-built brick public air-raid shelters, but many preferred the Anderson shelter or to stay in their own home protected in a Morrison shelter or in a cellar. People in London at first were not allowed to use the underground railway stations for fear they would get trapped under ground. But public pressure to use them forced the authorities to give way and they became popular places to shelter.

The air attacks and their effects are described on page 127. The British people, encouraged by the Prime Minister, Winston Churchill, coped well with the bombing. However, there was looting and some opposition from citizens, particularly in London's East End which took the brunt of the early bombing.

Source Air-raid wardens check on civilians in an Anderson shelter after a bombing raid.

Source A public information leaflet telling people what to do to protect themselves against gas attacks.

OFFICIAL INSTRUCTIONS ISSUED BY THE MINISTRY OF HOME SECURITY

GAS ATTACK

HOW TO PUT ON YOUR GAS MASK

Always keep your gas mask with you – day and night. Learn to put it on quickly. Practise wearing it.

1. Hold your breath. 2. Hold mask in front of face, with thumbs inside straps. 3. Thrust chin well forward into mask, pull straps over head as far as they will go. 4. Run finger round face-piece taking care head-straps are not twisted.

IF THE GAS RATTLES SOUND

1. Hold your breath. Put on mask wherever you are. Close window.
2. If out of doors, take off hat, put on your mask. Turn up collar.
3. Put on gloves or keep hands in pockets. Take cover in nearest building.

IF YOU GET GASSED

BY VAPOUR GAS Keep your gas mask on even if you feel discomfort
If discomfort continues go to First Aid Post

BY LIQUID or BLISTER GAS

1	2	3	4
Dab, but *don't rub* the splash with handkerchief. Then destroy handkerchief.	Rub No. 2 Ointment well into place. *(Buy a 6d. jar now from any chemist).* In emergency chemists supply Bleach Cream free.	If you can't get Ointment or Cream within 5 minutes wash place with soap and warm water	Take off at once any garment splashed with gas.

PRINTED FOR H.M. STATIONERY OFFICE BY FOSH & CROSS LTD., LONDON.

Air-raid precautions

At first, defences against air raids were very limited. Radar on the east and south coasts of Britain provided warnings of approaching enemy aircraft. However, searchlights were limited in their range, and the German bombers simply flew above them.

Air-raid wardens were active in enforcing the blackout regulations that had been issued before the war started, together with gas masks and instructions about air-raid warnings. The ARP (air-raid precautions) Wardens, mostly part-time volunteers, organised preparations for air raids and were also active when bombing actually began.

Source **P** Damage in the centre of Canterbury, Kent, after heavy bombing in 1942.

Source Q

Lighting restrictions

All windows, sky-lights, glazed doors, or other openings which would show a light, will have to be screened in war time with dark blinds or blankets, or brown paper pasted on the glass, so that no light is visible on the outside. You should obtain now any materials you may need for this purpose.

No outside lights will be allowed, and all street lighting will be put out.

Instructions will be issued about the dimming of lights on vehicles.

Fire precautions

An air attack may bring large numbers of small incendiary bombs, which might start up so many fires that the Fire Brigades could not be expected to deal with them all. Everyone should be prepared to do all he can to tackle a fire started in his own house. Most large fires start as small ones.

Clearing the top floor of all inflammable materials, lumber, etc. will lessen the danger of fire, and prevent a fire from spreading. See that you can reach your attic or roof space readily.

Water is the best means of putting out a fire started by an incendiary bomb. Have some buckets ready.

Extracts from a civil defence leaflet, issued in July 1939 by the British government.

Source R

We shall defend our island, whatever the cost may be, we shall fight on the beaches, we shall fight on the landing grounds, we shall fight in the fields and in the streets, we shall fight in the hills; we shall never surrender.

Churchill speaking in the House of Commons, 4 June 1940.

THINGS TO DO

1 How did the government prepare for the Blitz?

2 How does **Source N** show the value of an Anderson shelter?

Propaganda and censorship

The Ministry of Information was responsible for the poster campaigns which encouraged people to join the voluntary services and to work hard and save in order to help the war effort. It also produced posters which warned people of the dangers of 'careless talk'. There was a fear that German spies could be working in the country so people were told not to discuss the war in public. The Ministry of Information tried to keep in touch with the people through an organisation called Mass Observation whose members carried out surveys and reported on conversations they had heard in shops and pubs.

Other wartime propaganda was concerned with encouraging people to save for the war effort and not to waste. The 'squander bug' became a regular feature of messages to the housewife implying that wasting anything was helping the Germans.

Newspapers were also censored by the government during the war. They reported on the bombings but concentrated on the heroism of the rescuers rather than the deaths and injuries in an attempt to keep up morale. Publication of the left-wing *Daily Worker* was banned in 1941 because it was claiming that the war was being fought for the bosses rather than a battle for democracy. Newsreel films were made for the cinema and broadcasts were made over the radio. Both sides tried to influence the other by transmitting propaganda over the radio. The 'Lord Haw Haw' broadcasts from Germany were disturbing to some British citizens. 'Lord Haw Haw' (William Joyce) was a Briton living in Germany who was used by Radio Hamburg to mock the British war effort and to undermine morale. The BBC also made broadcasts to Germany which included enough truth to make them appear genuine but enough rumour to disturb the German war effort.

Source S

Everybody is worried about the feeling in the East End, where there is much bitterness. It is said that even the King and Queen were booed the other day when they visited the destroyed areas.

From the diary of Harold Nicolson, a minister in the Ministry of Information, 17 September 1940.

Source T

There were more signs of hysteria, terror, neurosis, observed than during the whole of the previous two months together in all areas. The overwhelming feeling on Friday was the feeling of utter helplessness. The tremendous impact of the previous night had left people practically speechless in many cases. On Friday evening (15 November), there were several signs of suppressed panic as darkness approached.

A Mass Observation report on the bombing of Coventry in 1940.

THINGS TO DO

1 List how some children benefited from evacuation and how others suffered from it.

2 What evidence is there in **Sources S** and **T** to show that the bombing did have some effect on morale?

3 List the ways in which Britain tried to defend itself from attack.

4 Why do you think so many people joined the Home Guard?

Internment

There was a worry that there were lots of secret spies in Britain. Soon after the war started, German and Italian citizens living in Britain were arrested and put in prisoner-of-war camps – even though some of them had fled Germany and Italy to escape fascism. By the summer of 1941 the scare had died down, and only about 5,000 were kept in prison.

Source **V** One of a series of posters intended to stop people carelessly giving away secret information to enemy spies.

Source **U** A Ministry of Information poster from early in the war. Some people thought this reinforced a 'them and us' attitude. The workers would win the war; the upper classes would benefit from the victory.

THINGS TO DO

1 In what way did women contribute to the war effort in Britain?

2 Choose three pieces of propaganda from this chapter. For each one explain why it is propaganda and how it was trying to influence public opinion.

Source **W** The intention of this poster was to make people think twice about spending money unnecessarily.

Exam-style assessment

This question follows the pattern of questions to be set by AQA in Paper 1, **Section B**, of its new Modern World History specification.

Study **Sources A**, **B**, **C** and **D**, and then answer all parts of the question which follow.

Source A: Work for women in the army, servicing a 6-ton truck

Source B: Changes in numbers of women employed, 1939–43

Changes in numbers of women employed, 1939–43	
Distribution	−6,000
Services	+58,000
Textiles	−165,000
Clothing	−149,000
Admin/clerical	+480,000
Engineering/aircraft/ships	+1,197,000
Manufacturing	−48,000
Food	−18,000
Chemicals	+220,000
Agriculture	+102,000
Transport	+147,000
Other	+531,000

From *Life in Wartime Britain* (1993) by RICHARD TAMES

Source C: Be careful about giving away secret information!

A government poster during the Second World War.

Source D: The importance of the Battle of Britain

> The Battle of Britain was an attempt by Hitler to destroy the fighters of the Royal Air Force so as to clear the way for an invasion of Britain in the autumn of 1940. The attempt failed. The failure was decisive for the future direction of the war.

From *The World at War* (1973) by MARK ARNOLD-FORSTER

Questions

(a) What can you learn from **Source B** about the numbers of employed women in the Second World War? **(3 marks)**

(b) Use **Source A** and your own knowledge to explain how attitudes towards women in the armed forces changed during the Second World War. **(6 marks)**

(c) How useful is **Source C** for studying propaganda and censorship during the Second World War? Explain your answer by using **Source C** and your own knowledge. **(8 marks)**

(d) How accurate is the interpretation in **Source D** of the importance of the Battle of Britain within Britain's role in the Second World War? Use **Source D** and your own knowledge to explain your answer. **(8 marks)**

Russia/USSR, 1914–41

INTRODUCTION

Russia saw great changes in the period 1914–41. In the early 1900s it was the most backward country in Europe ruled by a Tsar with complete power. Attempts to change Russia either by revolution or reform all failed in the period up to 1914. However, the First World War highlighted the weaknesses of Tsarist Russia and led to the collapse of Tsarist rule in 1917. But within eight months the new Provisional Government had been overthrown by the Bolsheviks/Communists under Lenin.

Despite a bitter civil war and severe economic problems, Lenin made sure that Communist rule in Russia survived. The Bolsheviks defeated their opponents, the Whites, in the Civil War, and introduced economic policies to rescue the economy – first, War Communism and then NEP.

Lenin's successor, Stalin, set about making Communist Russia – called the USSR (Union of Soviet Socialist Republics) – a much stronger economic power with his policies of collectivisation of agriculture and the Five-Year Plans for industry. The human cost and suffering to the Soviet people was immense but Stalin's reforms did allow the USSR to survive the Second World War.

Stalin also established a strong personal control of the USSR. Possible opponents, including those in the Communist Party, were 'purged' or 'liquidated' and this included many innocent victims. In many ways Stalin's control of the USSR was not unlike that of the Tsar in 1914.

1894	Nicholas II becomes Tsar
1904	Russo-Japanese War
1905	Revolution
1914	Russia enters the First World War
1917	Two revolutions in March and November
1918	Treaty of Brest-Litovsk with Germany
1921	New Economic Policy (NEP) introduced
1924	Death of Lenin
1928	Stalin introduces collectivisation and first Five-Year Plan
1934	Assassination of Kirov
1936	New constitution introduced
1940	Assassination of Trotsky
1941	Germany invades the Soviet Union

How strong was the Tsarist regime in 1914?

Source **A** Tsar Nicholas II and Tsarina Alexandra in 1903.

The government of Nicholas II

Nicholas II became Tsar in 1894 at the age of 26. He was modest and deeply religious, and took his responsibilities as Tsar of Russia seriously. However, he knew very little about his people. He never travelled around the country meeting them and relied on his advisers telling him what was going on. Nicholas believed in autocracy — government by one man. He believed his powers came from God. Therefore he did not tolerate criticisms of his rule. He ruled with the help of his wife, Tsarina Alexandra, and they were determined that their son, Alexis, should inherit their power.

Only Nicholas had the power to make laws in Russia. He appointed ministers, but they were often no more than advisers and were sometimes inefficient and corrupt. As there was no elected parliament in Russia, local councils (*zemstvos*) had to look after matters such as schools and hospitals. When there were calls for an elected parliament, Nicholas dismissed them as a 'senseless dream'.

Nicholas' rule was enforced by the secret police (Okhrana). Critics of the Tsar were arrested, imprisoned and often sent to labour camps in Siberia. Newspapers and books were censored and controlled to prevent criticism. The Russian Orthodox Church also supported the Tsar and preached to its congregations that it was a sin to oppose him. However, in spite of his complete control, there was opposition to Nicholas' rule.

The countryside

Russia was a rural society. Over 90 per cent of the people were poor peasants who were barely able to scratch a living from the land, which they rarely owned for themselves. Agriculture was in desperate need of modernisation. Peasants farmed with old-fashioned tools on strips of land in fields as they had done for centuries. This was inefficient and made it difficult for new methods to be introduced.

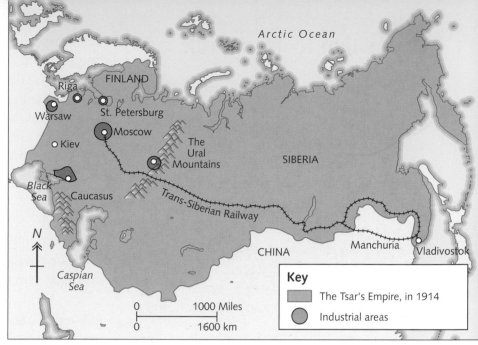

Russia in 1914.

Russia was a land of great contrasts. While the majority of peasants lived in abject poverty, at the other end of the scale was the aristocracy, or great landowners. They lived comfortably on huge estates. They controlled the local government, especially the local councils called *zemstvos*, and acted as a link between the people and the Tsar. Some ran their estates very inefficiently, although a minority saw the need for a more up-to-date agricultural system.

The towns

Compared to most western European countries in 1900, Russia was economically backward. This situation began to change with the onset of industrialisation. Large factories were springing up and industry grew faster in Russia than in any other European country. A whole range of industries, such as coal mining, iron and steel, and textiles, emerged. Large numbers of peasants flocked to the towns to work in the factories. This industrial working class was known as the proletariat. The number of workers grew rapidly as more factories were built, especially in the already large cities of Moscow and St Petersburg. Their living and working conditions were appalling. The proletariat often lived in slums or even in the factories where they worked. They earned very low wages and worked long hours. They were not allowed to form trade unions to fight for better conditions. The police or the army rapidly crushed any protests or strikes.

Source

Very often the peasants do not have enough allotment land. They cannot feed themselves, clothe themselves, heat their homes, keep their tools and livestock, secure seed for sowing and lastly pay their taxes.

From a police report on conditions in the countryside, 1905.

Source

The whole day we pour out our blood and sweat. Every minute we expose our life to danger. When there are accidents, they accuse us of carelessness. The greed of the bosses, the long working hours, the meagre wages – there is the cause of all the accidents.

A Russian trade union leaflet of 1898, describing the conditions of town workers.

Opposition to Tsarist rule

The **Liberals** were middle-class, educated Russians, such as doctors, lawyers and teachers. They wanted an elected parliament to help the Tsar run the country. In 1905 they formed the Constitutional Democratic Party (the Cadets). Other groups were more extreme.

The **Social Revolutionaries** (SRs) wanted the peasants to overthrow the Tsar and set up a republic. All the land of Russia would then be handed over to the peasants to farm together in communes. The SRs were prepared to use violence and assassination to further their cause.

The **Social Democrats** (SDs) also wanted to overthrow the Tsar. However, they believed the revolution would be made by the urban workers. They followed the ideas of Karl Marx and were called Communists. The party, however, was divided. In 1903 it split into two groups. The Bolsheviks ('majority group'), led by Lenin, believed that revolution in Russia should be planned secretly by a small group of committed individuals who would seize power. The Mensheviks ('minority group'), led by Trotsky, believed revolution should be a mass movement involving anyone. The Bolsheviks eventually dominated the party.

One major difficulty for these revolutionary groups was that their leaders were often in prison or in exile. Lenin, for example, lived in exile in London for years. Trotsky was exiled in London and Paris and other revolutionaries were in Switzerland. The 1903 Party Conference was held in a warehouse in Brussels.

Revolution in Russia seemed just a dream. But it was much closer than anyone realised.

Source D

How long have you been a member of the Communist Party?

Since 1894.

Have you ever belonged to any other parties?

No.

What sentences were you given for revolutionary activities?

1887 prison;
1898-1900 Siberia;
1900 prison.

How long did you spend in prison?

Several days and 14 months.

How long at hard labour?

None.

How long in exile?

Three years.

How long a political refugee?

9-10 years.

Extract from Lenin's answers to a Communist Party questionnaire.

THINGS TO DO

1 The government of Russia was an autocracy. Explain what this means and how it worked in Russia.

2 (a) What were the different aims and ambitions of the groups opposing the Tsar?

(b) Is there anything on which they agreed?

3 Using the map on page 149 and your own knowledge, explain the difficulties in ruling Russia in the early twentieth century.

4 What does **Source B** tell us about conditions in the countryside?

5 How reliable is **Source C** as evidence of working conditions in Russia in the early twentieth century?

The causes of the 1905 Revolution

In the years after 1902 there was economic depression in the towns and bad harvests in the countryside. This led to demonstrations, strikes and violence. These were brutally crushed by the Tsar's army, which only increased bitterness. In July 1904, the Minister of the Interior, Plehve, who controlled the police, was assassinated by revolutionaries. In the same year Russia and Japan waged war against one another. Nicholas welcomed the war as an opportunity to increase his popularity, but Russia's forces suffered humiliating defeats. The war revealed the weaknesses, not the strengths, of Tsarist rule. These events and the people's growing resentment at the Tsar's autocratic rule help explain why unrest in 1905 led to revolution.

Bloody Sunday, January 1905

On 22 January 1905, about 200,000 people in St Petersburg, carrying pictures of the Tsar, marched to the Winter Palace to petition him to help improve their working conditions. Led by Father Gapon, they sang hymns as they marched. But the Tsar was not in St Petersburg and the marchers' way to the Palace was blocked by troops. Fighting broke out and the troops opened fire. Official figures put the number killed at 96, but actually hundreds were killed.

Source **E** Bloody Sunday: the marchers' path to the Winter Palace is blocked by troops.

The 1905 Revolution

'Bloody Sunday' was crucial. The Tsar was blamed for the massacre. As news of it spread, strikes and violence broke out all over Russia. Strikers in towns demanded shorter hours and higher wages. Peasants attacked landowners' property, looting and burning their houses and seizing the land for themselves. There was a naval mutiny in June. Sailors on the battleship *Potemkin* seized the ship and sailed across the Black Sea to Romania. In September, the Tsar was forced to sign a humiliating peace with Japan. Part of the peace treaty involved losing Port Arthur and Korea to the Japanese.

This aroused even more anger and despair among the Russian people. In October Russian workers began electing soviets (workers' councils) to plan strike action. It was clear the Tsar was losing control. Even some of his own army were supporting the revolutionaries. He was forced to make changes to the way Russia was governed.

The October Manifesto and the end of the 1905 Revolution

Nicholas issued the October Manifesto by which he granted freedom of speech, the right to form political parties and agreed to the election of a parliament (Duma) by the people. The Cadets accepted the Manifesto and claimed a great victory. The more extreme revolutionary groups, however, rejected it. They wanted to overthrow the Tsar and install a completely new system of government. So revolutionary action continued. But by now the Tsar had recovered some of his authority and ruthlessly put down opposition. Revolutionary leaders, such as Trotsky, once more fled Russia. By the end of the year Nicholas was again in complete charge of Russia.

The Dumas

The elections for the first Duma were held in April 1906. But by now the Tsar had regained so much of his power that he was able to impose the Fundamental Laws. These allowed Nicholas to dismiss the Duma and call new elections whenever he wanted. Only he could appoint ministers and in an emergency he had the power to govern by decree without consulting the Duma.

The Dumas were a huge disappointment. No Duma managed to pass any meaningful laws to improve the position of the poor in Russia.

The October Manifesto and the creation of the Duma had promised so much. It was soon clear, however, that the Tsar was not prepared to give up any of his powers. The autocracy continued.

Source F

Sire – We, working men and inhabitants of St Petersburg, our wives and our children and our helpless old parents, come to You, Sire, to seek for truth, justice and protection. We are near to death.... We ask but little: to reduce the working day to eight hours, to provide a minimum wage of a rouble a day.... Do not refuse to help Your people.

The Workers' Petition, 1905.

Source G

The rioting in Our Empire fills Our heart with deep grief. We grant freedom of person, conscience and assembly. We include in the Duma those classes that have been, until now, deprived of the right to vote. No law shall go into force without the approval of the Duma.

Extract from the October Manifesto.

Source H

I created the Duma not to have it instruct me but to have it advise me.

The Tsar speaking in 1908.

Russia in 1914

By 1914 the Tsar seemed to be well in control of Russia. There were still some strikes and demonstrations but the army was loyal and troops crushed any disturbance. The Okhrana (secret police) rooted out trouble-makers and revolutionaries. Nicholas' opponents were also weak. Leaders of the revolutionary groups were in prison, in Siberian labour camps or living in exile in other countries. Lenin, then in Switzerland, doubted if he would ever return to Russia or live to see it change by revolution.

However, things were about to change dramatically with the outbreak of the First World War.

Why did the rule of the Tsar collapse in February/March 1917?

Military defeat

In 1914 Russia went to war with Britain and France against Germany and Austria-Hungary. The outbreak of war in 1914 was greeted with enthusiasm and increased patriotism. St Petersburg was renamed Petrograd, the 'Russian' name for the city, because the original name sounded too German. Crowds gathered outside the Winter Palace to cheer the Tsar. In other parts of Russia the strikes ended. In the Duma members swore to support the Tsar. It seemed as if the people were prepared to give Nicholas another chance.

But the Russian army suffered defeats at Tannenburg and the Masurian Lakes and the Germans invaded Russia. The Russian army was large but poorly equipped, with not enough ammunition and weapons (nearly a third of Russian soldiers marched into battle without rifles) and basic supplies, such as boots, medical supplies and food. Leadership was also weak, with officers drawn from the nobles and winning promotion more because of their birth than their military skills.

Effects of war on the Russians

The war affected those at home, who had to put up with serious food shortages. With millions of peasants conscripted into the army there were not enough people to produce food. Whatever food there was frequently did not make it to the cities where it was most needed because the railways were being used to transport troops and supplies to the front. Problems increased as food prices rose and wages stayed the same. Millions of Russian refugees flooding into the towns to escape from the advancing German armies created overcrowding and greater pressure on food supplies. Unemployment rose as factories closed down because of the shortage of manpower, coal and other raw materials.

Russia was in chaos. People were dying of starvation and cold. There was more despair as news from the front told of Russian defeats and the deaths of loved ones.

Russia/USSR, 1914–41

Source

Thousands of students and working men, carrying portraits of the Tsar, singing the national anthem and hymns, went towards the Winter Palace. Here, [they] fell on their knees singing 'God save the Tsar.' Never during the twenty years of his reign had the Tsar been so popular as at that moment.

A Russian describing the outbreak of war in 1914.

Source Russian prisoners of war under guard in May 1915.

The Tsar and the war

The people's support for the Tsar at the beginning of the war soon evaporated. As long as he remained in Petrograd it was difficult to blame him personally for the defeats suffered by the Russian army. However, in 1915 he took personal command of the armed forces even though he had little military experience. He did this because he believed it was his duty and that the army would fight better if he was leading it. The decision had two important consequences.

First, Nicholas was blamed for the continued defeats of the Russian army. Second, he was now out of Petrograd and therefore not running the government.

The day-to-day running of Russia was now in the hands of the Tsarina, Alexandra. This was a mistake. Alexandra was of German birth and was suspected, wrongly, by the people of being a spy. She was also incapable of governing Russia. She would not work with the Duma and came to depend more and more on Gregory Rasputin (see case study).

Source **K**   The Tsar blesses his troops.

THINGS TO DO

Look at the evidence in the case study and the sources. Why do you think Rasputin's relations with the royal family helped to weaken the Tsar's rule?

Case Study: Rasputin

Gregory Rasputin, a self-styled monk and 'holy man', was of striking appearance and claimed to have hypnotic powers. He became well known in St Petersburg, especially among upper-class women who came to him for advice and healing. Through them he met the Tsarina. After he appeared to heal a life-threatening injury to the heir to the throne, Alexis, the Tsar and Tsarina were convinced Rasputin had been sent by God to look after their family and the Russian people.

Rasputin's influence grew under the protection of the Tsar, who even asked his advice in the appointment of ministers and officials. Rasputin used his power to place his friends in important positions. When war broke out his influence increased, especially after the Tsar took charge of the army.

The Tsarina became completely dependent on Rasputin and ministers were appointed and dismissed on his direction.

She even wrote letters to her husband containing Rasputin's advice on how to run the war.

Rasputin's power and influence aroused envy and made him powerful enemies, particularly among the nobles. It was a group of nobles, led by Prince Yusopov, who assassinated him in December 1916.

Rasputin's influence weakened the royal family's standing in Russia but his murder came too late to save them.

The move towards revolution

By 1917 Russia was in chaos. The German army advanced across the country, sweeping aside the Tsar's forces. The Russians were increasingly disillusioned with the war. The economy was getting worse, especially the shortage of food and its high prices. The winter of 1916-17 was severe and the railways were badly disrupted by ice, making it difficult to get food and fuel to the towns. Bread queues were familiar sights. The government was increasingly unpopular and the murder of Rasputin did little to change this. Nicholas was losing control.

Conditions were now ideal for revolution. Russia was about to be engulfed by two revolutions within nine months. The first, in March 1917, ended not only the rule of Nicholas II, but also the rule of the Tsars in Russia.

Source **L**   A Russian cartoon of Rasputin with the Tsar and Tsarina.

SUMMARY

The effects of the First World War on Tsarist Russia:

- Russian army suffered military defeat.
- Russia invaded by Germany.
- Economic disruption.
- Starvation.
- Weak government.
- Growing unpopularity of Tsar and Tsarina.
- Russian people disillusioned.
- Revolution and collapse of Tsarist rule.

A queue of hungry people outside a bread shop in 1917.

The March Revolution and the abdication of the Tsar

With a severe winter, food shortages and rising prices, and the war going badly, the Tsar's government was under pressure in the first two months of 1917. By March it had lost control.

Workers demanding higher wages went on strike at the Putilov engineering works in Petrograd on 4 March. Three days later 40,000 were on strike and the factory closed down. As the strike spread there were clashes between striking workers and the army, with some of the strikers being killed.

As law and order broke down the Tsar, who was at the front, was told what was happening, but he chose to ignore the warnings and ordered the Duma to stop meeting.

The key date in the Revolution was 12 March. Soldiers in Petrograd refused to fire on demonstrators and joined them instead. Soldiers and strikers then marched together to the Duma to demand a new government.

Nicholas now realised how serious matters had become. He tried to return to Petrograd but his train was stopped outside the city. His generals made him aware of how grave things were and advised him to abdicate, which he did on the 15 March. Within a week he and his family were arrested and removed to Siberia.

Source **N**

The situation is serious. Petrograd is out of control. The government is paralysed; the food and fuel supplies are completely disorganised. Discontent is general and on the increase. There is wild shooting on the streets; troops are firing at each other.

Telegram from the President of the Duma to the Tsar, 11 March 1917.

THINGS TO DO

1 How useful are **Sources K** and **L** for studying Russian attitudes towards the Tsar?

2 Explain why the Tsar was forced to abdicate.

4.2 The Provisional Government and the Bolshevik Revolution

Why did the Provisional Government last for only eight months?

The Provisional Government and the Petrograd Soviet

The Duma formed a Provisional Government to run the country until elections could be held to choose a permanent government.

At the same time the Petrograd Soviet (a council representing the interests of workers and soldiers) met and other soviets were set up throughout the country. The Petrograd Soviet had more power in the city than the Provisional Government and set about organising the distribution of food and housing and running the rail services. More importantly, it took control of the armed forces of the city.

The weaknesses of the Provisional Government

At first the Provisional Government was popular, particularly through its granting of basic rights, such as freedom of speech and the right to strike. But problems soon emerged. The government itself was made up of members of different political parties – SRs, Cadets, Liberals and Mensheviks – with different views on how Russia should be governed. This often made it hard to make decisions. The Petrograd Soviet by contrast was more united and had a clearer idea of what it wanted to do.

Two issues made the Provisional Government more unpopular. The first was land. The government rejected the idea of peasants owning the land they worked until an elected permanent government was formed to decide on the matter. This infuriated the peasants, many of whom refused to wait and seized the land for themselves.

More crucial was the war. The government decided to go on fighting, fearing that any peace treaty worked out with the Germans would end in Russia having harsh conditions imposed on it. This decision was unpopular with the army and the people. Soldiers demoralised by defeat were deserting in even greater numbers. People were suffering food and fuel shortages and were desperate for the war to end. In this climate of discontent an alternative to the Provisional Government emerged – Lenin and the Bolsheviks.

Source

The Soviet of Workers and Soldiers' Deputies has decided:

- In all military units committees should be chosen.
- The orders of the Provisional Government shall be carried out only when they do not go against orders and decisions of the Soviet.
- All weapons must be under the control of the committees. They must not be handed over to officers.
- All ranks and titles in the army are abolished.

Order No. 1 of the Petrograd Soviet Army, issued on 14 March 1917.

THINGS TO DO

1 How much power did the Petrograd Soviet have?

2 Why did the Provisional Government become unpopular?

Lenin's return and the *April Theses*

Modern World History for AQA

Source **B** A painting of Lenin addressing a crowd who are shown as greeting him on his return to Petrograd in April 1917.

The Revolution in March caught the revolutionary groups unprepared, just as the 1905 Revolution had.

The Bolsheviks' leaders were in exile – with Lenin in Switzerland and Stalin in Siberia. So, the Bolsheviks were leaderless. Lenin made it back to Russia as fast as possible – with the help of the Germans! The Germans saw that with the Bolsheviks in power Russia would withdraw from the war, releasing German troops from the Eastern Front for fighting in the west. Even if the Bolsheviks failed to seize power the turmoil in Russia could only help Germany's war aims.

Lenin made it to Petrograd on 16 April, having travelled through Germany by train in a sealed carriage provided by the German government. He announced that the Bolsheviks would not co-operate with the Provisional Government, but would work for its overthrow. He also declared that Russia should withdraw from the war and that land would be distributed to the peasants. These announcements were published as the *April Theses*. They were summarised in slogans: 'Peace, Bread and Land' and 'All Power to the Soviets'.

The *April Theses* were popular with the people. Lenin also gave leadership to the Bolsheviks and a clear direction.

The July Days

In July the Provisional Government ordered a military attack on the Germans. It ended in a massive defeat. News of this reached Petrograd, and soldiers, sailors and workers demonstrated against the government on 16 and 17 July. The Bolsheviks eventually joined the demonstrators and their Red Guards joined in the rioting that followed.

Troops loyal to the government put down the rising and a warrant was issued for Lenin's arrest. Though he managed to escape to Finland, other Bolshevik leaders were arrested.

The July Days failed and the Provisional Government held on to power through the support of the army. However the problems of the Provisional Government persisted, with more military defeats and food shortages.

Source **C**

Week by week food became scarcer. The daily allowance of bread fell from a pound and a half to a pound, then three-quarters, half and a quarter of a pound. Towards the end there was a week without any bread at all. On the freezing front, miserable armies continued to starve and die without enthusiasm.

An American writer, John Reed, describes conditions in Petrograd in October 1917.

The Kornilov Affair

The commander of the Russian army, General Kornilov, tried to seize power and install a military dictatorship in September 1917. But he had little support and his troops were persuaded not to fire on fellow Russians. Kornilov was arrested and the rising crumbled.

This was another example of the unpopularity of the Provisional Government. In contrast, the Bolsheviks won popularity because they had refused to help Kornilov and were prepared to fight him, with arms supplied to their Red Guards by the government. Afterwards the Red Guards held on to the weapons.

Source ⓓ Leon Trotsky, a leading Menshevik, only joined the Bolsheviks in summer 1917, but he became a close colleague of Lenin and was given the task of organising the Bolshevik seizure of power.

SUMMARY

The Provisional Government failed to survive because:

- It was weak politically. It was not elected and was made up of different parties.
- It was challenged by the Petrograd Soviet.
- It was unpopular because it refused to hand over land to the peasants.
- It continued the war and was blamed for the defeats of the Russian army.
- It failed to solve food shortages and other economic problems.
- The Bolsheviks offered alternative policies which were more popular.

The Russian calendar

Until February 1918, Russia used the old calendar, which was thirteen days behind the rest of Europe. Then the new Bolshevik government decided to bring Russia into line. This means that alternative dates exist for events before the changeover. This book uses the new dates, but you might come across alternatives elsewhere. This makes a particular difference with the second revolution of 1917, which is known as either the October or the November revolution.

How were the Bolsheviks able to seize power in October/November 1917?

In November 1917 the Bolsheviks, led by Lenin and Trotsky, successfully overthrew the Provisional Government and set up their own government. The November revolution was partly caused by the failures of the Provisional Government. It was also due to the appeal and planning of the Bolshevik Party.

The Bolsheviks

Lenin had spent many years preparing the Bolsheviks for revolution. From the start he had criticised the First World War. He thought it was a capitalist war. Lenin soon became aware of the discontent among both soldiers and civilians. By 1917 he had a small group of dedicated revolutionaries ready and able to seize power. Leon Trotsky, a leading Menshevik, joined the Bolsheviks only in the summer of 1917, but he became a close colleague of Lenin and was given the task of organising the seizure of power.

Support for the Bolsheviks increased due to Lenin's slogans, the mistakes and failures of the Provisional Government and the part played by the Red Guards in the defeat of the Kornilov Rebellion. Lenin ensured that he gained the support of the influential Petrograd Soviet, which began to work against Kerensky and the Provisional Government. By late September, the Bolsheviks had won majorities in the Moscow and Petrograd Soviets for the first time.

Lenin still had to persuade the other leading Bolsheviks that the time was right to seize power. He returned secretly from Finland in October to attend a Central Committee of the Bolshevik Party. The Committee voted 10–2 in favour of carrying out a second revolution.

The events of the Bolshevik revolution

The Bolshevik revolution, contrary to later communist propaganda, was quite a small-scale affair. Although Lenin was in charge, Trotsky did most of the planning. The plan was for the Bolsheviks to strike at the same time as the All-Russian Congress of Soviets was meeting in Petrograd. The armed Bolshevik Red Guards were to seize the important buildings and bridges in Petrograd. They had already won over some of the troops in the Petrograd garrison. The cruiser *Aurora*, with a Bolshevik crew, was to sail up the River Neva and fire its guns as a signal for the Red Guards to capture their targets.

Trotsky was Chairman of the Military Revolutionary Committee. From his office in Room 10 of the Smolni Institute, he issued arms to the Red Guards and drew up the plans for the seizure of the key places in Petrograd. Kerensky knew of the Bolshevik plans and had closed down the Bolshevik newspaper offices. He did not, however, have enough loyal troops to protect his government.

There was little fighting during the November revolution, much less than in March. The Red Guards took control of the capital, seizing the Telephone Exchange, the Telegraph Agency, the State Bank and the bridges over the river. The *Aurora* sailed up the river ready to bombard the Winter Palace.

Kerensky went to the front line to try to find loyal troops who would save his government. He failed and went into hiding. The Red Guards took the Winter Palace the same night (7/8 November). The All-Russian Congress of Soviets was meeting while these events took place. The Mensheviks and most of the Social Revolutionaries walked out of the meeting in protest at the Bolshevik revolution. This left the Bolsheviks in control.

The ministers of the Provisional Government were arrested in the Winter Palace, apart from Kerensky, who managed to flee abroad. The following day, Lenin set up a new government called the Council of the People's Commissars. He issued a decree declaring that power had been taken over by the Congress in the name of the soviets of all Russia.

A few days later, on 15 November, the Bolsheviks seized control of Moscow. They now had control of the two largest cities, but little else.

Reasons for the Bolshevik success

Later Bolshevik propaganda portrayed these events as a 'popular revolution' brought about by mass support from the proletariat for communist ideas (see Source E). Nothing could be further from the truth. It was achieved by a relatively small group of dedicated revolutionaries.

The majority of Russians, even in Petrograd and Moscow, were unaware of the Bolshevik takeover. So why were the Bolsheviks successful?

This was due to a variety of factors. In many respects, Lenin and the Bolsheviks were fortunate because of the mistakes of the

Source **E**

A painting from 1937 showing the storming of the Winter Palace.

Provisional Government. But Lenin ensured that the Bolsheviks took advantage of these mistakes. The appeal of Bolshevism and especially Lenin's slogan 'Peace, Bread, Land' brought support, while Lenin ensured that the timing of the revolution was just right. The main reasons for success were the careful Bolshevik preparations, under Trotsky, and the tactics used to seize the key points in Petrograd.

Source **G**

The reality of the [November] Revolution was an armed rising by a revolutionary minority inspired by the political genius of Lenin against a government that had already lost control.

The view of a British historian in 1987.

Source **F**

The Bolshevik party was waging a determined struggle to win over the masses. The struggle was headed by Lenin, who frequently addressed mass rallies and meetings. Lenin's speeches, noted for their profound content and brilliant delivery, inspired the workers and soldiers. Bolshevik membership began to grow rapidly.

A Soviet historian, writing in 1981.

THINGS TO DO

1 How useful is **Source E** as a view of the Bolshevik revolution?

2 How do **Sources F** and **G** differ in their interpretation of the Bolshevik revolution?

How did Lenin impose Communist control on Russia?

Modern World History for AQA

Source A

A communist poster 'Lenin, Father of the Working People.'

Setting up a Bolshevik government

On 8 November the Bolsheviks set up their new government. Most of the commissars (ministers) of the government were Bolsheviks. Lenin himself was chairman of the Council of Commissars – in effect the leader. Trotsky was Commissar for Foreign Affairs and Stalin Commissar for Nationalities (that is, all the non-Russians living within the state of Russia).

Lenin announced an immediate end to the war, and peace talks with the Germans began in December. He also issued a land decree. This seized land owned by the Tsar, the Church and rich landlords and handed it to the peasants. They would form committees in their local areas to divide it up among themselves. These measures made the Bolsheviks popular throughout Russia in the days following the Revolution.

The Constituent Assembly

Before the Provisional Government fell from power, Kerensky promised an election to choose a permanent parliament, the Constituent Assembly. Lenin allowed the elections to go ahead.

Lenin renamed the Bolshevik Party as the Communist Party and tried to broaden its appeal to the mass of Russian people. However, most voters were peasants and were supporters of the SRs, which won 370 out of the 700 seats.

Lenin's Communist Party won 175 seats and with the support of other groups it could muster over 200 seats, but this was not enough to give it a majority. Lenin therefore shut down the Assembly after only one day. He was not prepared to hand over, or even share, his power with any other group. It was

When I made my speech in the assembly, every sentence of it was met with outcries, some spiteful, often supported by the brandishing of guns. Lenin showed his contempt for the Assembly by lounging in his chair and giving the impression of a man who was bored to death.

Written by Chernov, a Social Revolutionary.

Russia's losses in the Treaty of Brest-Litovsk, March 1918.

the first step in setting up a dictatorship by the Communist Party.

The communist dictatorship

Although the Revolution had been fought to end the Tsar's autocracy, Lenin intended to create a communist dictatorship with rule as strong as that of the Tsar. In December 1917, he set up the Cheka, a secret police force. The Cheka's agents worked in factories and villages all over Russia to spy on people. Anyone suspected of being anti-Communist would be arrested, tortured and could be shot without trial. When opponents tried to assassinate Lenin in 1918, he launched a Red Terror campaign against his enemies that summer. It is said that over 50,000 opponents of Communism were arrested and executed during this period.

Peace: the Treaty of Brest-Litovsk

Lenin was determined to end Russia's involvement in the war whatever the cost. He feared the war would bring about the overthrow of Communist rule, just as it had the Provisional Government. The Russian army in any case had been weakened by poor morale, massive desertions and a breakdown in discipline. It was incapable of resisting the

Germans. Defeat seemed inevitable. Peace negotiations with Germany ended on 3 March 1918, and the Treaty of Brest-Litovsk was signed. The terms were harsh. Russia lost a huge amount of land on her western frontier, which contained one-sixth of the population (over 60 million people), three-quarters of her iron and coal and over one-quarter of her farmland, some of it the best in Russia. The Communists had paid a high price, but Lenin knew he could not fight the Germans and his opponents in Russia at the same time.

THINGS TO DO

What were the advantages and disadvantages to Russia of the peace treaty with Germany? Do you think that Lenin was right to agree to it?

The Russian civil war, 1918–21

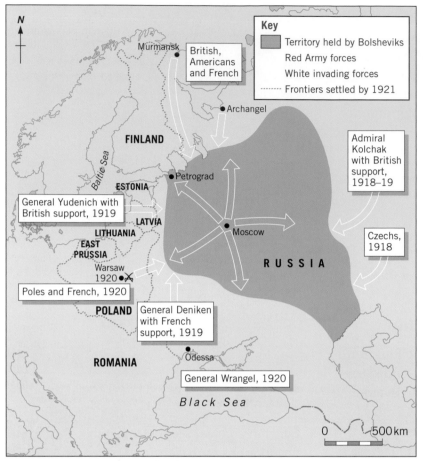

The main events of the Russian civil war.

The Bolsheviks faced a war of survival against supporters of the Tsar. This civil war lasted three years.

Causes of the civil war

The Bolsheviks had been able to seize power because their opponents were weak and poorly led. Once Lenin's enemies began to organise, the Bolsheviks faced a dangerous enemy. Opponents of the Bolsheviks were known as the 'Whites' and included many different groups: landowners who had lost land due to the Bolshevik revolution, religious groups who opposed the Bolshevik seizure of Church property, genuine royalists who wanted the restoration of Tsardom, and others. In the south of Russia, several army officers loyal to the old regime formed anti-communist armies. Admiral Kolchak and Generals Deniken and Wrangel became leaders of the White armies.

The threat to the Bolsheviks was increased by foreign intervention. The communist revolution and its threat of world revolution alarmed countries such as Britain, France, the USA and Japan. These countries were also annoyed by Lenin's decision to make peace with Germany and by his refusal to pay the Tsar's debts to foreign countries. They wanted Russia back in the war. These countries sent weapons. British troops landed at Murmansk in the north, and a combined British–Japanese force landed at Vladivostok in the far east. British and French troops landed in the south.

The Czech legion also joined the anti-communist crusade. This was a unit composed of Czechs who had been captured during the First World War and who had agreed to fight on the Russian side against their Austrian masters. They too wanted Russia back in the war. The Czech legion took control of the Trans-Siberian Railway.

Source C

Of all the tyrannies in history, the Bolshevik tyranny is the worst, the most destructive, the most degrading. The atrocities committed under Lenin and Trotsky are far more hideous and more numerous than anything for which the Kaiser was responsible.

Winston Churchill, British Secretary of State for War, giving his reasons for opposing Bolshevism in 1919.

The events of the civil war

In the north-west, the forces of General Yudenich threatened Petrograd. The British assisted him. By 1920 he was within a few kilometres of Petrograd, and he was only driven back after Trotsky's appearance at the front inspired the Bolshevik forces.

In the south-west, the threat came from General Deniken and his successor, General Wrangel. In 1919, Deniken's advance on Moscow was stopped, and in March 1920 his forces were finally destroyed, apart from a small number later commanded by Wrangel. The latter's forces were finally defeated in the Crimea in November 1920.

Admiral Kolchak threatened from the east. He was extremely cruel, filling 'death trains' with Red Army prisoners. Kolchak's forces were defeated in 1919 and the leaders were arrested and later shot.

Amidst this civil war, another war was being fought against the Poles. Anxious to seize further territory from their traditional enemy, they had invaded Russia in spring 1920. Their invasion, led by General Pilsudski, went seriously wrong. They were driven back to the gates of Warsaw. The Poles and Russians finally signed the Treaty of Riga in March 1921.

Reasons for Bolshevik success

Despite foreign support, the Whites were eventually defeated due to a combination of their own weaknesses and Bolshevik strengths.

The Whites had several weaknesses. Their geographical location made co-operation between the different armies difficult. They also lacked a single leader. The White generals were jealous of each other and refused to co-ordinate their offensives. The Reds never had to face an attack by all their enemies at the same time. Some White leaders, such as Kolchak, were brutal and established a harsh rule over their territories. General Deniken slaughtered 100,000 Jews in the Ukraine. This 'White Terror' encouraged many

Russians to support the Reds, especially when landlords were given back their lands.

The Whites did not have one aim and were unwilling to sacrifice their individual interests in order to form a united anti-Bolshevik front. Western aid did provide much-needed weapons, but made the Whites appear to be the puppets of foreign powers. The Red Army, through skilful propaganda, could claim that they were fighting for a Russia free from foreign control.

The Bolsheviks had several advantages. They controlled the industrial centres and the extensive railway network, which enabled the Reds to rush supplies and troops to any part of their front under threat. They also had the key administrative centres of Moscow and Petrograd, and were concentrated in a much smaller area than their rivals.

The Bolsheviks were also fighting for a cause – their communist revolution. They had superior morale, largely due to Trotsky's skills as an organiser and motivator. The Reds used extensive propaganda to portray the Whites as the tools of foreign powers. In contrast, the Reds were portrayed as defending Russia's national interests against foreign powers.

Trotsky's leadership of the Red Army proved decisive. He had formed this new army and turned it into a feared fighting force. When there were not enough officers, he conscripted Tsarist officers into the army. Discipline was harsh.

Victory also came due to Bolshevik ruthlessness. War Communism (see page 168) provided vital supplies. Cheka units in the countryside hanged, beat, shot and burned anyone who helped or fought for the Whites. The Tsar and his family were executed in case he was rescued from captivity and became a leader of the Whites.

Source D

This Bolshevik propaganda poster shows France, the USA and Britain as evil capitalists who were trying to control Russia.

Many Russians supported the Reds through fear. Others, however, genuinely preferred the Bolsheviks. The majority of peasants were annoyed when the Whites returned land to the landowners. Most of the proletariat did not want a return to the Tsarist regime.

The consequences of the civil war

The civil war had disastrous effects on a population already devastated by over three years of war. Atrocities were commonplace on both sides. Prisoners were often tortured and killed. There had been 21 million deaths between 1914 and 1921. The fighting had seriously hindered both agriculture and industry. Land was only 50 per cent cultivated; steel production was down to 5 per cent of its pre-war output. Dirt and rats led to disease, and there was a serious shortage of doctors and hospitals.

There was a serious famine in 1921 and at times food shortages in the towns were so acute that the ration of bread fell to 30 grams a day. Industrial production dropped as workers left the cities for the countryside in the hope of finding more food. Those who stayed behind salvaged what they could by using the black market. It is estimated that about 5 million deaths were caused by the famine.

Although the Reds won the civil war, they did not forget how close they had come to defeat by foreign armies. For years afterwards, the communist government remained suspicious of foreign, especially Western, governments. Many communists believed they would be safe only if they helped bring about communist revolutions in other countries. In March 1919, during the civil war, the Communist International (Comintern) was set up. Its task was to help set up communist parties in other countries and to work for an international communist revolution. This made some countries even more suspicious of Russia.

Source E

Sometimes a starving family eats the body of one of its junior members. Sometimes parents at night seize part of a body from the cemetery and feed it to their children.

Notes written by two doctors working in the Ufa region, one of Russia's worst famine areas.

THINGS TO DO

Was the Bolshevik success in the civil war due mainly to Trotsky's leadership?

Case Study: the assassination of the Tsar, July 1918

After his abdication in March 1917 Nicholas and his family were arrested, removed to Siberia, and then held at the Red-controlled town of Ekaterinburg. During July 1918, with a Czech army, part of the White forces, closing in on Ekaterinburg and the possibility that Nicholas would be freed to become a rallying point for White forces, the Communists decided to murder the royal family.

The White account of the murder is that on 16 July the Tsar and his family were taken to the basement of the house in which they were prisoners and were shot. Those who did not die instantly were finished off with bayonets. Eleven members of the royal household were murdered: the Tsar, his wife Alexandra, his son and four daughters, the family doctor and three servants. The bodies were then taken to a mine where they were soaked in acid and burned.

The Communists announced the Tsar had been executed but the rest of the family had been sent to safety. The Communist version of events never explained what eventually happened to the royal family, though an American, Anna Anderson, did in later years claim she was Nicholas' daughter, the Grand Duchess Anastasia, and that she had escaped from Russia.

In 1991 a burial pit in a bog was found in Ekaterinburg containing several bodies. The remains were examined using DNA tests and dental records and in 1994 the conclusions were made public. The bodies were those of the Tsar, his wife and three of their daughters. They had been shot and bayoneted. The report appeared to confirm most of the accepted accounts of the murders. There was no sign of the bodies of the Tsar's son, Alexis, and one of his daughters, Maria. Later, however, charred remains were found and identified as the missing son and daughter.

Source F

Shortly after one o'clock am, they were taken from their rooms. It seemed as if all of them guessed their fate, but not one of them uttered a single sound. I heard the firing and I returned to the house. I saw that all members of the Tsar's family were lying on the floor with many wounds in their bodies. The blood was running in streams. The heir [Alexis] was still alive and a soldier went up and fired two or three more times at him.

A Red Army soldier describes the murder of the royal family.

Source G The room where the assassination took place.

THINGS TO DO

1 Look at the evidence in the case study. What do you think happened to the Tsar and his family? Give reasons for your answer.

2 Why were they murdered?

How successful was Lenin in creating a new society in Russia?

War Communism

Lenin's greatest problem in fighting the war was to make sure the Red Army had enough food and supplies. This involved producing more weapons and food. To achieve this Lenin extended state control over the economy. This he called War Communism.

The state now took control of the factories, and appointed managers to run them. Factory workers had to work hard and long hours and trade unions were banned. Food was rationed and ration cards were issued only to those in work.

To get enough food to feed the Red army and the industrial workers, the Cheka seized all surplus grain from the peasants. The peasants resisted. They hid food, but they risked punishment if caught. Many peasants preferred to grow less grain than give it away free to feed the people in the towns. Grain production fell even more as a result. To make matters worse, drought and severe famine hit the country in 1921, and over four million Russians starved to death.

The Kronstadt Revolt

War Communism made the communist government very unpopular. Discontent among peasants led to violence in the countryside. In towns workers went on strike, in spite of the penalty for striking being death.

The most serious opposition to the government came in March 1921. Sailors at the Kronstadt naval base revolted. They accused the communists of breaking their promises of 1917 by failing to help the workers. Lenin ordered the Red Army to put down the revolt. This caused 20,000 casualties and the leaders of the revolt were executed.

The Kronstadt Revolt made Lenin realise how unpopular War Communism was and that he had to improve the economic situation in Russia. Failure to do so might end in the overthrow of the communist government.

Source

> Parties which were sent into the countryside to obtain grain by force might be driven away by the peasants with pitch-forks. Savage peasants would slit open a belly, pack it with grain, and leave him by the road-side as a lesson to all.
>
> ***A Communist describes unrest in the countryside.***

THINGS TO DO

Look at **Sources H** and **I** and the section on the Kronstadt Revolt. What reasons do they suggest to explain why Lenin ended War Communism?

Source   Starving children during the famine of 1921.

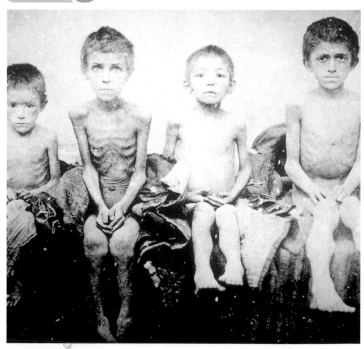

New Economic Policy

Lenin therefore introduced the New Economic Policy (NEP). State control of the economy imposed by War Communism was relaxed under the NEP. Smaller industries and factories were returned to private ownership. What was then produced was sold on the open market for profit. Grain was no longer seized from the peasants. Instead, they had to give a fixed amount to the government in tax, retaining for themselves any surplus, which could be sold in the open market at a profit. Important industries, such as coal, steel, railways and the banks, remained under state control.

Lenin hoped that the NEP would help increase industrial production and farm output, and put Russia back on its feet economically. He called the NEP 'a breathing space'. Most of the Communist Party saw the need for change and were prepared to go along with the NEP. However, there was some opposition to it from within the Party. Many communists thought that returning the idea of profit to trade and business was against communist principles.

On the whole the NEP was a success. Factories and peasants responded to the change by increasing their production of industrial goods and grain. The end of the civil war certainly helped. In fact the NEP was marked by seven years of relative stability compared to the previous seven years of world and civil war.

The NEP, though, did create problems. Some peasants – the Kulaks – became rich at the expense of others who often became hired labourers. Traders and businessmen in towns, called 'Nepmen', made huge profits by buying goods and food cheaply and selling them at much higher prices. To many this was a betrayal of communism and a return to the old system.

The creation of the USSR

By the end of the civil war in 1921 the communists controlled most of the Tsar's former empire. As areas were captured they were turned into socialist republics. By 1923 all of these socialist republics had come together as the Union of Soviet Socialist Republics (USSR). In theory the new state was a democracy with parliaments elected by the people. In practice the Communist Party was the only party, so the USSR was run by a dictatorship of the Communist Party.

By the time Lenin died in January 1924, having dominated Russia since 1917, he had made sure the Communist Party kept control of the country. He achieved this partly by introducing popular policies, but mainly by force and terror.

Output (in millions of tons)			
	1913	1921	1928
Coal	29.0	9.0	35.0
Oil	9.2	3.8	11.7
Iron	4.2	0.1	3.3
Steel	4.3	0.2	4.0
Grain	80.0	37.6	73.3

Production in the USSR, 1913–28.

THINGS TO DO

1 What was the New Economic Policy?

2 How successful was it?

SUMMARY

Communist control of Russia between 1918 and 1924 brought:

- State control of the key industries.
- State control of the banks.
- State control of the railways.
- Removal of grain from the peasants by seizure or taxation.
- A new constitution, creating the USSR.

How far did Stalin set up a personal dictatorship in Communist Russia?

The struggle for power with Trotsky

When Lenin died in 1924 a successor had not been appointed. Trotsky was most likely to succeed given that Lenin in his 'Political Testament' had warned the Party against appointing Stalin (Source B).

However, Stalin was in a strong position. Trotsky was unpopular with some members of the Party, partly because he had not joined the Bolsheviks until 1917 and partly because he was arrogant. In contrast Stalin was a loyal Party member.

Each man had different ideas on communism's future. Trotsky believed it could survive only if other countries became communist. The only way this could be done was to have a 'permanent revolution', which involved encouraging and helping revolution in other countries. Stalin believed communism in Russia must survive by itself, and that it was up to the Russian people, guided by the Communist government, to turn Russia into a modern, powerful state. This approach was called 'Socialism in one country'. It was more popular with the people because it involved them doing something about their own futures. Stalin was also General Secretary of the Communist Party, another strong advantage. He was responsible for making appointments to posts in the Party. This meant he could remove his opponents and replace them with his supporters.

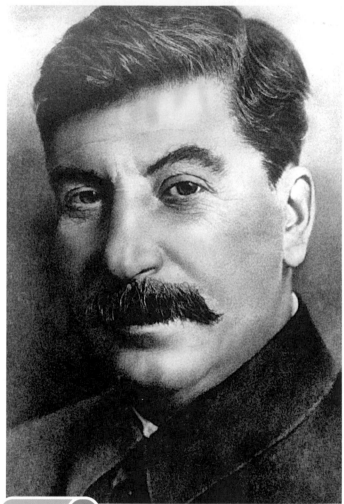

Source **A**   Joseph Stalin.

Source **B**

Comrade Stalin, having become General Secretary, has great power in his hands, and I am not sure that he always knows how to use that power with sufficient caution. Therefore, I propose to the comrades that a way be found to remove Stalin from that post.

An extract from Lenin's 'Political Testament', 1923.

The removal of Trotsky

After Lenin's death Stalin built support in the Central Committee of the Communist Party, the ruling body of the Party. The Party Congress of 1924 elected Stalin to the leadership of the Party. Trotsky's influence then swiftly declined. He was dismissed as Commissar for War in 1925 and the following year he was dismissed from the Central Committee. In 1927 he was expelled from the Communist Party and in 1929 exiled from the USSR.

Trotsky's exile took him to Mexico, where in 1940 he was assassinated by an agent of the Soviet secret police.

The removal of other communist leaders

Stalin did not want to share power and so moved against other leading communists who might threaten him. He got rid of left-wingers Kamenev and Zinoviev from the Central Committee in 1926 and the right-winger Bukharin in 1929. By removing his main political opponents and building up so much support within the Party Stalin had become the unchallenged leader of the Communist Party and the USSR.

Stalin's control of the USSR

The 1936 Constitution confirmed Stalin's and the Communist Party's control over the USSR. There was the appearance of democracy, with two chambers of parliament – the Soviet of the Union and the Soviet of Nationalities – with elections to them every four years. But there was only one political party – the Communists – so the elections were never contested. Real power was with the Central Committee of the Communist Party and its chairman, Stalin.

Stalin also controlled other parts of Russian life. The Churches were persecuted and religious services were banned. Priests were arrested and sent to labour camps. Art, music and literature were censored and directed to glorify the achievements of the Communist Revolution and the people of Russia. This was called 'Socialist Realism'.

In all these ways, the USSR was a totalitarian state, with the Communist Party having total control over the lives of the people.

The cult of personality

Hero-worship of the leader is another feature of the totalitarian state. This is called the 'cult of personality'. Propaganda was used to make people aware that Stalin was playing a part in every aspect of their lives – work, home, leisure. The message was that Stalin was looking after the people. Paintings, posters, statues and films all glorified him.

History was also re-written to show Stalin as Lenin's most trusted adviser during the Revolution. All mention of Trotsky was removed from Russian history.

In this way Stalin not only strengthened the communist dictatorship of the USSR, but he also established a personal dictatorship.

Source

> Stalin's face is seen everywhere. His name is spoken by everyone. His praises are sung in every speech. Every room I entered had a portrait of Stalin hanging on the wall. Is it love or fear? I do not know.
>
> *A foreigner describes the glorification of Stalin in the USSR.*

THINGS TO DO

Explain why it was Stalin rather than Trotsky who succeeded Lenin as ruler of the USSR.

Case Study: the Purges and Great Terror

By the 1930s, even with his main opponents removed, Stalin still felt insecure. To eliminate the criticism and opposition Stalin embarked on a policy of purges, which went on from 1934 to 1938. Millions of communists and non-communists were arrested and either executed or sent to labour camps.

Many of the arrested 'confessed' under torture to whatever charges were trumped up against them. The most important figures in the Party were tried in public, in what was known as 'show trials'.

The accused were always found guilty of treason and executed. This was what happened to Kamenev and Zinoviev in 1936 and to Bukharin in 1938. Thousands of other Party members were denounced and expelled. The Purges enabled Stalin to gain complete control of the Communist Party.

Stalin also purged the armed forces to make sure they stayed loyal to him. Nearly 90 per cent of the army's top officers and every admiral in the navy were purged. This ensured the loyalty of the armed forces to Stalin. However, it left Russia short of experienced officers to lead those forces in war against Nazi Germany.

This 'Great Terror' also extended to ordinary Russians, millions of whom were arrested. Without even being tried they were executed or sentenced to labour camps in far-off Siberia or the Arctic, where millions were worked to death or died of cold and hunger. The Terror was carried out by the secret police, the NKVD (formerly the Cheka), aided by informers who were encouraged to denounce their fellow-workers, neighbours, friends, and even their own families. The Russian people lived in terror.

By 1939 it was clear even to Stalin that the Purges and Terror were destroying Russian society and they were scaled down. No one knows how many suffered during this time. Some have estimated that 20 million people were sentenced to labour camps, over half of them dying there. The country lost many of its scientists, doctors, teachers, engineers, as well as military officers.

Source **D** A French cartoon of the 1930s showing a Russian with banner saying 'We are really happy'.

The prisoners were charged with every conceivable crime: high treason, murder, espionage and all kinds of sabotage. They had all signed written statements confessing to the crimes and incriminating themselves and each other. ... Yet what they said bore no relation to the truth. It became clear that the purpose of the trial was to show them not as political offenders, but as common criminals, murderers and spies.

A British diplomat describing a show trial.

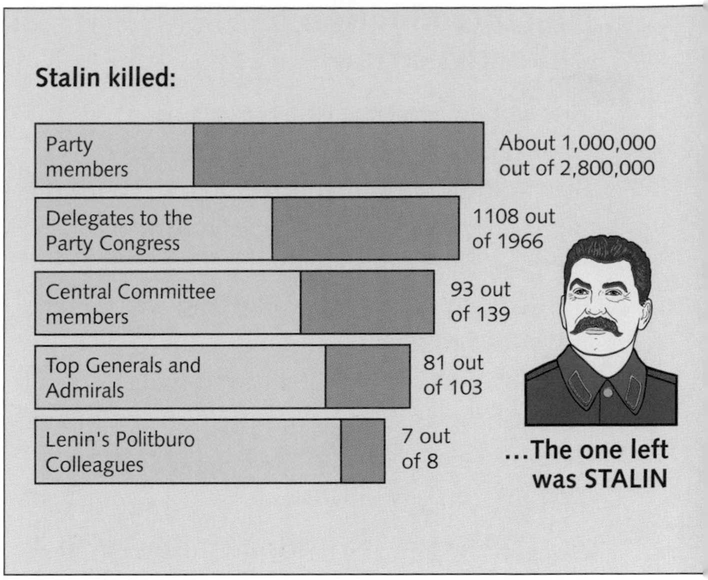

Stalin killed:

Party members	About 1,000,000 out of 2,800,000
Delegates to the Party Congress	1108 out of 1966
Central Committee members	93 out of 139
Top Generals and Admirals	81 out of 103
Lenin's Politburo Colleagues	7 out of 8

...The one left was STALIN

The purge of the Communist Party.

THINGS TO DO

1 Use **Source C** and the evidence on Stalin's control of the USSR to explain the cult of personality.

2 Use **Source D** and the evidence in this section to explain why Stalin used show trials to remove his opponents in the Communist Party.

3 Look at **Source E** and the chart above. What were the results of the Purges for: Stalin, the Communist Party, the Russian people?

SUMMARY

Stalin set up a personal dictatorship in the USSR by:

- Removing Trotsky.
- Use of the Purges to remove rivals in the Communist Party.
- Use of the Purges and Terror to remove other opposition.
- Securing control of the armed forces.
- Censorship of the media and the arts.
- The cult of personality.

To what extent did Stalin make the USSR a great economic power?

The need for economic growth

Under the NEP Russian industry made up much of the ground lost during world and civil war. Even so, in 1928 the country was still backward compared to other major powers.

Stalin wanted the USSR to be strong industrially, mainly because it would make it more able to resist invasion. Industry had to expand, especially heavy industries, such as coal, steel and oil. New factories and new towns would have to be built. To feed the workers and their families more food would be needed, so agriculture had to be made more efficient to meet this demand. For its industry the Soviet Union needed to buy machinery from other countries and to do this it needed to raise money from the export of grain to the West.

The introduction of collectivisation

Russian agriculture was backward in 1928. Most farms were small following the distribution of land among peasants after the Revolution. Peasants were still using old methods of farming. When a food crisis occurred in the late 1920s Stalin was forced to introduce rationing. To make sure the industrial workers of the towns had enough to eat, grain was seized from the peasant farmers. They were furious and hoarded or produced less, just as they did during War Communism.

Given that industry depended on an efficient agriculture to produce the food needed, Stalin in 1929 announced the collectivisation of Russian agriculture as the way to increase its efficiency.

The collective farm

Among the different kinds of collective farms, the most common was the Kolkhoz, where peasants joined their land together to form a larger farm. All their animals were also given over to the farm. It was run by a committee, and the peasants worked together and shared everything. Each farm produced a set amount of grain and sold this to the state at a low price. Anything they produced over this amount was for them to keep or sell. The state provided tractors and other machinery to help the peasants farm more efficiently.

The process of collectivisation

Stalin linked collectivisation to socialist policy to try to persuade the peasants to join the collective farms. In doing this he identified an enemy of the poor – the Kulaks, rich peasants who had prospered under the NEP. He claimed he was taking land from the 'greedy, capitalist Kulaks' and giving it to the poor peasants.

The Kulaks were arrested and 'liquidated' – that is, shot or deported to labour camps in Siberia.

Source F

The history of old Russia has consisted in being beaten again and again because of our backwardness. It is our duty to the working class to increase the pace of production. We are 50-100 years behind the advanced countries. We must make up this gap in ten years. Either we do it or they crush us.

Extract from a speech by Stalin in 1931.

Source G

Stock was slaughtered every night. As soon as dusk fell the muffled, short bleats of sheep, the death squeals of pigs, or the lowing of calves could be heard. Bulls, sheep, pigs, even cows were slaughtered, as well as cattle for breeding ....
'Kill, it's not ours any more ... Kill, they'll take it for meat anyway ... Kill, you won't get meat on the collective farm ....'
And they killed. They ate until they could eat no more.

An extract from the Russian novel, Virgin Soil Upturned, by M. Sholokhov.

Source H

Collectivisation achieved its main aims. The government could now take food from the peasants at incredibly low prices. Also it acquired an increased working force for industry. Mechanisation, especially tractors, released millions of young peasants for industries in the cities.

A modern British historian writing about collectivisation.

Many peasants were still not convinced about collectivisation and, rather than hand over their crops, stock and buildings, they destroyed them.

By 1930 over half the farming land was collectivised, but Stalin was worried about continuing resistance from many farmers. So he made changes to the system. Peasants could keep their own houses and a small plot of land for their own use. This encouraged more peasants to join the collective farms, though some still refused. By 1937 nearly all the farmland in the USSR was organised into collective farms.

Russian agricultural production, 1928–38.

THINGS TO DO

Use the graph above and the evidence in this section to make a judgement on whether collectivisation succeeded.

Results of collectivisation

Collectivisation had limited success. Grain production did not increase; actually it fell between 1929 and 1933. Bad harvests and peasants' destruction of crops in protest at collectivisation caused famine in 1932-33, with millions dying of starvation. Grain production did, however, increase after 1933 as the collectives became more organised.

Collectivisation had a high human cost. The Kulaks were eliminated, with almost five million being executed or deported, and over 13 million peasants died during collectivisation, many of them from the famine.

Source

A painting of Stalin with industrial workers.

Industry: the Five-Year Plans

Stalin believed industry could only develop through strong state control and planning. This was to be achieved by a series of Five-Year Plans. During these the state would decide what and how much would be produced.

Gosplan, the state planning agency, was responsible for the Plans. It set the targets an industry had to meet in five years. Each factory in an industry would have its own target to contribute to the overall target of that industry. Success in meeting targets was rewarded, failure was punished.

Between 1928 and 1941 there were three Five-Year Plans. The first concerned heavy industry – coal, iron and steel, oil and electricity. Though it failed to meet its targets, substantial industrial growth was achieved. At the end of the second Plan, 1933-37, which also involved heavy industry, even more industrial growth had taken place. The third Plan began in 1938 with the idea of producing more consumer goods. However, it was disrupted by the threat of war with Nazi Germany and the need to divert industry to the making of arms for war.

The growth of industry

Russian industry changed and expanded enormously because of the Plans. Old industrial areas were re-developed and expanded, and new ones were created to the east, in the Urals and Siberia, well away from areas most likely to be attacked by enemies, such as Germany.

New towns were built, such as Magnitogorsk in the Urals and Komsomulsk in Siberia. In eight years Magnitogorsk was transformed from a tiny village to a massive industrial city producing steel.

Other achievements included the construction of a hydro-electric dam on the River Dneiper, which by itself produced more electricity than was produced in the whole of Tsarist Russia.

Results of the Five-Year Plans

In all the key industries – coal, iron and steel, oil, electricity – the USSR grew to be a major industrial power in ten years. Though it was still well behind the most powerful Western countries, it was no longer an easy target for invaders, particularly the Germans.

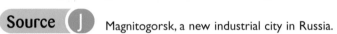

Source   **J**   Magnitogorsk, a new industrial city in Russia.

The human cost of this achievement was high. Forced labour killed millions of people. In the towns and cities, unable to cope with the mass influx of new workers from the countryside, slums and poor sanitation flourished. There wasn't enough food and rationing was common. Working conditions were poor and hours of work long. Improvements were made by the government, with more schools being built and social insurance schemes introduced. However, these could not meet the level of demand.

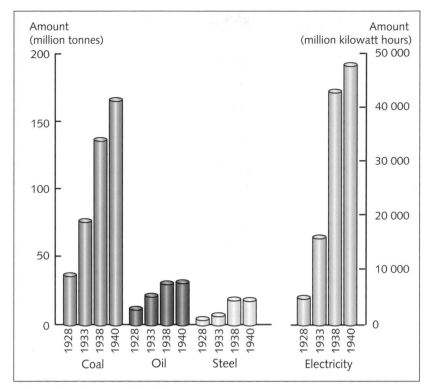

Industrial production, 1928-40.

Source

A quarter of a million people – communists, Kulaks, foreigners, convicts and a mass of peasants – were building the largest steelworks in Europe in the middle of the Russian steppe at Magnitogorsk. Here men froze, went hungry and suffered, but the construction went on with a disregard for individuals.

An extract from a book by an American engineer who worked in the USSR in the 1930s.

THINGS TO DO

Study **Sources J, K** and the graph above. What evidence do they give to show the effects of the Five Year Plans on Russian industry?

SUMMARY

The achievements of Stalin's economic policy were:

- Collectivisation of all farmland in USSR.
- Production of more grain for export.
- Increased industrial production in all key industries.
- Expansion of Russian industry to new areas.

The cost of Stalin's economic policies were:

- Elimination of the Kulaks.
- Disruption of agriculture because of peasant opposition to collectivisation.
- Poor condition of life in cities and towns.
- Death of millions of Russians through famine, starvation, overwork and forced labour.

Exam-style assessment

These questions follow the pattern of questions to be set by AQA for Paper 2 of its new Modern World History specification.

SECTION A: Industrialisation and Collectivisation under Stalin

Study **Sources A** to **E** and then answer all parts of Question 1 which follow.

Source A: Estimated figures for the First Five-Year Plan

Industry	1927-8 production	Target for 1932	1932 production
Electricity (milliard kWh)	5.05	17.0	13.4
Coal (million tonnes)	35.4	68.0	64.3
Oil (million tonnes)	11.7	19.0	21.4
Steel (million tonnes)	4.0	8.3	5.9

From *Russia and the USSR, 1900-1995* (1996) by R. RADWAY

Source B: A Soviet poster from 1931

The poster says 'We strike down lazy workers'.

Source C: Building the Moscow Underground in the 1930s

We got so dirty and we were such young things – small, slender, fragile. But we had our orders to build the metro and we wanted to do it more than anything else. We wore our miners' overalls with such style. My feet were size four and the boots were size eleven. But there was such enthusiasm.

From an interview with Tatyana Fyodorova in 1990 when she was 90 years old

Source D: The effects of industrialisation

Beginning with 1928 Soviet national economic development was based on five-year plans. The working people sought to implement them as soon as possible. Nationwide campaigns were launched for the speedy fulfilment of planned targets. By 1936 Russia had been transformed from an economically backward country into a mighty industrial state.

From *History of the Soviet Union* (1974) published by the Novosti Press Agency, an official Soviet government publisher

Source E: Another view of the effects of industrialisation

The Five Year Plans resulted in hunger, shortages and inefficiency. It is necessary to dwell on these many negative features. Even though there were achievements, they must be seen against a background of appalling difficulties.

From *An Economic History of the USSR* (1969) by ALEC NOVE, a British historian

Question 1

(a) What can you learn from **Source A** about Stalin's Five-Year Plans? **(5 marks)**

(b) Are **Source B** and **Source C** agreeing about the responses of the Russian people towards industrialisation? Explain your answer. **(6 marks)**

(c) How reliable is **Source C** for studying Russian attitudes towards industrialisation in the 1930s? Explain your answer using **Source C** and your own knowledge. **(9 marks)**

(d) Why do you think **Source D** and **Source E** give different interpretations of the Five-Year Plans? Explain your answer using **Sources D** and **E** and your own knowledge. **(10 marks)**

(e) In the same period, Stalin ordered the collectivisation of agriculture. Use your own knowledge to explain whether you think this policy was a success. **(15 marks)**

SECTION B: Russia 1917–28

Study **Sources F** and **G** and then answer parts **(a)**, **(b)**, **(c)**, and **either (d) or (e)** of Question 5 which follows.

Source F: Discipline in the Red Army

- Every scoundrel who incites anyone to retreat or to desert will be shot.
- Every soldier who throws away his rifle will be shot.

From *Orders to the Red Army* by TROTSKY during the Civil War

Source G: Russia in the Civil War, 1918–21

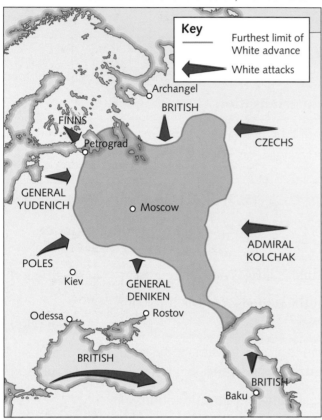

Question 5

(a) What can you learn from **Source F** about how Trotsky controlled the Red Army during the Civil War? **(3 marks)**

(b) Describe Lenin's policy of War Communism. **(5 marks)**

(c) Using the map (**Source G**) and your own knowledge, explain why the Reds were able to win the Civil War by 1921. **(7 marks)**

EITHER

(d) Explain why the Bolsheviks had been able to seize power in Russia in October/November 1917. **(15 marks)**

OR

(e) Why was Stalin able to defeat Trotsky in the struggle for power after Lenin's death? **(15 marks)**

5 Germany, 1918–39

INTRODUCTION

In 1918 Germany suffered defeat in the First World War. The Treaty of Versailles, which formally brought peace to Europe, proved humiliating to Germany. It weakened the Weimar Republic, the new government in Germany, and brought challenges to it. The impact of the Treaty played an important part in shaping post-war Germany, and it also brought economic hardship with hyperinflation in 1923.

In the later 1920s Weimar Germany recovered under Gustav Streseman. The country's economy was more stable and extremist groups attracted more support. However, following the Wall Street Crash of 1929, economic problems engulfed Germany, with huge unemployment, and many people looking to political extremes – the communists and the Nazis.

Hitler and the Nazi Party were brought to power by the votes of the German people. However, in a short time, a fascist dictatorship was established in which the Nazi Party controlled all aspects of German life such as education, the law, religion and the media. Those who disagreed, or who were not accepted by the Nazis, were persecuted – none more so than the Jewish people. Hitler brought benefits to the German people, most importantly in employment, but the Germans paid a heavy price for such gains.

1918	Kaiser Wilhelm II abdicates New republic set up
1919	Weimar constitution set up Germany signs the Treaty of Versailles
1920	Kapp *Putsch*
1923	French occupation of the Ruhr Munich *Putsch*
1924	Dawes Plan
1925	Germany signs the Locarno Pact
1929	Death of Gustav Stresemann Wall Street Crash
1930	Brüning becomes Chancellor
1932	Nazis win 230 seats in Reichstag elections
1933	30 January: Hitler becomes Chancellor
1934	30 June: 'Night of the Long Knives'
1936	Olympics held in Berlin
1938	9 November: Kristallnacht
1939	1 September: Germany invades Poland

How far do the early problems of the Weimar Republic suggest that it was doomed from the start?

The abdication of the Kaiser

In 1918, the final year of the First World War, conditions in Germany were poor. There was starvation and hunger among the people. The army was demoralised. In November, the sailors at Kiel mutinied, refusing to obey orders to leave the port for battle with the British navy. The Kaiser failed to send the army to crush the mutiny. The result was that it spread – to other sailors, to soldiers and to workers who went on strike. Within days there were strikes and risings all over Germany as the country fell into chaos. The Kaiser found himself without support, even from his army generals. On 9 November he abdicated and fled to Holland. On 11 November 1918 Germany signed the armistice with the Allies. The war was over.

However, the Kaiser had departed so suddenly that a new government had not been appointed or elected. The lead was taken by Friedrich Ebert, the head of the Social Democratic Party. This was the largest single party in the Reichstag (the German Parliament) so it could claim that it represented the people. Two days after the Kaiser's abdication, Ebert declared a new German Republic with an elected parliament.

Source (A) An ex-soldier begs in the streets of Berlin in 1923.

The Spartacist Uprising

Causes

The Spartacus League, led by Rosa Luxemburg and Karl Liebknecht, was made up of German communists who opposed everything that Ebert did. They wanted Germany to be ruled by the soviets that had been created in the November revolution. On the last day of 1918 they renamed themselves the German Communist Party and made plans to seize power. Many Germans, especially the middle and upper class, feared a communist takeover in which they would lose their property, businesses and land.

Events

On 5 January 1919 the Spartacus League staged a revolt in a bid for power. A strike was organised and a revolutionary committee was formed to take control.

Ebert did a deal with the army commanders that allowed the army to put down the Spartacists. In return, the Social Democrats agreed not to set up a new army that was sympathetic to the republic. The old army of the Kaiser's Germany remained in existence. Thousands of Spartacists were killed and Karl Liebknecht and Rosa Luxemburg were both shot.

Results

Ebert's government had been saved, but at a cost. The army, which never fully supported the republic, remained unchanged. The communists never forgot the Spartacist Uprising, and throughout the history of the republic, they saw the Social Democrats as their deadliest enemies. This was later to be of vital importance.

The creation of the Weimar Republic

On 19 January 1919, four days after the defeat of the Spartacists, a general election was held for a new parliament. The Social Democrats were elected as the largest party and Ebert was appointed the first President of the German Republic. However, it was felt that Berlin was too unsafe for the government to meet there. Instead, it moved to the safer town of Weimar.

Revolts in Berlin and Bavaria

Any hopes that the newly elected government would be accepted by all Germans were quickly ended. In March 1919 the communists organised riots and strikes in Berlin. Again the Free Corps destroyed this opposition.

A further threat to the Weimar Republic was the setting up of a Socialist Republic in Bavaria in November 1918. On 7 April 1919 it was made a Soviet Republic like Russia with Munich as its capital. Food, money and houses were taken from the rich and given to the workers. The government sent soldiers to besiege Munich. In May the soldiers, helped by the Free Corps, broke into the city. The revolt was crushed and its leaders massacred.

The Weimar government had established its control of Germany by defeating opposition with the help of the Free Corps. Now it had an even greater problem to face – the peace treaty to end the First World War.

Source B

The Spartacus League is now fighting for total power. The government, which wants the people to decide their own future freely, is to be overthrown by force. The people are not allowed to speak. You have seen the results. Where Spartacus rules, all personal freedom and security is abolished. The newspapers are suppressed. Traffic is at a standstill. Parts of Berlin are the scenes of bloody battles. Others are already without water and light. Food warehouses are being attacked. Food supplies are being stopped. The government is taking all measures necessary to destroy this rule of terror.

An extract from a document published by the Ebert government in January 1919.

THINGS TO DO

Look at **Source B** and the evidence in this section. Explain why the Weimar government was able to defeat the opposition to it in 1919.

The problems of the Weimar Republic

German reactions to defeat

In later years, many Germans argued that Germany could have won the war in 1918. They said that the politicians of the new republic, who became known as 'the November criminals', had betrayed them when they agreed to an armistice. This 'stab in the back theory' won support among the army and German nationalists. In fact, the army commanders knew they were close to defeat and encouraged the government to sign the cease-fire. The new republic, however, was associated with defeat and this made it unpopular.

The Treaty of Versailles

When the Germans signed the armistice, they believed that the treaty would be based on the Fourteen Points devised by President Wilson of the USA (see page 21) and would be fair and democratic. However, the Germans were not allowed to attend the Paris peace conference. They were not even told anything about the talks that took place there. But most German people still expected a reasonable peace treaty.

The hopes of the German people were dashed on 7 May 1919 when they were presented with the peace treaty. Germany was held to be 'guilty' of causing the First World War and all the damage resulting from it. This was used to justify demands for reparations or compensation. Most Germans argued that Germany, alone, had not caused the war. However, the reparations were fixed at £6600 million in 1921.

Germans were equally angry about losing a large amount of territory in the peace settlement (see page 23). All Germany's colonies and over 70,000 square kilometres of its land were taken away and given to nearby countries. Germany was also severely cut back as a military power, with its army and

Source **C** This cartoon was published in a German magazine in 1919. It was called 'Clemenceau the Vampire' and shows the French Prime Minister sucking the blood from Germany.

navy greatly reduced in size and its air force scrapped. Further humiliation came when the area of western Germany known as the Rhineland had to be demilitarised by the Germans and was occupied by the Allies.

The Germans were horrified with the terms of the treaty and anti-treaty protests took place all over Germany. The German government insisted that it had no choice but to accept the treaty, as otherwise the Allied armies would occupy and possibly partition Germany. The popular press, however, called for revenge. On 28 June 1919 two German representatives signed the Treaty of Versailles.

The new republic had got off to a bad start. Not only was it blamed for German defeat in 1918, but also many Germans did not forgive it for signing the Treaty of Versailles.

The Weimar Constitution

In August 1919, the Weimar government published its constitution. Many people welcomed it, as it was one of the most democratic in Europe. Germany was to be one of the most advanced democracies in Europe.

At a time when few other countries gave women the right to vote, the Weimar Constitution gave all men and women over 20 years old the right to vote for members of the lower house of parliament, the Reichstag. The number of seats for each party in the Reichstag was to be based on the total number of votes won by that party. This is known as proportional representation. It gave small as well as large parties a share of seats. The head of government, or chancellor, had to have the support of a majority in the Reichstag.

Germany was to be a federation. This meant that each German state, such as Bavaria and Prussia, had its own state government. Each state sent a representative to the upper house of parliament, the Reichsrat.

The head of state, the president, was elected by the people. Finally, the constitution granted the German people a wide range of human and civil rights, for instance free speech and the freedom of movement and religion.

Weaknesses of the Constitution

The new Constitution, however, had several fundamental weaknesses. The president had the power to appoint and dismiss the chancellor. If he considered that there was an emergency, he could use Article 48 to suspend democracy for a time and rule by issuing decrees or laws. This was to prove decisive in the breakdown of democracy in Germany after 1930. In addition, one of the German states, Prussia, had an overall majority of

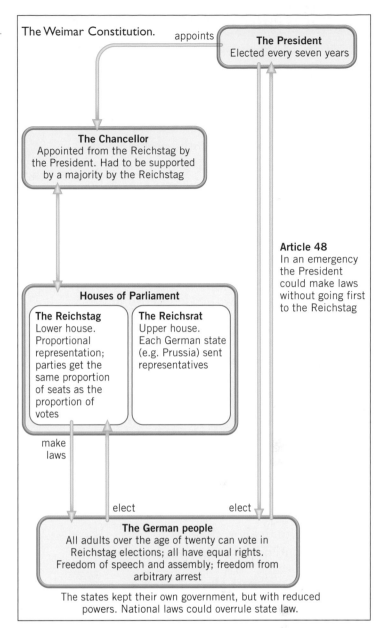

The Weimar Constitution.

The President
Elected every seven years

appoints

The Chancellor
Appointed from the Reichstag by the President. Had to be supported by a majority by the Reichstag

Houses of Parliament

The Reichstag
Lower house. Proportional representation; parties get the same proportion of seats as the proportion of votes

The Reichsrat
Upper house. Each German state (e.g. Prussia) sent representatives

Article 48
In an emergency the President could make laws without going first to the Reichstag

make laws

elect   elect

The German people
All adults over the age of twenty can vote in Reichstag elections; all have equal rights. Freedom of speech and assembly; freedom from arbitrary arrest

The states kept their own government, but with reduced powers. National laws could overrule state law.

representatives in the Reichsrat. This meant that Prussia alone could veto (block) any changes in the constitution.

In addition, because of proportional representation, no party ever had an overall majority in the Reichstag. This meant that all governments were coalitions, which had to be put together from several parties. This, in turn, often led to weak governments that could not agree on policies. It proved disastrous in times of crisis, such as 1929–30. Proportional representation also encouraged the growth of extremist parties such as the Communists and National Socialists.

The Kapp *Putsch*, 1920

The Treaty of Versailles had ordered the reduction of the German army. Many of the soldiers who had been demobbed joined the Free Corps. These had supported the government in defeating socialist and communist risings, often with great violence. In early 1920 the Allies put pressure on the government to break up the Free Corps, who, led by Wolfgang Kapp, marched into Berlin to seize power. This was a *putsch* – an attempt to take power by force. Kapp was supported by the army and the police in Berlin. By this time Ebert and his government had returned from Weimar to Berlin. Now they left Berlin and fled to Dresden. From here the government appealed for support from the workers in Berlin. The workers supported the government and organised a general strike. Within a day there was no water, gas, coal or transport in Berlin. The *putsch* quickly collapsed and Kapp fled to Sweden. Ebert and the government returned to Berlin. Order had been restored. The Weimar government now hoped for a period of calm to allow the new constitution to be put into operation.

Reparations and the occupation of the Ruhr

Under the Treaty of Versailles, Germany was forced to pay reparations, which were fixed at £6600 million in 1921. Germany made the first payment in 1921 but declared in 1922 that, due to severe economic problems, it could no longer make the payments. On 9 January 1923, the French responded to this by sending in approximately 60,000 French and Belgian troops to invade the Ruhr, Germany's main industrial area. They took raw materials and goods in place of reparations.

The German army, limited in size under the Treaty of Versailles, was unable to prevent this action so the government called for the workers to carry out passive resistance. This meant the workers went on strike and refused to collaborate with the French. The French reacted angrily and removed 150,000 strikers from the Ruhr, even shooting people when they refused to work. Industrial production in Germany ground to a halt.

Source D — A German poster from 1923. It says 'Hands off the Ruhr!'

Hände weg vom Ruhrgebiet!

Hyperinflation, 1923

The effect of a government printing money is that the value of the money goes down and prices go up. As more and more money is printed, so prices rise higher and higher. More money then has to be printed to meet the increasing prices. As a result, money becomes worthless. This is called hyperinflation.

Hyperinflation affected the German people in different ways. For those in work, wages rose higher and higher – sometimes twice a day. Workers were seen collecting their weekly wages with wheelbarrows. However, the price of goods always tended to rise faster than wages. People on fixed incomes suffered the most. The rises in prices meant that their incomes were now too low to live on.

Source **E** Children playing with worthless money, 1923.

They struggled to buy food and clothes, and to heat their homes. Many of these people were pensioners and they now faced starvation. People with savings in the bank also suffered as the money they had saved was now worthless. Surprisingly, some Germans gained from the hyperinflation. Those who had debts or had taken out loans could now pay the money back with ease.

However, many more Germans suffered from the hyperinflation than gained from it. They laid the blame for their problems on the government. The Weimar Republic became even more unpopular. Some of this anger turned into violence. For example, in November 1923, the Nazi Party tried to seize power in Munich (see page 194 on the Munich *Putsch*). Yet the Weimar Republic survived. This was largely because of the work of Gustav Stresemann who was Chancellor for a few weeks in 1923, and then Foreign Minister until his death in 1929.

(see page 194 on the

Source **F**

As soon as I received my salary I rushed out to buy what I needed. My daily salary was just enough to buy one loaf of bread and a small piece of cheese .... A friend of mine, a vicar, came to Berlin to buy some shoes with his month's wages for his baby. By the time he arrived, he only had enough to buy a cup of coffee.

A German woman writing about the effects of hyperinflation.

How far did the Weimar Republic recover under Stresemann?

The crisis facing the Weimar Republic reached its peak in November 1923. For the next six years Germany went through a period of prosperity that is sometimes called the 'golden age of the Weimar Republic'.

The role of Stresemann

Gustav Stresemann was leader of the German People's Party (DVP). He became Chancellor briefly in 1923 and Foreign Minister from 1923 to 1929. As Chancellor, he introduced a new currency, the Rentenmark, to replace the old worthless mark. He ordered the striking workers in the Ruhr back to work and agreed that Germany should start paying reparations again. This made him unpopular and he was forced to give up the post of Chancellor in November 1923.

As Foreign Secretary, Stresemann did more than anyone else to make Germany acceptable again to the European powers. In 1929 he was awarded the Nobel Peace Prize. Stresemann was also important in countering extremism within Germany and did much to keep governments going during the 1920s. It was a tragedy that he died in October 1929 – at a time when Germany needed his special qualities.

Source G

Gustav Stresemann.

Economic recovery

The introduction of the Rentenmark stabilised the German currency. To avoid another financial collapse in the future, other measures were also taken. In 1924 Germany agreed the Dawes Plan with the USA, Britain and France, in which the USA lent Germany 800 gold million marks. The Germans could use this to build new factories that would produce jobs and goods, and which would raise the standard of living of the German people. The Dawes Plan also spread the load of the reparation payments according to Germany's ability to pay. Over the next few years, Germany would make repayments starting at £50 million and rising to £125 million. Afterwards, payments would be linked to the prosperity of the German economy. The Dawes Plan did much to restore confidence in the German economy, and investment poured in

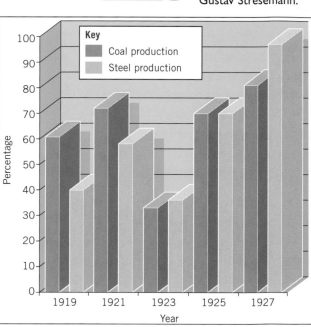

Steel and coal production in Germany, 1919–27 (100 stands for production in 1913, so a figure of 40 means that production had fallen to 40 per cent of what was produced in 1913).

from abroad. By 1925 all French and Belgian troops had been withdrawn from the Ruhr.

This seemed to be a period of economic prosperity as German industry produced more goods, exports rose, unemployment fell and most Germans were better off. The Young Plan of 1929 extended the deadline for payments of reparations for a further 59 years.

Modern World History for AQA

International relations

Other countries began to treat Germany as an equal. In 1925, Germany and France signed the Locarno Pact, in which they agreed never to try to change the border between them. In the following year, Germany was allowed to join the League of Nations. In 1928, Germany signed the Kellogg–Briand Pact with over 60 other countries. This said that these countries would never go to war against one another.

Impact of recovery

The republic was now more stable than at any time since 1919. The result was a decline in support for extremist parties such as the Communists and National Socialists. The moderate Social Democrats, on the other hand, increased their support after 1924. It seemed that the Weimar Republic was safe.

People also had more money to spend. Berlin became the pleasure capital of Europe. Going to clubs and cafés became an important part of Berlin life. Artists flocked to Berlin. There was little censorship and people could do whatever they wanted.

The late 1920s saw a huge cultural revival in Germany. As the economy and politics became more stable, writers and artists had more chance to try out new ideas. The artist George Grosz used art to criticise society. Erich Remarque wrote the anti-war novel, *All Quiet on the Western Front*. Later it was made into a highly successful film.

A golden age?

Although Germany did experience economic recovery after 1923, there were still problems. The German economy now became very dependent on US loans. This was to have disastrous consequences in 1929 (see page 190). Much of the money borrowed from US banks was invested in projects that in the long term would pay off the loans and the interest. What was needed was time. Even as early as 1927, however, industrial growth

Source H A painting by the artist George Grosz.

had started to slow down and there was a depression in farming.

Some critics saw the new Weimar Republic as 'decadent' and unpatriotic. Its new culture did not seem to represent the more traditional virtues of Germany. Many blamed the new wave of art for a decline of moral standards in the 1920s. Berlin had a huge number of nightclubs and there was more emphasis on sex in entertainment than there was in Paris.

THINGS TO DO

1 Which is more useful to a historian studying the recovery of the Weimar Republic, 1924–9, the charts of industrial production on page 188 or **Source H**?

2 Was the recovery of the republic due to the leadership of Stresemann?

The Great Depression

In October 1929, Stresemann, the most able minister in the government, died. Shortly after, the American financial market on Wall Street in New York crashed. The effects of the collapse were felt not only in the USA, but across the world. Germany was hit particularly badly because of the scale of its loans from America after 1924. American bankers and businessmen whose stocks and shares had collapsed now wanted their money back from German businesses. They demanded repayment of their loans and, of course, were not in a position to lend any more money. The result was a disaster for Germany. Businesses closed down as loans were repaid and trade slumped. Unemployment shot up. By 1932, six million Germans were unemployed. Millions of others became homeless, and set up camps on the outskirts of towns. They became dependent on charity food and soup kitchens to avoid starvation.

Source I

This German cartoon from 1927 attacks the disregard of the poor by the world's financiers, while they themselves were on the brink of a massive crash.

Unemployment in Germany 1925–33.

Source J

Men standing hopelessly on the street corners of every industrial town in Germany; houses without food or warmth; young people without any chance of a job. All these things explain the bitterness which burned in the minds of millions of ordinary Germans.

A description of the effects of unemployment in Germany in 1932.

The Weimar government and the Depression

The government was taken by surprise at the speed and extent of the Depression. It also had very few answers as to how to deal with it. To increase government expenditure to help the poor could be done only by printing money – and after 1923 this was unthinkable. So the government introduced a series of limited measures which often made things worse. It raised taxes to obtain money to help the needy, but this caused further problems for the businesses and companies being taxed. It reduced the wages of public officials, but this made life more difficult for them. Finally, it reduced unemployment benefit at a time when the growing numbers of unemployed needed all the help they could get. These policies also caused the collapse of the government as political parties withdrew from the coalition. It proved impossible to put together another coalition of parties that could form a government. In such a political emergency, the Constitution allowed the President to take control of

Source K This Nazi election poster of 1932 says 'Our last hope: Hitler!'

the government. So the 84-year-old Hindenburg became the ruler of Germany.

The Depression brought out all the weaknesses of the Weimar Republic which seemed to be incapable of doing anything to end the Depression. It is not surprising that the German people began to listen to parties promising to do something. In particular, they began to look to the Nazis.

SUMMARY

The Great Depression of 1929–33:

- It ended the recovery of Germany from the 1923 depression.
- It was caused by Germany's dependence on American loans.
- It brought unemployment and hardship to the German people.
- It was blamed on the Weimar Republic and increased its unpopularity.
- It increased the support of extreme parties who promised to end it.

THINGS TO DO

Explain why the German people turned away from the Weimar politicians.

How did the Nazi Party develop its ideas and organisation up to 1929?

Hitler's life in Vienna

Adolf Hitler was born in Austria in 1889. His father, a customs officer, died when he was fourteen, his mother when he was eighteen. With little education and no job, Hitler drifted to Vienna, the capital of Austria. He wished to become an art student but the Academy of Art would not enrol him. He was forced to live in poverty in hostels for tramps and take whatever jobs he could find. He developed an interest in politics and supported nationalist parties. He also came to dislike foreigners and, especially, Jewish people. He became convinced that it was Jews who had caused him to be a failure in Vienna. This early political interest would become important later on.

Source **A** Adolf Hitler.

Source **B**

The news came through that we were about to surrender, I broke down completely. Darkness surrounded me. I buried my head between the blankets and the pillow. I had not cried since the day that I stood beside my mother's grave.

Hitler's reaction to the German surrender in 1918.

Hitler and the First World War

In 1913 Hitler left Austria to avoid military service. When war broke out he immediately joined the German army. He was promoted to corporal and won the Iron Cross, First Class – the highest award for a German soldier. In 1918 he was gassed. It was in hospital that Hitler learned that Germany had surrendered and signed the armistice. He was furious at this and, like many other Germans, he blamed the defeat not on the German army but on Communists and Jews – the 'stab in the back' idea examined on page 184 of this chapter.

After the war Hitler returned to Munich. However, he remained in the army and worked in the intelligence service as a spy. His job was to find out if political parties, including the newly-formed German Workers Party, were a threat to the new goverment.

The foundation of the Nazi Party

The German Workers Party was small. Hitler found he agreed with its ideas and decided to join. He became its seventh member. Soon he became its leader and began to reorganise the Party to increase its popularity.

One of the first things he did was to change its name to the National Socialist German Workers Party – shortened to the Nazi Party. In 1920 he drew up the party programme which summarised the ideas of the new party (see Source C). In 1921 he set up a private army, the SA (Stormtroopers), also known as the Brownshirts because of their uniforms. The SA consisted of young men and some former members of the Free Corps. Their role was to protect Nazi speakers at rallies. In practice they usually went much further and beat up opponents. For example, Social Democrat and Communist meetings were often broken up by violence. Hitler also devised a symbol for the new party – the swastika. The Party began to publish its own newspaper to put forward its ideas.

The Nazi Party was based in Munich, the capital of the German state of Bavaria. Hitler was well known here, mainly because of large public meetings held throughout the state. However, the Nazi Party was relatively small in Germany as a whole. Even so Hitler was confident that Nazi ideas would appeal to the German people. In 1923, as economic crisis and hyperinflation hit Germany and brought despair to millions of Germans, he became convinced that now was the time to seize power.

Source C

1 We demand the union of all Germans to form a greater Germany.

2 We demand the abolition of the Peace Treaty of Versailles.

3 We demand land and territory for the nourishment of our people.

4 None but those of German blood may be members of the German nation.

....

25 We demand the creation of a strong central government in Germany.

From the Twenty-Five Points of the Nazi Party programme, 1920.

THINGS TO DO

Study **Source C**. Who might be attracted by each of the points set out in the source?

The Munich *Putsch*, November 1923

Although the Nazi Party was small and its support was largely limited to Bavaria, Hitler thought that the conditions in Germany in 1923 and the unpopularity of the government gave him a good chance of success. He expected support from the right-wing Bavarian government, led by Gustav Von Kahr. He also thought that the German army could be persuaded to desert the government and support the Nazis. He was encouraged in this by General Ludendorff who had shown sympathy with Nazi ideas.

On 8 November 1923, as Kahr addressed a meeting at a beer hall in Munich, Hitler arrived with 600 Stormtroopers. He stopped the meeting and tried to persuade Kahr at gunpoint to support the putsch. The arrival of Ludendorff at this point appeared to win over Kahr. The next day the SA seized key positions in Munich and Stormtroopers from other parts of Bavaria began to arrive. However, Kahr had been freed after agreeing to support the *putsch* but had alerted the army and the police.

As the Nazis marched to the city centre, their route was blocked by armed police and soldiers. Firing broke out – 16 Nazis and 3 policemen were killed. Hitler, Ludendorff and other Nazi leaders were arrested.

The *putsch* failed largely because Hitler over-estimated his support and the army and police stayed loyal to the government.

In February 1924 Hitler was put on trial on a charge of treason. He used the trial as a public platform to put forward his ideas and to condemn the Weimar Republic. The trial made Hitler a national and international figure. Despite the seriousness of the charge, Hitler was sentenced to only five years imprisonment. He served less than nine months. The other leaders received even lighter sentences.

Source D

Police about to disperse Hitler's supporters in Munich, 9 November 1923.

Mein Kampf

While in prison Hitler wrote a book about his life and ideas called *Mein Kampf* ('My Struggle'). This became the 'bible' of the Nazi movement. It contained many of the ideas

Source E

I am not a criminal. There is no such thing as high treason against the traitors of 1918. History will judge us as Germans who wanted only the good of their people and fatherland.

From Hitler's speech at his trial, 1924.

which Hitler later put into practice. The ideas in *Mein Kampf* were nothing new. However, they did give a clear indication of what the Nazi Party stood for. When Hitler came to power, the book became compulsory reading for all Germans – at home, in school and, even, in church.

The Nazi Party, 1924-29

The years between 1924 and 1929 were difficult ones for the Nazi Party. After the Munich *putsch*, the party was banned by the government and its supporters began to drift away. On Hitler's release from prison in December 1924 the ban was lifted and the party re-formed.

However, it struggled to attract the support of the German voters. These were the Stresemann years (see pages 188–9), when employment was high, business was doing well and Germany at last seemed to be recovering from the war and its effects. The extremist policies of the Nazi Party were not attractive in such stable conditions. This decline in the Nazi Party is seen in its performance in elections. In May 1924 it won 32 seats in the Reichstag, in December this had fallen to 14 seats, and in 1928 there was a further fall to 12 seats.

Yet the Nazi Party did not fade away in these years. A number of developments of importance took place. Hitler increased his control of the Party, Nazi organisations were set up and public meetings and rallies were held throughout Germany. It was activities like these which brought an increased membership to the Nazi Party. In 1925, it had 27,000 members, in 1928 over 100,000.

Even so, this was a long way off becoming a major national party which could take power in Germany. Something was needed to push the Nazi Party forward. It was at this point in 1929 that Germany was hit by a severe economic depression.

THINGS TO DO

Look at **Source E** and the evidence on the Munich *putsch*. Was the *putsch* a failure or success for Hitler?
Give reasons for your answers.

Source F

- Germany should be ruled by a strong leader with total power – the Führer.
- The Aryan race of which the Germans are part is the 'master race'. All other races are inferior to them.
- Jews have weakened the German race and brought Germany's defeat in the war. They must be destroyed.
- Communism must also be destroyed.
- The Treaty of Versailles must be destroyed and the land which Germany lost must be returned.
- Germany needs more land to live and work in (*Lebensraum*). If necessary, it must take this by force.

The main ideas of **Mein Kampf.**

SUMMARY

The development of the Nazi Party from 1919 to 1928:

1919	Hitler joined the German Workers Party.
1920	Hitler became its leader and renamed it the National Socialist German Workers Party – the Nazi Party.
1921	SA was set up.
1923	The Munich *putsch*.
1924	Hitler imprisoned; wrote *Mein Kampf*.
1928	Nazi Party won 12 seats in the Reichstag.

How was Hitler able to become Chancellor in January 1933?

The Nazi Party and the Great Depression

Support for the Nazi Party was due to the growing belief that it was a party with a leader who could do something about Germany's problems.

The Nazis promised much: jobs for the unemployed in state-financed public works programmes, help for employers to increase their profits, help for farmers and shop-keepers. They also promised that Germany would be great again. The Nazis were prepared to promise anything to win votes.

Source G

A Nazi election poster of 1932 saying 'Women! Millions of men out of work! Millions of children without a future! Save our German families. Vote for Hitler.'

Only the Jews and Communists, who were blamed for all Germany's problems, were left out of the Nazis' plans for Germany.

The Nazis were also well organised. They were disciplined, and portrayed Hitler as a strong leader who would 'save' Germany. Mass rallies enabled Hitler to speak to thousands of people at one time. Joseph Goebbels, who was in charge of propaganda, ran a 'Hitler over Germany' campaign, which involved flying Hitler from one rally to the next, allowing him to make speeches all over Germany. This was supported by a poster campaign, strong in emotional appeal (Source G).

The SA also played an important role. They beat up opponents, especially the Communists, and smashed up their election meetings. This made it very difficult for the Communists to run a free election campaign. In contrast to the strong campaign of the Nazi Party, the Social Democrats and other parties who supported the Weimar government seemed to have little to offer.

Nazi election gains, 1930–2

Nazi election campaigning was effective. In 1930 they won 107 seats and in July 1932 this had increased to 230 seats. Although this fell to 196 in the November election, they remained the largest single party in the Reichstag.

In the presidential elections of April 1932 Hitler stood against Hindenburg for the presidency of Germany. Hindenburg won with 19 million votes against Hitler's 13 million.

Unlike the Munich *putsch*, the Nazis were using the democratic process to win power. By the summer of 1932 Hitler was in a position to demand that he should become Chancellor of Germany.

Hitler becomes Chancellor

Hindenburg disliked the Nazi Party and its leader. He refused to make Hitler Chancellor despite the fact that after the July 1932 elections the Nazis were the largest party in the Reichstag. Instead, he used his emergency powers to appoint the leader of the smaller Centre Party, von Papen, as Chancellor. However, one of Hindenburg's advisers, von Schleicher, told him that the army opposed von Papen and might take action unless he was replaced. Hindenburg was forced to back down but again he did not summon Hitler.

In December 1932 he asked von Schleicher to become Chancellor. Von Schleicher failed to get much support in the Reichstag and resigned after only eight weeks. Finally, on 30 January 1933, Hindenburg summoned Hitler to his office and invited him to become Chancellor. Even then Hindenburg showed his distrust of Hitler. He persuaded Hitler to accept von Papen as Vice Chancellor and put von Papen's supporters into the government. In this way Hindenburg expected to be able to control Hitler. However, he had underestimated Hitler's political ability. Hitler accepted the arrangement but immediately called another election to the Reichstag. He wanted to get full control of the Reichstag by making the Nazis the majority party.

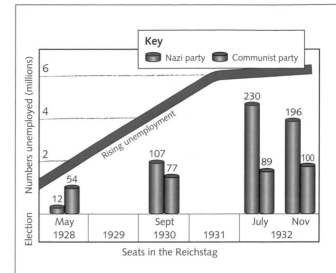

Growth of support for the Nazi Party in Reichstag elections.

Source **H** Hitler as Chancellor being presented to President Hindenburg.

5.3 Establishment of a Nazi Dictatorship, 1933–4

How did Hitler change Germany from a democracy to a Nazi dictatorship, 1933–4?

Case Study: the Reichstag fire and its results

On 27 February 1933, the Reichstag building was set on fire. Inside the building a young Dutch Communist, Marinus van der Lubbe, was found by the police with matches in his pocket. He was charged with the crime and later confessed. At his trial he was found guilty and then executed. Firm evidence still does not exist to prove the case. Van der Lubbe was known to have been of limited intelligence and his interrogation by the Nazi-controlled police force may well have resulted in a forced confession. It is possible, although again not proven, that the Nazis themselves planned and set fire to the Reichstag.

There was an underground passage that ran from the SA offices into the Reichstag building, and so access to the Reichstag would have been easy. A few days before the fire the SA had picked up Van der Lubbe after hearing him boast that he planned to set fire to the Reichstag. It would have been easy to set him up to take the blame.

If there is a doubt over who was responsible for the Reichstag fire, its results are not in doubt. Hitler immediately claimed that the fire was proof of a Communist plot to take control of the government. It was the signal for a bloody uprising.

He persuaded President Hindenburg to sign an emergency decree, the Law for the Protection of People and the State. It ended all the freedoms guaranteed in the Constitution and gave the police total control. Working with the SA the police arrested Communist leaders and detained them without trial. Communist meetings were broken up, and their newspapers closed down. Other political opponents of the Nazis also suffered.

At the same time as all this violence, the Nazi propaganda machine encouraged the German people to vote for the Nazis. There were mass rallies, torchlight parades and radio broadcasts.

Source

This act of arson is the most outrageous act yet committed by Communism in Germany. The burning of the Reichstag was to have been the signal for a bloody uprising and civil war.

Statement by Hitler, issued the day after the Reichstag fire.

At a luncheon on the birthday of the Führer in 1942 the conversation turned to the topic of the Reichstag building. I heard with my own ears when Goering interrupted the conversation and shouted: 'The only one who really knows about the Reichstag is I, because I set it on fire!

The Nazi general, Halder, speaking at the Nuremberg War Crimes trial, 1945.

THINGS TO DO

Look at **Sources A**, **B** and **C**, and the evidence in the case study on the Reichstag fire. Who do you think set fire to the Reichstag? Give reasons for your answer.

Source The Reichstag buildings on fire, 27 February 1933.

The 1933 election

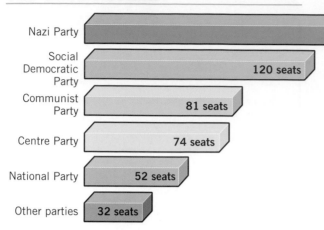

Nazi Party	288 seats
Social Democratic Party	120 seats
Communist Party	81 seats
Centre Party	74 seats
National Party	52 seats
Other parties	32 seats

Results of the March 1933 election.

The election results of March 1933, not unexpectedly, brought victory to the Nazis. More people voted for them than ever before (44% of the voters) and the Party won more seats (288) than ever before. However, the Nazis still did not have control of the Reichstag – 359 seats went to parties other than the Nazis. But they were now helped by one of the smaller parties, the Nationalist Party. It decided to join with the Nazis. Its 52 seats were added to the 288 of the Nazi Party, and this gave the Nazis control of the Reichstag.

Hitler was finally in a position where he could move for complete power.

The Enabling Law

The elections of March 1933 and the decision of the Nationalist Party to join with the Nazis had given Hitler control of the Reichstag. He lost no time in using this to his advantage. On 23 March he introduced an Enabling Law which would allow him to have complete power in Germany. However, this law needed to be approved by the Reichstag. Because it also changed the Constitution of the German Republic, it had to be approved by a two-thirds majority in the Reichstag. Hitler did not have this – the Nazis and the Nationalist Party together held just over half the seats. Great pressure was now put on the other parties in the Reichstag. The first step was to ban the 81 Communist members of the Reichstag

from taking their seats. This was done easily by using the emergency powers Hitler had already been given by the Law for the Protection of the People and the State. The next largest party in the Reichstag was the Social Democrats. Its members were threatened and attacked by the SA as they turned up on the day of the vote for the Enabling Law. Many did not even turn up. Other parties gave in to Nazi pressure. The result was that the Enabling Law was passed by 444 votes to 94. Over a hundred members of the Reichstag were absent for the vote.

The Enabling Law destroyed the Weimar Constitution. It gave Hitler the power to pass any laws without consulting the Reichstag and without the approval of the President. He could even make treaties with foreign countries on his own authority. After March 1933, and for the rest of Hitler's rule of Germany, the Reichstag did not meet very often, and then only to hear a speech from Hitler. In November 1933 new 'elections' were held to the Reichstag. The Nazis were the only party allowed to stand.

Source

Our leader, Otto Wels, gave our good wishes to the persecuted and oppressed in the country who were already filling up prisons and concentration camps because of their political beliefs.

Hitler was furious. The SA and SS who surrounded us shouted at us 'Traitors' and 'you'll be strung up'.

A Social Democrat describes the scene when the Enabling Law was passed.

The removal of opposition

With the powers given to him by the Enabling Law, Hitler now moved against any opposition to the Nazi Party. The Communists had already been destroyed. In June 1933 the Social Democrat Party was banned. Other political parties soon followed. This removal of political parties became formal in July when Hitler introduced the Law against the Formation of New Parties. This stated that the Nazi Party was the only party allowed to exist in Germany. It also laid down severe punishment for anyone who tried to set up another party. Germany was now a one-party state. Trade unions, which tended to be anti-Nazi, were also abolished and their offices destroyed. The leaders of political parties and trade unions were arrested and imprisoned. Many were to die in labour camps.

At the same time Hitler also ensured that Nazis were placed in important positions in the state and the government, and that opponents of the Nazis were removed. When Hitler became Chancellor, there were only three Nazis in his government. Now all the ministers were Nazis. Nazi officials were also put in charge of the local governments which ran the states of Germany. Many civil servants, who administered the government departments, were Nazis or sympathised with the Nazis. Those who did not were removed from office. The same was true for the judges.

All these actions gave Hitler complete control of Germany and its political, administrative and legal systems.

However, Hitler now identified one more threat to his power – and it came from within his own party.

Source E

The Law against the Formation of New Parties.

Article I: The National Socialist Party is the only political party in Germany.

Article II: Whoever tries to maintain another political party or form a new party will be punished with penal servitude and imprisonment up to three years, if not a greater penalty.

The Law against the Formation of New Parties, July 1933.

THINGS TO DO

Look at **Sources D** and **E** and the evidence in the section. What methods did Hitler use to remove the opposition to the Nazi Party?

Source F

Nazi Stormtroopers arresting suspected Communists in 1933.

Case Study: the Night of the Long Knives

Now that Hitler was in control of Germany, he did not need the SA. Hitler also realised that the SA might be a threat to his control. It was an undisciplined body, with many of its members no more than thugs. Its leader, Ernst Roehm, held views that were more socialist than those of Hitler. He wanted to remove big business and allow the state to take over the major industries. Hitler had won the support of the leading industrialists in his rise to power and, at this stage, could not afford to lose that support.

Above all, Roehm wanted the SA to take control of the German army. This alarmed Hitler because it would make Roehm more powerful than he was. Throughout 1933 Hitler had met with the army leaders to win their support for the Nazi take-over. Now he was in danger of losing that support. Hitler had to make a decision – whether to support Roehm and the SA or the army. Hitler decided to support the army.

He moved quickly against the SA. On 30 June 1934, the Night of the Long Knives took place. Hitler claimed that the SA was plotting to seize power. He ordered the SS to arrest them. Over the next few days hundreds of leaders of the SA were arrested. Many, including Roehm, were shot. Hitler also took the opportunity to remove other opponents. For example, von Schleicher, the former Chancellor, was murdered. In July, Hitler explained his actions to the Reichstag. It accepted that he had 'saved the nation'.

The event removed any opposition to Hitler from within the Nazi Party.

Source **G** A British cartoon published after the Night of the Long Knives in 1934.

THEY SALUTE WITH BOTH HANDS NOW.

The Death of Hindenburg

The one person with a higher position than Hitler in the German state was the President, Hindenburg. On 2 August 1934, Hindenburg died at the age of 87. Immediately, Hitler declared himself President as well as Chancellor and took the new title of 'Führer and Reich Chancellor'. At the same time the German army – the only group with the power to remove Hitler – swore an oath of personal loyalty to him and promised to support him.

The Nazi control of Germany was now complete.

Source

I swear by God this sacred oath that I will give complete obedience to the Führer, Adolf Hitler ... and will be ready as a brave soldier to risk my life at any time for this oath.

The German army's oath of loyalty to Hitler.

Source

It became clear that my SA were planning a revolution to seize power. I alone was able to solve the problem. In order to save the state the SA had to be destroyed.

Hitler explains his reasons for removing the SA.

THINGS TO DO

1 Explain the meaning of the following:

Enabling Law ;
Führer;
Law against the Formation of New Parties;
Night of the Long Knives.

2 Look at **Sources H** and **I** and the evidence in the case study. What reasons are given by Hitler for the removal of the SA?
Why do you think he removed the SA?

SUMMARY

The establishment of the Nazi dictatorship in Germany, 1933-34:

1933	March	Nazi Party took control of the Reichstag.
		Enabling Law passed.
	May	Trade unions abolished.
	June	Social Democratic Party banned.
	July	Law against the Formation of New Parties made the Nazi Party the only legal party in Germany.
1934	June	SA eliminated in the Night of the Long Knives.
	August	Death of President Hindenburg.
		Hitler declared himself Führer.
		Army swore oath of loyalty to Hitler.

Hitler was able to establish a dictatorship in Germany because:

- He was underestimated by leading politicians like Hindenburg.
- The opposition to him was weak and divided.
- The Nazis used violence to crush political opposition.
- He removed any opposition to the Nazi Party and within the Nazi Party.

What were the main features of the totalitarian dictatorship in Nazi Germany?

The one-party state: law and order

Nazi Germany was a police state. This meant that the power of the authorities was supreme. These powers were used not only to prevent crime and punish criminals but also to arrest and punish people simply because they had said or done something against Hitler and his party. The organisation which enforced law and order was the SS.

When it was first set up, the SS (or *Schutz-Staffel*) had been a small private bodyguard for Hitler. Later, it had played a major part in the removal of the SA in the Night of the Long Knives. By 1934 it consisted of 50,000 highly trained men. Its leader was Heinrich Himmler, a devoted Nazi totally loyal to Hitler. Under him the SS was given unlimited powers. It could search houses, confiscate property and arrest people without charging them with any offence. It could send people to concentration camps without a trial. These camps were run by a branch of the SS called the Death Head Units. Conditions were brutal and harsh and, as one prisoner later wrote, 'death took place daily'.

By 1939 there were many camps in Germany and prisoners were being used as slave labour. Later, during the war, these camps would also become extermination camps.

Another branch of the SS was the Gestapo, the state secret police. The Gestapo had the power to arrest anyone it wanted. It could also spy on people, read their mail and tap their telephones. The Gestapo was helped by a system of informers whereby local party members were encouraged to spy on their neighbours and fellow workers, and to report anything that might be anti-Nazi. Children were even encouraged to spy on their parents. The Gestapo became the most feared organisation in Germany.

The old systems of law and order still remained but were now under Nazi control. The police were controlled by the SS and all judges were reappointed after taking an oath of loyalty to Hitler. The courts could, therefore, be used for political as well as criminal cases.

Source **A** Jewish shops were boycotted as part of the Nazi persecution of Jews.

Case Study: Persecution

The Jews

The people who suffered most under Nazi rule were the Jews. Hitler blamed them for Germany's defeat in the First World War by 'stabbing the German army in the back'. Nazi ideas on the Aryans as a master race excluded the Jews. The Nazis believed that Jews were an inferior race who should not be allowed to mix with true Germans. In their minds the inter-marriage of Jews and Germans over the years had weakened the German people. The Jews were also resented for their influence in Germany. Although they were less than 1 per cent of the German population, Jews were prominent in the professions as lawyers, bankers and doctors. The Jews were an obvious target – they were the scapegoats for all Germany's problems in the 1920s.

Once in power, the Nazis made life difficult for the Jews. In 1933 a boycott of all Jewish shops and businesses was ordered. In 1934 Jewish shops were marked with a yellow star to show that they were Jewish. Jews were also dismissed from important jobs in the civil service, education and the media. In parks and public transport, Jews had to sit apart from other Germans. These actions were humiliating for the Jews. However, they were just the start of the persecution.

In 1935 Hitler passed the Nuremberg Laws. The Citizenship Law stated that Jews were no longer German citizens. As a result, they could not be employed in any public position nor would they be protected by the law. The Law for the Protection of German Blood and Honour banned marriages between Jews and non-Jews and outlawed sexual relations between the two groups outside of marriage.

Persecution was now official, directed by the state. Many Jews saw the warning signs and started to leave Germany. However, most Jews stayed and for them life became much worse. They found it difficult to buy the necessities of life – food, clothes, medicine – because German shopkeepers would not serve them. They were dismissed from their jobs and unable to get other work. They were banned from entering public places, such as hotels and cinemas. Jewish doctors, dentists and lawyers were forbidden to look after Germans. Between 1935 and 1938 more Jews left Germany, and even more would have done so if other countries had been prepared to accept them.

In November 1938 a Jew shot dead a Nazi official in Paris. Hitler ordered the SS to begin a campaign of terror against the Jews on Kristallnacht (the Night of Broken Glass). In a week of violence, Jewish shops, synagogues and homes were destroyed and looted. Thousands of Jews were arrested, nearly a hundred were killed. This was followed by a collective fine on the Jews of one billion marks. Jews were further humiliated by being forced to clean the streets on their hands and knees. This was followed by the mass arrest of Jews at the beginning of March 1939. Within weeks 30,000 Jews had been sent to concentration camps.

The Second World War brought the Nazi treatment of the Jews to its terrible conclusion. Hitler began his 'Final Solution' with its aim of the total extermination of the Jewish people. Six million Jews died in the Nazi Holocaust.

Other groups

Not only the Jews were persecuted under Nazi rule. Anyone who did not fit into the ideal of an Aryan was suspect. The result was that many Germans found themselves excluded from the 'master race', and therefore persecuted.

Gypsies were an obvious target. They did not look like Aryans and, because they were homeless and tended not to have permanent jobs, they were not 'socially useful'.

Black people were another 'inferior race' and a target of persecution, even though there was relatively few of them in Germany.

Others who suffered because they were not 'socially useful' included tramps and beggars, alcoholics, the mentally and physically disabled. Many of them were sent to concentration camps. Other measures were also taken. In 1933 the Nazis passed a Sterilisation Law. This allowed the sterilisation of people with certain illnesses, especially mental illness. The law was extended to other groups. By 1939 the Nazis had also begun a euthanasia programme to kill the mentally ill, including babies and children.

The Church

Hitler tried to get the churches to encourage their congregations to support the Nazis. At first Hitler tried to reach agreement with the churches. In 1933 a Concordat was signed with the Catholics by which the Church promised to keep out of politics and, in turn, the Nazis would not interfere with the Church. A harder line was taken against Protestant churches. They were brought together in one Reich Church – a Nazi-dominated church. Ministers who opposed this, such as Martin Niemoller and Paul Schneider, were arrested and put in concentration camps.

THINGS TO DO

Look at evidence in the case study. Explain the different ways that Jewish people suffered under the Nazis.

Education

Hitler wanted to create a 'Thousand-Year Reich', in which the Nazis would rule forever. He believed this could be done only by winning the support of the young people of Germany. Hitler therefore began a programme of indoctrinating young people, getting them to believe in Nazi ideas. This could be done by controlling the education system.

Teachers were instructed and trained to put across Nazi ideas in their lessons. They had to belong to the German Teachers' League, a Nazi organisation. Any teachers who refused were dismissed.

The teaching of school subjects was controlled in order to indoctrinate the young. For example, in history children were taught about the failures of the Weimar Republic and its betrayal of Germany. The Nazi Party was shown as saving Germany. Biology was used to explain Nazi ideas on race, that Germans were the 'master' Aryan race and that others were inferior. Physical education was stressed and extra time was found for it in the time-tables of schools. It was important to have fit, healthy young people.

Some subjects were taught to girls only to prepare them for the role of wife and mother. They studied domestic science and child care.

Children were not only indoctrinated through the education system, they were also indoctrinated through the Hitler Youth Movement.

PERIODS	Monday	Tuesday	Wednesday	Thursday	Friday	Saturday
1. 8:00–8:45	German	German	German	German	German	German
2. 8:50–9:35	Geography	History	Singing	Geography	History	Singing
3. 9:40–10:25	Race Study	Race Study	Race Study	Race Study	Party Beliefs	Party Beliefs
4. 10:25–11:00	Break – with sports and special announcements					
5. 11:00–12:05	Domestic Science with Mathematics – Every day					
6. 12:10–12:55	The science of breeding (Eugenics) – Health Biology					
	2:00–6:00 Sport each day					

Source B A 1935 timetable for a girls' school in Nazi Germany.

Hitler Youth Movement

The Hitler Youth Movement was organised and run by members of the SS. Its aim was clear: to indoctrinate young people into accepting Nazi ideas, to train them for future service and to ensure that they were loyal and obedient to Hitler.

The Movement was set up in 1925. After 1933 young people were encouraged to join it and other youth organisations were forced to shut down. After 1935 it was compulsory to join it. By 1939 eight million young Germans belonged to the movement. As they became older they progressed through different groups in the movement.

THINGS TO DO

Look at **Source B** and the text. How did the Nazis use education to 'indoctrinate' young people?

The movement was attractive to young people. They wore smart uniforms and paraded through their towns. They took part in a range of leisure activities, such as sport, gymnastics, walking and weekend camps. The older members were trained to use rifles. Every young person had a 'performance book' in which the marks gained in these activities were recorded. Those with the best marks were sent to special schools – the Adolf Hitler Schools – where they were trained to be the future leaders of Germany.

Women

In the new Nazi order, women were encouraged to have children. The Nazis were worried about the declining birth rate in Germany and believed that Germany needed more people if it was to become great again. So they encouraged marriage through the Law for the Encouragement of Marriage, which was introduced in 1933. This granted newly married couples a loan of 1000 marks. To encourage married couples to have children they allowed them to keep 250 marks for each child they had. Mothercraft classes were introduced. Homes for unmarried mothers were set up to allow unmarried women to become pregnant, often by a 'racially pure' member of the SS. These measures to encourage more children worked. The birth rate rose throughout the 1930s.

Women were also encouraged to stay at home to look after their husbands and children, and many women teachers, civil servants and doctors were dismissed from their jobs. Women were given advice on what to cook and were even advised on how to appear: no make-up or plaited hair and dieting was frowned upon.

Source C

Age	Boys	Girls
6-10	The Little Fellows	
10-14	The Young Folk	Young Girls
14-18	Hitler Youth	League of German Girls

The organisation of the Hitler Youth Movement.

Source D

A 1930s painting representing the Nazi image of the ideal family.

THINGS TO DO

Look at **Sources C** and **D**. What message do they give to young people and women about their places in Nazi Germany? Give reasons for your answer.

Propaganda

The Nazis continued to use propaganda to encourage the German people to have the same ideas and beliefs of the Nazi Party and to ensure they stayed loyal to Hitler. Joseph Goebbels was responsible for propaganda as the Minister for Propaganda and National Enlightenment. He used all the resources of the state to carry out his task.

Newspapers were allowed to print only stories which were pro-Nazi and were given detailed instructions about what to write. Newspapers that did not support the Nazis were closed down – over 1,500 were closed by 1934.

The Nazis saw the advantages of radio for reaching mass audiences. Goebbels took control of all the local radio stations and used them to send out the Nazi message. Cheap radio sets were produced so that every German household could afford one. They were called the 'People's Receivers'. They were made so that foreign stations could not be picked up, so that the only view of the world they received was the Nazi one. Loudspeaker pillars were set up in streets and public squares all over Germany to make sure that people could hear the radio wherever they were.

The cinema also reached a mass audience and the Nazis made use of it in their propaganda campaign. The German film industry made over a hundred films a year. They included comedies, adventures, love stories and many political films. Special films carrying the Nazi message were made for the young. A typical programme at the cinema would also include newsreels and documentary films with a Nazi slant.

Mass rallies, which had been used by the Nazis in their rise to power, became even grander and more spectacular. The most famous was the Nuremberg rally held every year for a week in August. There were army

Source E

As the time for the Führer's arrival drew near, the crowd grew restless. Suddenly the beat of the drums increased and a fleet of black cars rolled into the arena. The stadium looked like a sea of swastikas. Hitler began to speak. The crowd hushed into silence, but the drums continued their steady beat. Hitler's voice rasped into the night and every now and then the crowd broke into a roar of cheers. Some began swaying back and forth, chanting 'Sieg Heil' over and over again. I looked at the faces around me and saw tears streaming down people's cheeks.

A description of a Nuremberg rally.

parades, gymnastic displays, bands and choirs, firework displays and fly-pasts by the airforce. Above all, it had Hitler to address the mass of people gathered in the arenas. The Nazis also used the 1936 Olympic Games in Berlin as a massive propaganda event to demonstrate the superiority of the Aryan race. The black American athlete Jesse Owens winning four gold medals, however, dampened some of the Nazi celebrations.

All German culture was controlled by the Nazis. Goebbels formed the Reich Chamber of Culture. Musicians, actors, writers and artists had to be members of the Chamber before they could work or perform. Membership depended on supporting the Nazis. Many could not accept this and left Germany.

Music had to be German and composers like Wagner, Beethoven and Mozart were in favour. German folk songs and marching music were also encouraged. However, the work of Jewish composers was banned, as was jazz because it was black American music.

Source **F** A Nazi rally at Nuremberg during the 1930s.

Books written by Jews or by authors opposed to the Nazis were banned. In 1933 students were encouraged to burn huge piles of banned books looted from libraries.

The theatre, cinema and art were all censored in the same way.

By force, persuasion and propaganda the Nazis firmly controlled the German people. Yet something more was required for the Nazis to retain power. They had to deal with the economic problems which helped them to power.

THINGS TO DO

Look at **Sources E** and **F**. Why do you think the Nuremberg rallies made such a great impression on the German people?

SUMMARY

The main features of the Nazi dictatorship were:

- Creation of a police state.
- Control of law and order by the SS and Gestapo.
- Arrest and internment of political opponents.
- Persecution of the Jews, gypsies and other groups.
- Control of the Church.
- Indoctrination of young people by education and the Hitler Youth Movement.
- Brainwashing of the German people by propaganda.
- Censorship of all forms of culture.

To what extent did the German people benefit from Nazi rule in the 1930s?

Economic policy

When Hitler came to power in 1933, Germany was still in the economic depression which had begun in 1929. It was Nazi promises to end the Depression that won them so much support. Hitler was now expected to make good these promises. The control of economic policy was the responsibility of Dr Schacht, who was Minister of the Economy from 1934 to 1937. His 'New Plan' for Germany had clear aims: to reduce unemployment, to build up the armaments industry and to make Germany self-sufficient.

Increasing employment

In 1933 five million Germans were still out of work. It was vital that the Nazis find them jobs. National Labour Service was immediately set up. This was for young men between 18 and 25 years. They did various jobs, such as digging ditches and planting forests. The men had to wear uniforms and live in camps. They were given pocket money rather than wages. These schemes were then extended to ambitious public works programmes organised by the German Labour Front. New motorways (autobahns) were built, as were hospitals, schools, sports stadiums and other public buildings. These schemes created thousands of jobs.

However, the greatest fall in unemployment was brought about by rearmament. In 1935 Hitler ignored the Treaty of Versailles and started to rearm Germany. He then introduced compulsory military service (conscription). The army alone increased by over one million men between 1935 and 1938. To support this rearmament, an armaments industry grew up to make the weapons and equipment needed. This also employed thousands of men.

There were other ways the Nazis reduced the statistics of unemployment. Women were

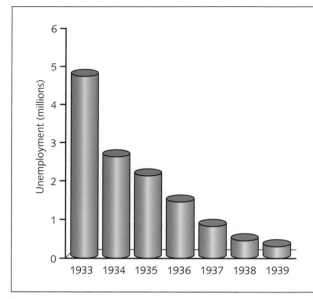

Unemployment in Nazi Germany during 1933–39.

forced out of work to look after their homes and families. Jews were dismissed from their jobs but they were not recorded as unemployed. More and more people were being sent to labour camps and concentration camps but were not recorded as unemployed.

So unemployment in Germany fell. By 1939 the Nazis were even declaring that there was a shortage of labour.

THINGS TO DO

Look at the graph above and the evidence in the section on increasing employment. Give at least five ways in which the Nazis reduced unemployment. Which way do you think was the most successful?

Improving the economy: self-sufficiency

Hitler wanted to make Germany self-sufficient – that is, the country should be able to produce its own food and raw materials so that it did not have to depend upon other countries. This policy was called autarky. A Four-Year Plan was drawn up in 1936 with the aim of making Germany self-sufficient in four years. More raw materials, such as coal, oil, iron and other metals were produced and synthetic (artificial) raw materials, such as rubber, fuel and textiles, were developed. New factories and industrial plants were built.

The Four-Year Plan was expensive and needed massive state investment in industry. By 1939 it had not succeeded in making Germany fully self-sufficient. Over a third of its raw materials was still being imported from other countries.

Nazi economic policy also aimed to strengthen the military power of Germany. This is clear from the rearmament programme, the building of autobahns and the attempt to achieve self-sufficiency. When it was obvious that Germany could not achieve full self-sufficiency, the Nazis decided to take over countries with the raw materials and food it needed. This was the policy of *Lebensraum* (living space). Nazi economic policy and foreign policy began to overlap.

The German Labour Front and Strength through Joy

All German workers were forced to be members of the German Labour Front run by Dr Robert Ley. This controlled the workers in a number of ways. Trade unions were abolished. Strikes were made illegal. Workers could not bargain for higher wages and there was no limit on the number of hours they had to work in a week. Workers could not leave a job without the permission of the Front.

The Nazis also tried to control people's leisure time. A branch of the German Labour Front, called 'Strength through Joy', organised people's leisure activities so that free time was not 'wasted'. Cheap holidays were arranged, including foreign travel and Mediterranean cruises. 'Strength through Joy' was also involved in the plan to manufacture a car cheap enough for workers to buy. This was the Volkswagen ('People's Car'). Workers could pay for it on a hire purchase scheme into which they paid weekly sums in advance. Actually, very few German workers managed to buy a Volkswagen and the whole scheme was a failure.

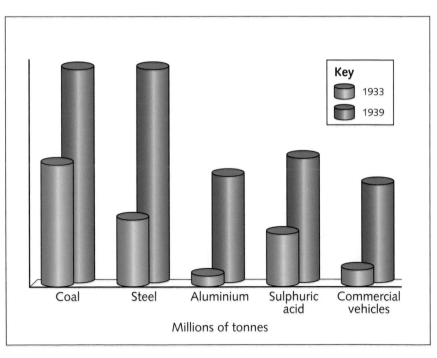

Industrial growth in Nazi Germany.

Nazi rule in the 1930s

Many German people benefited from Nazi rule. The economic problems which had affected the nation from 1929 to 1932 ended. In their place there was employment and financial stability. The Nazis also restored Germany's honour and pride. There was more optimism and self-confidence.

However, the price was heavy. The German people lived in a police state where their whole lives were controlled by the Nazis – their education, their religion, their work, even their leisure time.

It is difficult to judge exactly what the German people thought about Nazi rule. There was very little open opposition or underground resistance, and what did exist was soon destroyed. The powers of the SS and the Gestapo terrified most Germans from saying or doing anything against the Nazis. The censorship and propaganda of the Nazis meant that people did not have the information on which to make reliable judgements.

On balance, it would seem that most Germans were prepared to accept Nazi rule in the 1930s. They were now to be faced by even bigger changes as Hitler took the nation into war.

Source **G**

A poster of 1938 encouraging German workers to 'Save five marks a week and get your own cars'. The Volkswagen ('people's car') was introduced by the Nazis.

THINGS TO DO

Look at the graph on page 212, **Source G**, and the evidence in the text on improving the economy. Do you think the Nazis improved the economy?
Give reasons for your answer.

SUMMARY

In their economic policy, the Nazis:

- Reduced unemployment by public works and the rearmament programme.
- Controlled German workers in the German Labour Front and National Labour Service.
- Controlled the leisure time of German workers in 'Strength through Joy'.
- Tried to make Germany self-sufficient (autarky) in raw materials.
- Used economic policy to prepare for war.

Exam-style assessment

These questions follow the pattern of questions to be set by AQA for Paper 2 of its new Modern World History specification.

SECTION A: Germany, 1919–29

Study **Sources A** to **E** and then answer all parts of Question 2 which follow.

Source A: The rising price of a loaf of bread in Berlin

Year	Price
1918	0.63 marks
1922	163 marks
January 1923	250 marks
July 1923	3645 marks
September 1923	1,512,000 marks
November 1923	201,000,000,000 marks

From a British school text-book (1995)

Source B: A German view of the cause of inflation

Germany complains: 'My sons have taken everything away. All they left me is a paper Mark with which to cover my nakedness.'

A German cartoon of 1920
published in a magazine

Source C: A British view of the German economy

Germany is teeming with wealth. She is humming like a beehive. The comfort and prosperity of her people absolutely astound me. Poverty is practically non-existent.

And yet this is a country that is determined that she will not pay her debts. They are a nation of actors. If it wasn't for the fact that the Germans are without a sense of humour, one might imagine the whole nation was perpetrating an elaborate practical joke.

From *The Times*, 18 April 1922

Source D: A British view of the cause of German inflation

The Weimar Republic was burdened with economic problems arising out of the war.

Defeat left her saddled with a huge internal debt of 144,000 million marks and with a currency which had lost over one-third of its pre-war value.

From *A History of Germany* (1972) by WILLIAM CARR, a British historian

Source E: Another British view

Reparations cost Germany only about 2 per cent of her national output per year.

This suggests that the annual payments were not too harsh and that the Allies were right in claiming that Germany simply did not want to pay.

From *Germany 1815-1939* (1992) by FINLAY McKICHAN, a British historian

Question 2

(a) What can you learn from **Source A** about prices in Germany in the years 1918–23? **(5 marks)**

(b) Compare the state of the German economy that is suggested in **Source B** with what is suggested in **Source C**. **(6 marks)**

(c) How useful is **Source C** for studying the state of the German economy in the early 1920s? **(9 marks)**

(d) **Sources D** and **E** give different interpretations of Germany's ability to pay reparations in the early 1920s. Which do you think is the more accurate interpretation, **Source D** or **Source E**? Explain your answer using **Sources D** and **E** and your own knowledge. **(10 marks)**

(e) In the period up to 1929, the Nazi Party was regarded as weak and not worth serious consideration. Use your own knowledge to explain how far this was actually true. **(15 marks)**

SECTION B: Germany, 1929–39

Study **Source F** and then answer parts **(a)**, **(b)**, **(c)** and **either (d) or (e)** of Question 6 which follow.

Source F : Unemployment and Nazi seats gained in elections to the German Parliament, 1928–33

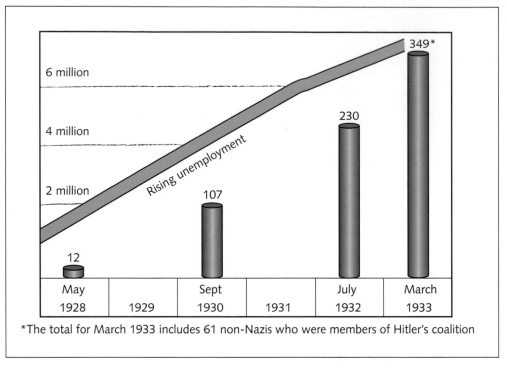

*The total for March 1933 includes 61 non-Nazis who were members of Hitler's coalition

From *The Twentieth Century* (1983) by M. N. DUFFY

This textbook was written for use in British schools.

Question 6

(a) What can you learn from **Source F** about the Nazi Party in the years 1929-33? **(3 marks)**

(b) Using **Source F** and your own knowledge, why did rising unemployment help the Nazi Party in the years 1929–33? **(7 marks)**

(c) Describe how Hitler used the incident of the Reichstag Fire of February 1933 to gain support. **(5 marks)**

EITHER

(d) Did the German people benefit from Nazi rule in the period 1933–39? Explain your answer. **(15 marks)**

OR

(e) Explain how the Nazis treated the Jews in the period 1933–39. **(15 marks)**

6 The USA, 1919–41

INTRODUCTION

When the First World War ended so did American involvement in European and world affairs. Although President Wilson played a major part in drawing up the Treaty of Versailles, America adopted a policy of isolation after the war.

For many Americans the time between the wars was a period of suffering and intolerance. Immigration was reduced and racism increased. This reached its peak in the activities of the Klu Klux Klan. Conditions for black people and groups like farmers were never good. The USA also saw the introduction of Prohibition and, with it, the violence of organised crime.

However, throughout the 1920s the USA enjoyed a period of economic prosperity. Industries thrived with mass production and many Americans bought consumer goods using credit facilities. Many bought shares in the stock exchange. All this allowed many Americans to achieve a life-style European workers could only have dreamed about.

It lasted only a relatively short time. Depression hit the USA in 1929 as the stock market collapsed. The result was mass unemployment. The 1930s saw President Roosevelt in his New Deal try to bring 'relief and recovery' to the American economy. Although the New Deal had its successes, including creating millions of jobs, it was the Second World War which finally ended the Depression in America.

1918 End of the First World War

1919 Treaty of Versailles

1920 US Senate votes for America not to join the League of Nations Prohibition introduced

1925 Ku Klux Klan has 5 million members

1927 First 'talkie' at cinema Lindbergh flies solo across the Atlantic

1929 Wall Street Crash starts Great Depression

1932 Election of President F. D. Roosevelt

1933 Beginning of the New Deal

1936 Problems between the New Deal and the Supreme Court

1939 Second World War begins with USA isolationist

1941 (December) USA declares war on Japan and Germany

The USA, 1919–41

217

How did the USA react to the end of the First World War?

The USA in 1919

By 1919 the USA had grown into one of the world's greatest powers. Throughout the 19th century the USA was seen as a 'land of opportunity'. Between 1850 and 1914 over 40 million people left Europe and emigrated to the USA. One result of this was that the USA had become a mixed society – it has been estimated that people from 100 different nationalities were living in America in 1914.

In the First World War American forces played a key part in the campaigns of 1918 and the extra resources they brought helped in the final defeat of Germany. The USA did not enter the war until April 1917 and so lost just 100,000 men. Unlike the other powers involved in the war, the USA was strengthened by it. Throughout the war, the countries of Europe had paid the USA to provide them with their war needs – food and raw materials as well as weapons. The USA had also gained many of the overseas markets of European countries.

Source **A**   An immigrant family arriving at Ellis Island in New York in 1905.

US reaction to the end of the First World War

President Woodrow Wilson had taken the USA into the war. He also played an important role in the peace talks. The Fourteen Points drawn up by him in 1918 were the basis for the peace settlement. Wilson saw it as the USA's duty to help preserve world peace and proposed an international body to do this.

So the Treaty of Versailles committed all countries which signed the Treaty to join the 'League of Nations'.

The mood of isolation grows

However, the mood of the American people was different from Wilson's. To many Americans the war seemed remote, fought thousands of miles away about issues that did not really concern them. They did not want more American soldiers to be killed trying to keep peace around the world. They were afraid that America's entry into the League of Nations would lead to just that. Furthermore they were worried that the USA, as the strongest and richest country in the world, would end up paying the cost of keeping world peace. It would be better to keep out of other countries' problems.

Rejection of the Treaty of Versailles and the League of Nations

President Wilson hoped that the USA would sign the Treaty of Versailles and join the League of Nations. Unfortunately for Wilson, his party – the Democrats – did not have control of Congress. Their opponents, the Republicans, rejected the Treaty of Versailles and with it America's entry into the League. Wilson refused to accept defeat and though he did not run again for President in the election campaign of 1920 the Democrat candidate, James Cox, fought for Wilson's ideas. His opponent, the Republican Warren Harding, campaigned with a slogan of 'America First'. He also talked about a return to 'normalcy', a word he had invented, but one which was attractive to Americans – the idea of life getting back to normal, to what it had been before the war. It is not surprising that Americans voted in Harding as the new President. The rejection of the Democrats meant the final rejection of the Treaty of Versailles and the League of Nations. America was to follow a policy of isolation.

THINGS TO DO

1 What was the impact of the First World War on America?

2 Why did some people
  (a) want America to be isolated?
  (b) oppose isolationism?

3 What can you learn from **Source B** about American society in 1918?

Source B

The First World War revealed some alarming facts in regard to our foreign population.

1 Many immigrants neglected to become American citizens.

2 Radical labor agitators were suspected of 'taking their orders from Moscow'.

3 Over one thousand newspapers in the United States were printed in foreign languages.

4 Over 10 per cent of the people here could not speak English.

5 American labor leaders were disturbed over the incoming foreigners who were used to working for low wages.

Adapted from an American school textbook published in 1961.

How did the policies of the American government encourage isolation?

Isolation did not apply only to foreign affairs; it also meant limiting foreign trade and immigration.

Tariffs against foreign goods

Action was taken to make sure that foreign goods would not be able to compete with home-produced goods on the US market. In 1922 Congress introduced the Fordney-McCumber tariff. A tariff (or tax) was placed on foreign goods coming into the USA. This made them more expensive than the same American products and so 'protected' American industry. This policy worked well in the 1920s and helped to bring about the 'boom' conditions (see pages 222–4). However, there was a danger: foreign governments retaliated by putting high tariffs on American goods exported abroad, which made them harder to sell.

Restricting the flow of immigrants

It was inevitable that the mood of isolation would bring with it some re-thinking of the open-door policy of immigration. This was starting to happen before 1919. It was partly the result of the war and an increased feeling of nationalism in the USA. There was also an increasing fear that new immigrants, especially from poor countries, would provide cheap labour. This would take jobs from Americans. There was a further fear that new immigrants would bring with them political ideas, such as communism, which were against the spirit of democracy that existed in the USA. This fear, called the 'Red Scare', became especially strong after the communist revolution in Russia in 1917.

In 1917 Congress passed an Immigration Law which required all foreigners wishing to enter the USA to take a literacy test. They had to prove they could read a short passage in English before they would be allowed into the

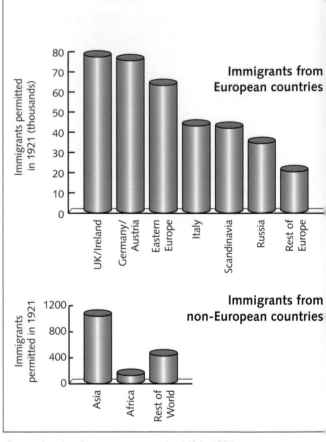

Quota levels of immigrants to the USA, 1921.

country. Such a test prevented people from the poorer countries of Europe and Asia entering the USA, as they could not afford to learn English in their own country.

In 1921 the Immigration Quota Act was introduced. This limited the maximum number of immigrants allowed into the USA to 357,000 each year. It also stated that the number of people emigrating to the USA from any country should not exceed 3 per cent of the number from that country already living in the USA in 1910. This 'quota' system worked in favour of people from western and northern Europe because they had a larger number of immigrant American citizens in 1910. This was almost certainly the intention.

In 1924 the quota limit was further reduced to 2 per cent of the population in 1890.

In 1929 the number of immigrants into America each year was reduced to 150,000 – under half of the 1921 figure. In addition, no immigrants from Asia were allowed.

More distrust of foreigners

For those foreigners fortunate enough to be allowed into the USA, there were still problems to face. The fact that many could find only low-paid jobs in the cities meant that they lived in poor housing. Immigrant ghettos began to appear where violence and crime were high. This only increased Americans' distrust of foreigners and led to growing intolerance. The 'Red Scare' of the early 1920s added to these suspicions. Sacco and Vanzetti were victims of the anti-immigrant feelings of the time.

THINGS TO DO

1 Use the information in this section to explain:
   (a) how the US government reduced the number of immigrants.
   (b) how the government encouraged immigration from some countries but not others.
2 Explain the following terms: isolation, tariff, immigration, normalcy, quota system.

Case Study: the Sacco and Vanzetti Case

Nicola Sacco and Bartolomeo Vanzetti were immigrants from Italy. They were self-confessed anarchists and openly said they hated the American system of government.

In 1920 they were arrested and charged with the murder of two guards in an armed robbery. The evidence against Sacco and Vanzetti was based on four points. At the time of their arrest, they had been carrying guns. They were identified by over 60 eye-witnesses. Sacco's bullets were identical to the ones found in the bodies of the dead guards. Finally, Vanzetti had a proven conviction for armed robbery in 1919.

The defence pointed to the fact that the prosecution eyewitnesses could not agree on the details of the crime or even on the descriptions of the killers. The defence also produced 107 witnesses who said Sacco and Vanzetti had been somewhere else at the time of the crime – although most of these witnesses were recent Italian immigrants.

The jury found both men guilty of murder. Appeals were made against the verdict. Petitions were organised by people convinced that the two men had been found guilty because they were foreigners. All failed. Sacco and Vanzetti were executed in 1927.

In 1977 the verdict against the men was declared unjust because the judge presiding over the case was strongly opposed to the political views of Sacco and Vanzetti.

THINGS TO DO

What does the Sacco and Vanzetti case tell us about the USA in the 1920s?

How far did the USA achieve prosperity in the 1920s?

During the 1920s the USA experienced increasing economic prosperity – a boom – in which many Americans, though certainly not all, shared. A plentiful supply of raw materials, the boost provided by the First World War and the policy of protection all helped America become the richest country in the world.

Mass production

Mass production helped boost the number of goods made. The principle behind the system of mass production was simple and effective. Huge new factories were built in the towns of America. In the factories, assembly lines were set up. The parts of the product being made travelled along the lines so that a worker did the same small job in fitting the part for which he was responsible on to the product. By the end of the assembly line the product was complete. The job was quick and straightforward and production rose dramatically.

The car industry

The motor car industry was one of the first to use the method of mass production. One of its pioneers was Henry Ford. Ford had the idea of making a car for the ordinary man and his family. In 1911 the first Model T

was produced by methods of mass production.

The use of mass-production methods meant that by the 1920s a Model T was being produced every ten seconds.

Source

The operations are sub-divided so that each man and each machine do only one thing ... the thing is to keep everything in motion and take the work to the man, not the man to the work.

Henry Ford speaking in 1926 about mass production.

Source **B**   The assembly line in the Ford Motor Company.

This allowed Ford to reduce his prices: in 1911 a Model T cost $1200; by 1920 it was $295. One Model T was identical to another – the same colour, the same engine size. This did not bother the American people. The 'Tin Lizzie', as it was known, became the most popular car in America. By the mid-1920s one out of every two cars sold was a Model T.

It was not only the car industry which expanded during the 1920s, although it did help other industries to grow – steel, rubber, glass, leather and oil were all in greater demand because of the car industry. The construction industry provided roads for the increased traffic. Consumer goods were also produced using mass-production methods: radio sets, telephones, refrigerators, vacuum cleaners, washing machines, ovens. These new 'gadgets' were attractive to the American people and sales rocketed.

Cycle of prosperity

This growth created a 'cycle of prosperity'. The increased production of consumer goods created increased employment. This meant that people had more money to spend on consumer goods, especially as their prices were falling. This in turn created an increased demand for goods and encouraged further increased production. So the cycle went on.

Government policy

Other factors also helped to maintain the boom. The Republican governments of the 1920s encouraged the growth of business by a policy of non-interference (called *laissez-faire*) and did not place any controls on industry or financial institutions. They also lowered taxes on people's incomes and on company profits: this gave people more money to spend on consumer goods and companies more money to invest in new factories and buildings.

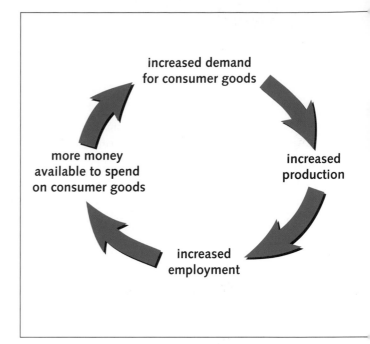

The cycle of prosperity.

Credit facilities

The ability to buy consumer goods was greatly helped by the introduction of hire purchase – buying on credit. This allowed people who did not have enough cash to pay the full cost of a product to obtain it by paying for it in instalments over a period of time. Mail order also increased the market for goods beyond the towns and cities into the more remote country areas.

Advertisements appeared in magazines, newspapers, on the radio, in cinemas and on billboards – all trying to convince Americans that they should 'keep up with the Jones" and buy the products that every other American now had.

	1920	1929
Motor cars on the roads	9 million	26 million
Kilometres of roads	620,000	1 million
Radios	60,000	10 million
Telephones in homes and offices	13 million	20 million

Some changes in the USA during the 1920s.

Confidence

Throughout the 1920s there was a feeling of confidence among the American people, which encouraged them to buy goods by cash or by credit. It encouraged them to invest some of their wages in companies by buying shares. Even this could be done on credit by buying 'on the margin'. A person could buy shares by paying 10 per cent of their total value in cash and borrowing the remaining 90 per cent from the banks. Share prices soared as more and more were bought. It seemed that the good times were here to stay.

Americans who did not share the prosperity

However, in reality there were still many Americans living in poverty. The new wealth in the USA was not shared by everyone. Some sections of the population suffered more than others.

Farmers

Farmers had a hard time in the 1920s – and almost half the American people were engaged in agriculture. Farmers were able to grow more crops because of inventions such as combine harvesters. So much was produced that supply outweighed demand. As a result of this surplus, food prices dropped and many small farmers suffered from lower incomes. As incomes fell, farmers found it difficult to keep up with their mortgage payments – some farmers were evicted, others were forced to sell their land. Farm labourers also found themselves out of work and drifted to towns or areas such as California where the fruit farms promised work.

Black people and immigrants

Black people had a similar experience. Almost one million black farm workers lost their jobs in the 1920s. Many moved from their homes in the south to the cities of the north. Here they were able to find jobs, but they were usually the lowest paid. The same was true for new immigrants.

Workers in older industries

Not all industries benefited from the boom. For example, the coal industry suffered as new forms of power – oil, gas, electricity – became more widely used. The overproduction of coal led to wage cuts or, worse, loss of jobs as mines closed down. Other older industries, such as cotton and textiles, suffered in a similar way.

THINGS TO DO

1 Why did the USA have a consumer boom in the 1920s?

2 Which people did not share the boom of the 1920s? Why not?

Source This cartoon comments on the situation of farmers in the 1920s.

'The Roaring Twenties' – is this a good description of the USA in the 1920s?

Although many Americans prospered in the 1920s there was also a dark side to life. This was seen most clearly in the intolerance and racism of the Ku Klux Klan and the organised crime which exploited the unpopularity of Prohibition.

Ku Klux Klan

The Ku Klux Klan stirred up racial and religious hatred in what they believed was a moral crusade to save the USA. It would only accept as true Americans those people who were WASPs (white, Anglo-Saxon, Protestant) – that is, people who had originally come from northern Europe and whose families had lived in America for several generations. All other people were condemned as not being true Americans: Jews, Catholics, immigrants from southern Europe (such as Italians), from eastern Europe (such as Russians), from Asia and, especially, black people.

During the 1920s membership of the Ku Klux Klan grew from 100,000 members in 1920 to 5 million members in 1925.

Members of the Klan were often poor whites who felt that their jobs were threatened by black people and immigrants who were willing to work for lower wages. However, the Klan also had rich and influential members including state politicians. The Klan was strongest in the southern states where there was a large black population and a history of oppression of blacks.

Source **D**

1. Are you a native-born, white, gentile [*non-Jewish*] American?

2. Are you absolutely opposed to and free of any allegiance to any government, people, sect or ruler that is foreign to the United States of America?

3. Do you believe in the Christian religion?

...

8. Will you faithfully strive for the eternal maintenance of white supremacy?

Extracts from the Kloran, the Klan's book of rules

THINGS TO DO

Look at **Sources D** and **E**. What do they tell us about the Ku Klux Klan?

Source **E**

A Ku Klux Klan parade in 1925.

Klan members held ceremonies in which they dressed in long white robes and hoods and Klansmen spoke to each other in secret codes known as 'Klonversations'.

Torture and violence were used against people who were not 'true Americans', with black people suffering the most. Victims were beaten, whipped, tarred and feathered, or lynched (where victims were put to death without trial). Their homes were set on fire and their property destroyed.

In many cases, the Klansmen were not punished for these activities. They were often protected by the authorities – the police or judges – who were themselves members of the Klan. It was also true that juries made up of white people were reluctant to find people guilty of Klan activities.

However, there were successful prosecutions against the Klan, especially for the most violent activities. The trials were widely reported and helped to produce a reaction against the Klan. After 1925 its membership fell and, while it continues to exist in the USA, the Klan has never again achieved the influence it had in the early 1920s.

Prohibition

In January 1920 the USA introduced Prohibition – the making, selling or transporting of alcoholic drink in the USA became illegal. This was made part of the American Constitution in the 18th Amendment. This measure, often referred to as the Volstead Act, declared that any drink with over 0.5 per cent of alcohol in it was illegal.

Prohibition marked the final success in a long campaign by groups such as the Women's Christian Temperance Union (1875) and the

Daddy's in There---

And Our Shoes and Stockings and Clothes and Food Are in There, Too, and They'll Never Come Out.
—*Chicago American.*

WANTED--A FATHER; A LITTLE BOY'S PLEA
JULIA H. JOHNSON

A shy little boy stood peering
  Through the door of a bright saloon;
He looked as if food and clothing
  Would be thought a most welcome boon.

And one of the men, in passing,
  As if tossing a dog a bone,
Asked, "What do you want this evening?"
  In a rude and unkindly tone.

"I am wanting"—the boy's lips trembled—
  "I am wanting my father, sir."
And he gazed at the little tables
  Where the careless onlookers were.

It was there that he saw his father,
  But the man only shook his head,
And the boy, with his thin cheek burning,
  Ran away with a look of dread.

Oh, the fathers'—the fathers wanted!
  How the heart-break, and bitter need,
With the longings, deep and piteous,
  For the wandering children plead.

May the children's call arouse them,
  May the fathers arise and go
With the young souls waiting for them,
  For the little ones need them so!

SERIES G. NO. 23.

The American Issue Publishing Co
Westerville, Ohio

Anti-Saloon League (1895) to have alcohol banned. They claimed that alcohol brought poverty, broke up marriages, caused crime and insanity, and disrupted industry. By 1917, alcohol had been banned in 18 American states and in 1920 the ban became national.

Effects of Prohibition: illegal alcohol, speakeasies and bootlegging

The ban on alcohol was not popular. Most people saw nothing wrong with having a drink and found ways to get round the law. Many people produced their own alcoholic drink – called moonshine – from home-made stills. The results were usually of poor quality and often caused illness and even death.

Others, especially in the towns, looked to others to provide the alcohol they wanted. A whole new 'industry' was created. People went to secret illegal drinking clubs called speakeasies which were set up behind locked doors. By 1930 there were nearly a quarter of a million speakeasies in America – over 30,000 in New York alone. The speakeasies sold alcohol smuggled by bootleggers from abroad – such as rum from the West Indies and whisky from Canada.

Organised crime

It was not long before the vast profits to be made attracted groups of gangsters to the illegal alcohol trade. Rival gangs in cities fought to take over the other's 'territory' – and the rackets within it. Gangland murders increased. In Chicago, 227 gangsters were murdered in four years without anyone being convicted. In 1929, during the St Valentine's Day massacre, Al Capone's men killed seven of the rival 'Bugs' Moran gang. The gangsters also operated protection rackets, prostitution and drugs trafficking. They were helped by the inability of the authorities to do anything about it. Many police, judges and state officials were bribed to turn a blind eye to the gangs' activities. Organised crime also bought its way into legal business activities and into trade unions.

Reasons for the failure of Prohibition

Drinking illegal alcohol was too popular and too profitable. It could not be controlled without huge numbers of enforcement agents.

Yet in the face of organised crime the Prohibition Bureau employed about 4,000 agents to stop bootlegging and close speakeasies for the whole of America. While agents like Eliot Ness achieved some success, most were ineffective. Some were also guilty of taking bribes from the criminals who ran the trade – nearly 10 per cent of the agents were sacked for taking bribes. However, perhaps the most important reason why Prohibition failed was that, despite the strength of the temperance groups, the vast majority of the American people did not agree with Prohibition. They were prepared to break the law in order to consume alcohol.

Prohibition ended in December 1933 when President Roosevelt repealed the 18th Amendment. His feelings summed up those of most Americans: 'Let's all go out and have a drink.'

THINGS TO DO

Look at **Source F**. What message is the poster presenting about the evils of drink?

Source G

I loved speakeasies. If you knew the right ones, you never worried about being poisoned by bad whisky. I'd kept hearing about a friend who had been blinded by bad gin. I guess I was lucky. The speaks were so romantic. …. They had that marvellous movie-like quality, unreality. And the food was great, even though some pretty dreadful things did occur in them.

This is what the songwriter Alex Wilder said about speakeasies.

Source H

I was one of the women who favoured Prohibition when I heard it discussed, but I am now convinced it has proved a failure. It is true we no longer see the corner saloon: but in many cases has it not merely moved to the back of a store, or up or down one flight [of stairs] under the name of a speakeasy?

An American journalist writing in 1928.

Case Study: Al Capone and Organised Crime

Al Capone's parents were Italian immigrants. Capone was brought up in New York but moved to Chicago as part of a gang run by 'Terrible Johnny' Torrio. In 1925 Torrio retired after being badly injured by the 'Bugs' Moran gang, and was replaced by Capone. In a short space of time Capone brought other gangs under his control. Soon his gang had 700 men, armed with shotguns and sub-machine guns. Opponents and rivals were 'rubbed out' (killed). He used corruption to bribe the authorities in Chicago, including police, judges and politicians.

Capone became a celebrity. His photograph appeared on the front cover of *Time*, America's leading weekly magazine. He mixed with businessmen, politicians and movie stars. Capone was responsible for murders, extortion and corruption. Yet the only charge the authorities could make stick against him came in 1931 when he was sentenced to eleven years in prison for tax evasion.

Source **I**

Al Capone on the front cover of *Time* magazine, 1930.

Source J

All I do is supply a public demand. I do it in the best and least harmful way I can.

This was Al Capone's attitude to Prohibition.

	1921	**1925**	**1929**
Illegal distilleries seized	9746	12,023	15,794
Gallons of distilled spirit seized	414,000	1,103,000	1,186,000
Arrests	34,175	62,747	66,878

Attempts by the authorities to enforce prohibition, 1921–9.

THINGS TO DO

1 Look at **Sources G** and **H**. How do they help us to explain why Prohibition failed?

2 Using the information provided in the case study do you think Al Capone was a criminal or a businessman?
Give reasons for your answer.

Developments in entertainment

In the 1920s, young people wanted to forget about the First World War and have a good time. They were better off and had more leisure time than their predecessors. They spent vast amounts of money enjoying themselves and so stimulated industry and business. The decade became known as 'the Roaring Twenties' largely because of the pace of social and economic development.

The jazz age

Jazz was a new form of music that developed from early kinds of black music. It was played in night clubs like the well-known Cotton Club in New York, by black musicians such as Duke Ellington and Louis Armstrong. It appealed to young people because it was often played in 'speakeasies'. These bars and clubs sold illegal alcohol and were therefore seen as daring and exciting places. The jazz too seemed wild and dramatic and it soon became a craze.

The radio

Young men and women listened to jazz on the radio. In 1920 only $2 million worth of radios were purchased. By 1929 this figure had increased by over 300 times and 10 million homes had their own radio. Local and national commercial stations were set up. They made money by advertising and, as people bought the consumer goods they heard about on the radio, so industry and business boomed.

Source K

The parties were bigger, the pace was faster, the shows were broader, the buildings were higher, the morals were looser and the liquor was cheaper.

From **Echoes of the Jazz Age**
by F. Scott Fitzgerald, 1931.

New fashions and crazes

A flapper.

Young people turned away from old-fashioned dances such as the waltz. New dances like the Charleston, the sexually suggestive Tango and the Bunny Hug became very popular. Young Americans went to the cinema and watched basketball, baseball and American football. Many young women became 'flappers'. Their hair was short and bobbed. They wore skirts that rose to the knee and tried to achieve a flat-chested appearance. They used lipstick and rouge, smoked cigarettes and drove cars such as Henry Ford's Model T 'Tin Lizzy'. Young men wore pin-stripe suits, trilby hats and spats on their shoes.

The older generation disliked what was happening. The Anti Flirt Association was set up to try to control the excesses of the young by distributing badges and making speeches.

This was a time of 'crazes' and 'fads', when youngsters joined in never-ending dance marathons, or sat on top of a flagpole for weeks just to break a record. Popular heroes appeared, such as Charles Lindbergh, who in 1927 became the first man to fly solo across the Atlantic. Other famous personalities included sportsmen, such as the boxer Jack Dempsey and the baseball player 'Babe' Ruth.

Film and Hollywood

The movie industry was established before the First World War, but its popularity soared during the 1920s when 'going to the movies' became a national habit. Soon nearly every town had its own cinema. By 1929, over 110 million Americans were going to the cinema each week. At first they watched silent films in black and white. Words were shown on the screen and cinemas employed piano players to provide the background music. In 1927, people flocked to see *The Jazz Singer* starring Al Jolson, which was the first 'talkie'. By the mid-1930s, films were also being produced in colour and Walt Disney had made cartoon characters like Mickey Mouse and Donald Duck into household names.

This is the great picture upon which the famous comedian has worked a whole year.

6 reels of Joy.

Charles Chaplin IN "THE KID"

Source **L** A poster of the film star Charlie Chaplin in *The Kid*.

Most of the films shown were made in the USA. The new film industry mushroomed in Hollywood, which became the film capital of the world. Great movie companies such as United Artists, MGM and Paramount churned out over 500 new films annually. They created international film stars like Charlie Chaplin, Gloria Swanson and Mary Pickford.

When the heart-throb Rudolph Valentino died in 1926, thousands of fans attended his funeral. However, some of these famous stars had their careers destroyed by technological developments. They had looked good on the screen in silent films, but their voices were unattractive and their careers ended when sound arrived.

Why did the USA fall into depression in 1929?

During the 1920s the American economy appeared to be strong and healthy but there were some serious weaknesses which would bring a change from prosperity to depression – these were the long-term causes of the Depression.

Overproduction

Mass-production methods meant that goods could be produced quickly and in large amounts. However, the market was becoming saturated. Once Americans had bought their cars, radios, vacuum cleaners and other consumer goods, the demand for these items fell. Factories were forced to produce fewer goods – and this meant cutting back on their workforces, which meant fewer people could afford to buy consumer goods!

Unequal distribution of wealth

The fall in demand was also a result of the unequal distribution of wealth. Many Americans no longer wished to buy new consumer goods, but there were millions more who could not afford to do so. In 1928, many American families lived on less than $2000 a year which was barely enough to survive. So even during the boom years more than half of Americans lived 'below the poverty line'. Worst affected were farmers and farm workers, black workers, new immigrants and workers in the old industries. For such people the boom had never been a reality.

THINGS TO DO

1   Explain why America went into an economic depression after 1929. Use the information on pages 231–2 to answer the question.

2   Explain how the factors which produced prosperity could lead to depression.

The USA, 1919–41

231

Tariff policy

One way of selling surplus goods was to find new markets overseas. However, when the Americans put tariffs on foreign goods in the 1920s many foreign governments responded by doing the same to American goods. So American businessmen found it difficult to sell their manufactures abroad.

Soon a 'cycle of depression' set in. Reduced demand led to factories closing down and workers being made unemployed. So there was less money to spend on consumer goods which further reduced demand and led to more closures.

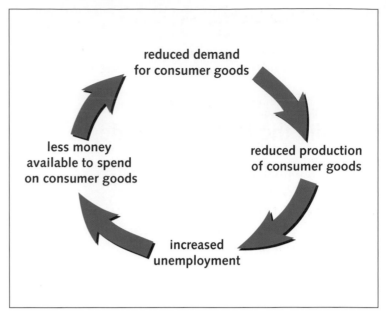

The cycle of depression.

Financial crisis: speculation

The confidence that had helped produce prosperity was now shaken. It led to the final reason for the Depression – the collapse of the financial markets.

During the 1920s more and more Americans were buying shares on the stock exchange in Wall Street. Share prices kept rising and there was confidence that they would keep doing so. People bought shares on credit expecting to sell them for a profit and settle their debts. This is called 'speculation'. However, during 1928, share prices did not rise as much as in previous years. Many companies were not selling as many goods, so their profits fell and people were less willing to buy their shares. Some, more experienced, investors began to sell their shares before values fell. When other smaller investors saw this they began to sell too.

The Wall Street Crash, 1929

Prices began to fall dramatically as investors tried to sell increasing numbers of shares. On Thursday 24 October – Black Thursday – nearly 13 million shares were sold. Prices dived as few buyers could be found. A group of bankers spent nearly $250,000,000 buying shares in the hope that this would encourage investors to buy rather than sell shares. It seemed to work and share prices stopped falling. However, on Monday 28 October, there was renewed panic and over 9 million shares were sold at falling prices. Finally on Tuesday 29 October, over 16 million shares were sold by panic-stricken investors for whatever price they could get. As a result prices tumbled – shareholders lost a total of $8000 million on that day alone. Although this was the worst single day on the stock market, share prices continued to fall for the next few weeks until they 'bottomed out' (stopped falling) in mid-November. By then the damage was done.

Effects of the Wall Street Crash

The effects of the Wall Street Crash were as dramatic as the Crash itself. Confidence in America's economy was gone and many rich Americans lost all their money in the Crash. Companies had to cut back and dismiss some of their workforce. During the period of the Depression (1929-33) over 100,000 businesses shut down completely.

Banks too suffered in the Crash. Many had invested in shares and lost the money customers had placed with them. People lost confidence in the banks and withdrew their money. This caused a 'run on the banks', which began to run out of money. In 1929 alone nearly 700 banks collapsed. In an attempt to try to recover some of their money banks began to call in loans from companies and the ordinary people who had borrowed money from them. But they were being asked to repay money which they did not have and so more companies closed and some people had to sell their homes and possessions.

Company	Share Prices	
	3 September	13 November
Anaconda Copper	131.5	70
General Electric	396	168
Radio	101	28
United States Steel	261	150
Woolworth	100	52
Electric Bond & Share	186	50

Share prices of some leading US companies in 1929.

SUMMARY

The causes of the Depression were:

- The production of more goods than were needed.
- Many Americans did not share in the economic prosperity of the 1920s.
- Failure to find markets abroad.
- Speculation in shares.
- Loss of confidence.
- Wall Street Crash.

THINGS TO DO

Look at the table of share prices and the information in this section. Imagine you are a shareholder. How would you explain to people who don't own shares what happened in the Wall Street Crash?

Source B Unemployed workers in New York queuing for free bread in 1930.

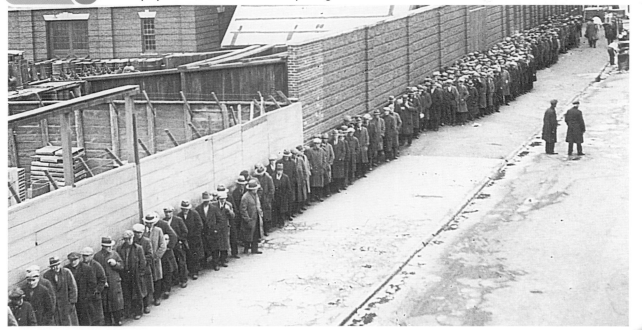

What were the effects of the Depression on the American people?

Unemployment

The financial crash affected nearly every American in some way as depression hit the USA. In 1929 the unemployment rate in America was just over 3 per cent of the workforce; by 1933 it was 25 per cent. In the industrial cities of the North, the rate was even higher as factories and businesses cut down on production or shut down completely. In Chicago, for example, nearly half the labour force was unemployed in 1933. For those in work wages were cut by 25 per cent. Some Americans took to the roads, travelling from place to place trying to find work wherever they could. They became tramps or 'hobos'. The exact number of hobos was not known but it was estimated to have been hundreds of thousands.

Homelessness

The Depression made many Americans homeless. When people became unemployed, there was no dole to help them. They had to sell their possessions to pay back loans or credit taken out during the good years. If they had mortgage payments they could not meet, their homes were re-possessed. If they fell behind with their rents, they were evicted. In 1932 alone a quarter of a million Americans lost their homes.

The homeless ended up on the streets, sleeping on park benches or in bus shelters. Some deliberately got themselves arrested so that they could spend the night in jail. Many moved to the edge of towns or to waste grounds in towns. There they built shelters from whatever they could find – corrugated iron, scrap metal, old wood. They called these collections of shelters 'Hoovervilles' as an insult to the President, Herbert Hoover.

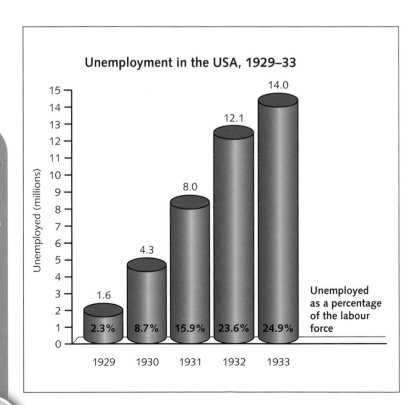

Unemployment in the USA, 1929–33

Year	Unemployed (millions)	Unemployed as a percentage of the labour force
1929	1.6	2.3%
1930	4.3	8.7%
1931	8.0	15.9%
1932	12.1	23.6%
1933	14.0	24.9%

THINGS TO DO

Look at the statistics on this page, **Source C** on page 235 and the other information in this section. Describe how people in cities like New York suffered in the Depression.

A 'Hooverville' in the centre of New York.

Farmers

The Depression made life even more difficult for farmers. Unemployment in the towns meant that farmers sold less of their produce. Prices of farm produce fell so much that it was not profitable even to harvest the crop. Wheat was left to rot in the fields and farmers went bankrupt. In 1932 one farmer in every twenty was evicted for failure to make mortgage repayments.

Around 1930 another problem hit some farmers – the dust bowl. In the states of the South and Midwest, such as Kansas and Oklahoma, farmers had changed from cattle farming to growing crops during the First World War. This continued in the 1920s but the land was being farmed too much and was becoming infertile. Then in the years after 1930 there was drought. Strong winds and little rainfall turned the top soil to dust. The land became like a desert. Thousands of farmers were ruined. They were left with no choice but to abandon their farms and look for work elsewhere. Many drifted to California where the fruit farms seemed to offer new opportunities.

Help from charities

The homeless needed help. It did not come from the state because the USA did not have a social security system, as in Britain, which would pay unemployment benefit to those who had lost their jobs. Some towns and cities decided to run their own public relief programmes which organised temporary homes, food, clothes and even jobs for the unemployed. Private charities run by bodies like the Salvation Army were also set up. In some cases, wealthy individuals gave help (even the gangster Al Capone provided food in Chicago). These charities set up soup kitchens, bread kitchens or cheap food centres to feed the hungry. 'Breadlines', long lines of men and women queuing for free bread and soup, became a common sight in most American towns.

America was in deep depression. One of the most popular songs of the time sums up the mood: 'Buddy, Can You Spare A Dime?'.

Source D

In the State of Washington I was told that forest fires were caused by bankrupt farmers trying to earn a few dollars as fire-fighters.

In Oregon I saw apples rotting in orchards. I saw sheep farmers feeding mutton to the buzzards.

An American journalist writing in 1932.

The USA, 1919–41

The Republican government and the Depression

The Republican government of Herbert Hoover believed in 'rugged individualism' – that is, the government should not involve itself in people's lives, and should let people sort out their own problems. The government was convinced that the Depression would not last long and that America would return to the boom of the 1920s.

But Hoover's government did take some action to try to improve the situation. In 1930 taxes were cut to increase people's spending power. The government provided over $4000 million for major building projects in the construction industry to provide new jobs. For example, in 1931 work began on building the Hoover Dam on the Colorado River. In 1932 an Emergency Relief Act gave $300 million to the states to help the unemployed. Also in 1932 the Reconstruction Finance Corporation provided loans of $1500 million to businesses to help them recover from the Depression. However, these actions were not enough to halt the Depression. Resentment of the government sometimes turned to violence. In the cities the unemployed held marches and demonstrations, which often turned into riots.

Millions of Americans blamed Hoover for the Depression and all the problems that came with it. With bitterness they said: 'In Hoover we trusted, now we are busted.'

They also talked of such things as 'Hoover leather' (cardboard soles for shoes) and 'Hoover blankets' (newspaper that people slept in). They were looking for a more positive approach in dealing with the Depression. They found it in F. D. Roosevelt, who promised 'a New Deal for the American people'.

Case Study: the Bonus Army

At the end of the First World War, soldiers had been promised a 'bonus', or pension, by the government which would be paid in 1945. By 1932 many veterans of the American army had been hit by the Depression and wanted the government to pay the bonuses early. In the summer of 1932 between 15,000 and 20,000 veterans reached Washington to protest to the government. There they set up a camp, or 'Hooverville' as they were known.

Congress refused to pay the bonuses. Nonetheless, the 'Bonus Army' decided to stay and protest. Hoover first used the police to contain the veterans. Then he called in the army. Armed troops, using tanks and tear gas, forced the Bonus Army out of the camp and burned the tents and shelters, killing two veterans and injuring nearly a thousand. The Bonus Army had been defeated but Hoover became even more unpopular.

Source Fighting between the police and the Bonus Army, in 1932.

What measures did Roosevelt introduce to deal with the Depression?

The 1932 Presidential election

By 1932 the American people felt badly let down by the Republican government of Herbert Hoover. In the 1928 Presidential election Hoover had promised that the economic prosperity of the 1920s would continue. The opposite had happened and the USA had been hit by depression. The policies of the government had done little to ease the suffering caused by the Depression. In the 1932 Presidential election campaign, Hoover offered only the hope that the Depression would soon end and that the USA had 'turned the corner' back towards prosperity.

Source **A** F. D. Roosevelt.

Source **B**

A cartoon, dated 3 March 1933, showing President Roosevelt throwing out the policies of the previous government, which are seen as rubbish.

F. D. Roosevelt, promised 'a New Deal for the American people'. He outlined policies which would provide jobs and relief for the poor and unemployed, action to help industry and agriculture and resolve the banking crisis.

The result of the 1932 Presidential election was never in doubt. Even so the scale of Roosevelt's victory surprised many Americans. He won 42 of the 48 states of the USA. It was the biggest victory in a Presidential election that anyone had ever won.

The New Deal

During the period between the election victory of November 1932 and taking office in March 1933 – the 'lame duck months' when the new government is not in place – Roosevelt worked out the New Deal in greater detail. To carry it out the government would put money into the economy to provide new jobs. This would give people money to spend and the demand for goods would increase. This in turn would lead to more employment. The 'cycle of prosperity' would be restored.

The Hundred Days

The New Deal required massive state involvement in the economy and the setting up of government-controlled agencies. Roosevelt was given the authority to do this when Congress granted him 'emergency powers' – the sort of powers he would have if the USA had been at war. Roosevelt acted quickly during his first 'Hundred Days' in office and set up a number of agencies which became known as the 'Alphabet Agencies' because the people found it easier to remember them by their initials than by their full names. Roosevelt also realised the need to explain to the American people what he was doing. They needed to have trust and confidence in his measures and in the recovery of the economy. As he said when he was sworn in as President: 'The only thing we have to fear is fear itself.'

He used the radio to reach a large audience of millions of Americans and to talk directly to them. In his 'fireside chats', in which he sat in a chair by a fire in his office, he explained in simple terms why the USA had fallen into depression and what he proposed to do to end it. The broadcasts were hugely successful – especially the first one which dealt with the banking crisis.

The cycle of recovery.

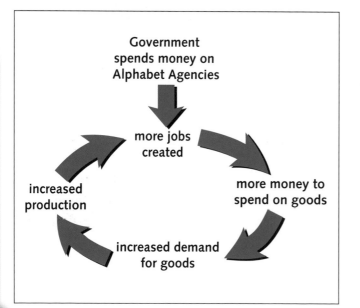

The banking crisis

During the Depression, people lost confidence in the banks. Many banks had closed as savers withdrew their money and businesses were unable to pay back bank loans. In March 1933 Roosevelt introduced an Emergency Banking Act. All banks were closed for four days. During that time government officials inspected the accounts of every bank. Only those banks that were properly managed were allowed to re-open – and these were supported by government loans. When the banks re-opened after the four-day 'holiday', savers kept their money in them and customers who had withdrawn their money even started to put it back into their accounts. The banking crisis was over.

Agriculture: the AAA

In May 1933 Roosevelt set up the Agricultural Adjustment Administration (AAA) to help farmers to increase their income. It was controversial because it paid farmers to produce less food, either by ploughing less land or by reducing their livestock. This meant that food prices went up and farmers' income increased. Any loss of profit was made up by government subsidies. Government money was also used to help farmers who were having difficulty in meeting their mortgage payments. As a result of these measures farmers' income doubled in the period up to 1939. However, it failed to help farmworkers. Many of these were evicted as there was less work for them to do.

Source **C** Roosevelt meeting a farmer in Georgia in 1932.

Dealing with unemployment: FERA, CWA, PWA, WPA

The key to the success of the New Deal was the creation of jobs to reduce the high level of unemployment which the USA experienced in the Depression. A number of agencies were set up to deal with this problem.

As a start, the Federal Emergency Relief Administration (FERA) was created in 1933 to give quick relief to the hungry and homeless. $500 million was spent on providing soup kitchens and clothing, and setting up employment schemes.

The Civil Works Administration (CWA) aimed to provide as many jobs as possible in the short term – especially before winter arrived. During the winter of 1933-4 over four million jobs were created in areas such as building and improving roads, schools, airports and other public buildings. People were paid to sweep up leaves in local parks or even to frighten pigeons away from public buildings. Once the winter of 1933-4 was over, the CWA ended – and so did the four million jobs it created.

In the meantime, another agency was set up to provide work – the Public Works Administration (PWA). This aimed to organise long-term work schemes that would be of lasting value to Americans: building schools, hospitals, airports, dams, bridges, battleships. All were built under the direction of the PWA, which also directed improvements in sewage and drainage systems. Such schemes created jobs, but generally they were for skilled workers rather than for the millions who lacked a skill or trade.

To help meet this need, the Works Progress Administration (WPA) was set up in 1935. In some ways it was similar to the PWA. It helped to build roads, schools and other public buildings, but the schemes were on a small scale. It also gave work to writers, artists, photographers and actors. For example, artists were paid to paint pictures showing how the New Deal was working. The WPA became the country's biggest employer – two million Americans were employed each year by it.

The three agencies, CWA, PWA and WPA, provided work for millions of Americans. The money they earned from this work could be used to buy food, clothing and other goods. This increased demand and in turn helped businesses to provide more jobs.

Source **D** 'Yes, you remembered me,' a cartoon of 1933.

THINGS TO DO

1 What point was the cartoonist making in **Source D**?

2 Outline the work carried out by:
(a) CWA (b) PWA (c) WPA.

Helping the young: CCC

Some of the agencies set up in the New Deal had more than one aim. For example the Civilian Conservation Corps (CCC) not only provided work but also helped agriculture and the environment. This agency gave work to single, unemployed young men between the ages of 18 and 25 for a limited period – usually six months. They lived in camps in the countryside, planted trees to stop soil erosion, cleared land, created forests and made reservoirs. In return they received food, clothing and shelter, and pocket money of one dollar a day. By 1938 over two million young people had served in the CCC. It was criticised by some Americans as being cheap labour but it was not compulsory and, through it, many young men learned skills which later allowed them to get a job.

Helping industry: NRA

Roosevelt tried to help both sides of industry, employers and workers, through the National Recovery Administration (NRA). Employers and businessmen were invited to follow codes fixing fair prices for the goods being sold, setting the minimum wages to be paid to workers, and laying down conditions of work including maximum hours of work. Child labour and cheap 'sweated' labour were forbidden. Businesses that signed the NRA code could advertise using the Blue Eagle with the motto 'We Do Our Part'. Americans were encouraged to buy goods with the Blue Eagle on them. The scheme was a success. By the end of 1933 two million employers, employing 22 million workers, had agreed to the codes.

Other measures of the New Deal

The New Deal introduced a number of measures which tried to help the American people in other ways. The Home Owners Loan Corporation (HOLC) helped people who were having difficulty meeting their mortgage repayments. The government, through the Corporation, lent money to people at low interest rates to prevent them from losing their homes.

The Social Security Act was introduced in 1935. It set up a national system of state pensions for people over 65, for widows and for the disabled. It also provided for an unemployment insurance scheme to be run by each state with financial support from the government. The National Labour Relations Act, or the Wagner Act, was also introduced in 1935. It gave American workers the right to join and form trade unions. It also stopped employers from dismissing workers who were members of a union.

SUMMARY

The Alphabet Agencies:

AAA Helped farmers by paying them to produce less food.

FERA Provided relief for the hungry and homeless in 1933.

CWA Created jobs on public work schemes, 1933-4.

PWA Created jobs in public work schemes, including construction.

WPA Created jobs in public work schemes, including community schemes.

NRA Introduced codes of fair competition for industry and business.

CCC Provided jobs for unemployed young men in the countryside.

TVA Brought improvement to states in the Tennessee Valley.

HOLC Helped people in difficulties with their mortgage repayments.

Case Study: The Tennessee Valley Authority (TVA)

The TVA aimed to bring relief to the Tennessee Valley – what Roosevelt called 'the nation's number one economic problem'.

The Tennessee river caused massive problems across a large area of south-east America. During the wet season it flooded, removing fertile soil while in the dry season it almost dried up, causing soil erosion and dust-bowl conditions. As a result the people of the Tennessee Valley lived in poverty. As the Tennessee river ran through seven different American states, it was also difficult to get common agreement on what actions to take to solve the problems. So Roosevelt set up the Tennessee Valley Authority (TVA) which developed a detailed scheme to improve the whole area. Trees were planted and forests created to improve the soil. Twenty-one dams were built to control the river and prevent flooding. Power stations were built at the dams to provide cheap electricity for homes and industry. The dams also created lakes and these were used for water transport which linked into the major river systems of the USA. The cheap source of power and good transport facilities attracted industries to the Tennessee Valley. The lakes also provided sporting and leisure facilities. As a result the Tennessee Valley recovered and became wealthier. Thousands of jobs were created, the land became fertile and the quality of life of the people who lived there greatly improved.

THINGS TO DO

Use the information in the case study to explain why Roosevelt thought that the TVA was his greatest achievement.

Source **E** A dam built by the TVA.

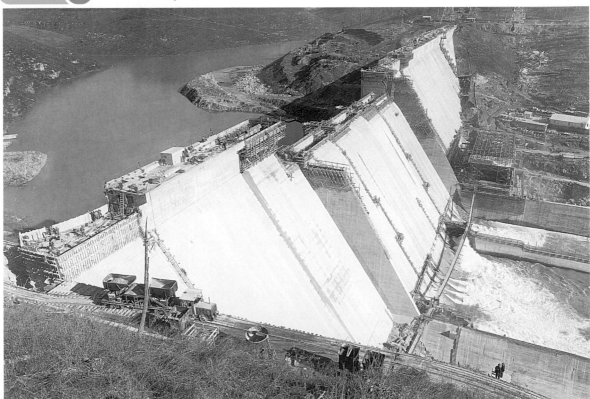

How far was the New Deal successful in ending the Depression in the USA?

In 1936 Roosevelt's first term of office as President was coming to an end. He sought re-election for a second term and based his campaign on the promise to continue with the New Deal. Only two states out of the 48 voted against Roosevelt. He had received a clear vote of confidence for his policies from the American people.

Opposition to the New Deal

Despite his landslide victory, 16 million Americans had not voted for Roosevelt. Many of these were Republicans who continued to believe in the old ideas of self-reliance and 'rugged individualism'. They felt that Roosevelt was behaving like a dictator, forcing Americans to do what he wanted. Republicans also objected to the huge cost of the New Deal and felt that the people's money was being wasted on worthless jobs. Businessmen also did not like government interference in their affairs. Many opposed the codes of fair competition set up by the NRA. They objected to the support for trade unions and the attempts to increase wages. This was the government interfering in business, which was not its job.

But there were also other Americans who felt that he was not doing enough. For example, Huey Long, Senator for Louisiana, launched the 'Share Our Wealth' programme. By taxing the rich and confiscating personal fortunes of over $5 million, this scheme planned to provide every American family with $4000–

Source F

In this 1933 cartoon Roosevelt said he was 'priming the pump' of the American economy. Priming a pump is getting it started.

$5000. In addition, all Americans would be entitled to other benefits such as free education and an old age pension. His ideas were popular, especially in Louisiana. However, they did bring opposition for being too extreme. When he was assassinated in 1935 support for his movement collapsed.

THINGS TO DO

Study **Source F**. What criticism does it make of the New Deal?

The Supreme Court

It is the responsibility of the Supreme Court to decide if any measure passed by the President and Congress is unconstitutional – that is, whether it goes against the American Constitution. If it feels that this is the case, the Supreme Court can block the measure and declare it illegal.

Roosevelt was unfortunate in that a majority of the judges on the Supreme Court were Republicans. They felt that the New Deal and the increased powers it gave the government were against the Constitution. As a result, a number of the Alphabet Agencies were declared illegal.

In 1935 the NRA and all the codes it had introduced had to be withdrawn because the Supreme Court ruled that they were unconstitutional. In 1936 the AAA was declared unconstitutional because the Supreme Court ruled that it was the responsibility of each state, not the federal government, to help agriculture. All the help that the AAA had given to farmers stopped. In another eleven cases the Supreme Court ruled against the Alphabet Agencies.

Roosevelt was furious at the actions of the Supreme Court. After his 1936 election victory he tried to add six judges to the Supreme Court so that there would be a Democrat majority. This threat to 'pack' the Court made Roosevelt unpopular throughout America, even among Democrats. He backed down – but so too did the Supreme Court. After this no more of Roosevelt's measures were rejected by the Court.

Source **G** In this 1936 cartoon Roosevelt shows 'Uncle Sam' the achievements of the New Deal.

Was the New Deal a success?

The New Deal achieved much and helped millions of Americans who had suffered in the years of depression, but there were areas where it was less successful.

Black people generally benefited less from the New Deal than white people: in 1935 about a third of black people were dependent on relief payments. Many farmers and especially farm labourers continued to have a low standard of living. Those who lived in the areas affected by the dust bowl were even worse off.

It is also true that the New Deal was not successful throughout the 1930s. In the first phase, from 1933 to 1936, it did bring recovery as the government pumped millions of dollars into creating jobs and reviving American industry. In 1933, 14 million Americans were unemployed; in 1938 it was 11 million. During 1937 Roosevelt reduced the amount of money the government was spending on the New Deal. He believed that enough had been done to bring recovery. However, production began to fall again as demand decreased. Share prices fell sharply on Wall Street. Businesses started to collapse once more. Unemployment in 1938 stood at 10.5 million. Roosevelt was again forced to pump more money back into the economy and unemployment fell in 1939 – but only to 9.5 million. It seemed as if the New Deal, with its massive amount of public spending, had achieved all it could.

The Second World War

What did help the American economy to recover was the Second World War. Although the USA did not enter the war until December 1941, its impact was felt from 1939. America sold goods to Britain and France which increased the demand for American manufactured goods and food produce. The level of unemployment fell. Finally, when the USA entered the war, its full resources – manpower, industry and agriculture – were absorbed in the fight against Japan and Germany. The economy was lifted out of depression.

Roosevelt and the New Deal had brought great changes to America. The federal (central) government became much more involved in people's lives than it had been in the 1920s. Most Americans now accepted that the federal government had a role to play in making sure that the weaker sections of society – the unemployed, the homeless, the old, the poor – were looked after. Roosevelt had helped to redefine the role of government in America.

Source H

The New Deal certainly did not get the country out of the Depression. As late as 1941 there were still six million unemployed and it was really not until the war that the army of the jobless finally disappeared.

An historian writing in 1963.

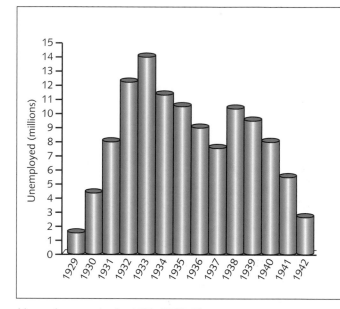

Unemployment in the USA, 1929-42.

THINGS TO DO

1 Was the New Deal a success? Explain your answer.

2 'Roosevelt was only trying to do his best for the country, so people were wrong to oppose his New Deal measures'. Explain whether you agree with this statement.

Exam-style assessment

These questions follow the pattern of questions to be set by AQA for Paper 2 of its new Modern World History specification.

SECTION A: The USA, 1929–33

Study **Sources A** to **E** and then answer all parts of Question 3 which follow.

Source A: Roosevelt's pledge for a New Deal

I pledge you, I pledge myself, to a New Deal for the American people. This is a political campaign; it is a call to arms. Give me your help, not to win votes alone, but to win in this crusade to restore America.

From a pre-election speech by F. D. ROOSEVELT in 1932

Source B: Why Hoover lost the 1932 election

Millions of Americans blamed Hoover for the Depression and all the problems that came with it. With bitterness they said: "In Hoover we trusted, now we are busted".

They were looking for a more positive approach in dealing with the Depression.

From Modern World History (1999) by T. HEWITT, J. McCABE and A. MENDUM

Source C: New York during the Depression

The visitor would be surprised to discover that, at first and even at second glance, New York City is much the same as it was in pre-depression days. Wandering about the city looking for disaster, the visitor will very likely find no more than he would have in New York in any other winter.

From the American magazine Fortune, in the winter of 1931

Source D: One view of the New Deal

An American cartoon of 1936.

Source E : Another view of the New Deal

A cartoon in an American newspaper, 1933.

Question 3

(a) How does **Source A** help to explain why many people voted for F. D. Roosevelt in the 1932 election? **(5 marks)**

(b) What are the strengths and weaknesses of **Source B** as an interpretation of why Hoover lost the 1932 election? **(10 marks)**

(c) How useful is **Source C** for describing the effects of the Depression on New York in late 1931? Explain your answer using **Source C** and your own knowledge **(9 marks)**

(d) Compare what the two cartoons (**Sources D** and **E**) are saying about the likely effects of the New Deal. **(6 marks)**

(e) Using your own knowledge, what were the causes of America's Great Depression that started in 1929? **(15 marks)**

SECTION B: The USA, 1919–29

Study **Sources F** and **G** and then answer parts **(a)**, **(b)**, **(c)** and **either (d) or (e)** of Question 7 which follow.

Source F: Bootleg liquor being dumped

From a photograph of the 1920s.

Source G: The beliefs of the Ku Klux Klan

> There are three great racial instincts which must be used to build a great America: loyalty to the white race, to the traditions of America and to the spirit of Protestantism.
>
> The pioneer must be kept pure. The white race must be supreme.

From a speech in the 1920s by HIRAM WESLEY EVANS,
the Imperial Wizard (leader) of the Ku Klux Klan

Question 7

(a) What can you learn from **Source F** about Prohibition in the USA in the 1920s? **(3 marks)**

(b) Describe the effects of Prohibition in the USA in the 1920s on law and order. **(5 marks)**

(c) Use **Source G** and your own knowledge to explain why the Ku Klux Klan attracted substantial support in the 1920s. **(7 marks)**

EITHER

(d) The USA in the 1920s was seen as being very prosperous. Did all Americans share in the prosperity of the 1920s? Explain your answer. **(15 marks)**

OR

(e) The years 1929–32 are labelled as the Great Depression. Did all Americans suffer equally in the Depression in the years 1929–32? Explain your answer. **(15 marks)**

Britain, 1905–51

INTRODUCTION

In 1900 Britain was a nation divided by class. Booth and Rowntree had shown that something needed to be done to living and working conditions. Poverty was no longer seen as the fault of the poor. It was the fault of the society Britain had created. From 1906 the Liberal government attempted to tackle these problems with a wide range of social and economic reforms. By 1918 the beginnings of the welfare state had been established, the system of government reformed, women had gained the vote and the Labour Party was establishing itself as the opposition to the Conservatives.

Industrial relations were poor in the first part of the century. These were made worse by the economic and social problems after the First World War, culminating in a nine-day General Strike in 1926.

A world depression in the 1930s proved difficult to overcome despite the growth of new industries in the south of the country and government attempts to solve the problems facing towns such as Jarrow. The National Governments of 1931 onwards failed to reduce unemployment by much.

It was only after the Second World War when nationalisation of key industries and further welfare reforms, such as the establishment of the National Health Service, took effect that further progress was made to overcome the economic and social problems which affected Britain in the twentieth century. The Labour Governments of 1945–51 benefited from the new mood in Britain after the Second World War.

1906	Beginning of school meals
1908	Beginning of Old Age Pensions Act
1911	National Insurance Act Parliament Act
1918	Women over 30 get the right to vote
1926	General Strike
1929	Wall Street Crash leads to Depression
1936	Jarrow Crusade
1939	Second World War starts
1942	Beveridge Report
1944	Education Act
1945	Labour Party elected
1946	National Health Service Act
1947	Transport and coal nationalised
1951	Labour Party defeated in election

How far was the welfare state established by 1914?

Life in Britain in 1900 was very different from life in Britain today. A very rich upper class or a 'well to do' middle class enjoyed a lifestyle which even people today would envy. Despite the number of inquiries which were held between 1890 and 1910 many of the governing classes still believed that most problems had been solved by providing workhouses for the very poor to live in and Public Health Acts to improve the health of the poor by ensuring cleaner water and better housing.

Living conditions for a London East End family at the beginning of the 20th century.

Source **B** Pupils exercising at a school in 1908.

This was not the case. Many people needed help urgently. A Royal Commission in 1895 revealed that most working people were not earning enough for the basic necessities of life. The findings of the Commission were supported by surveys carried out by Charles Booth (in London) and Seebohm Rowntree (in York) which showed shocking poverty in England's cities.

In 1906 the Liberal government was elected and set about introducing a series of reforms which provided the foundation of the modern welfare state.

Children's health

From the late nineteenth century education was compulsory. As children entered education in large numbers teachers complained that many of them were inadequately clothed and hungry. Voluntary charities had raised money to provide some clothing and meals but it was clearly not enough.

In 1906, the Education (Provision of Meals) Act enabled local education authorities to provide school meals for children. In Bradford, food centres were set up to feed pupils with broth, pies, vegetables, puddings and, occasionally, meat and fish!

In some areas meals were even provided during the school holidays. But it was not until 1914 that the provision of school meals was made compulsory.

The Liberal government also introduced the School Medical Inspection Service (1907) which allowed doctors and nurses to visit schools regularly and inspect each child once a year.

The first school clinics were opened in 1912, to treat childhood problems of the eyes, ears and teeth. This was the main way children's health was monitored and treated until after the Second World War.

THINGS TO DO

1 What evidence was there to suggest that many people were living in poverty at the beginning of the 20th century?

2 How reliable do you think **Source A** is in showing us what it was like to be poor?

3 How did the Liberal governments of 1906–14 try to help young people?

Old age pensions

The Old Age Pensions Act (1908) was passed to provide pensions from the 6 January 1909 to people 70 years of age or over. Pensioners were entitled to 5 shillings (25 pence) each a week provided they had less than £21 income a year from any other source. This included about 60 per cent of all people over 70. Over 650,000 people applied for a pension in the first year, and by the start of the First World War in 1914 there were almost a million pensioners.

Until now old people with no support from relatives and too poor to support themselves were often forced to rely on the workhouse for accommodation and food. With the pension the fear of the workhouse almost disappeared. By 1912 the number of people over 70 years old in workhouses dropped by 5590. At last many parents who had depended on their sons and daughters for food and shelter in their old age felt much less of a burden. As one pensioner exclaimed, 'Now we want to go on livin' for ever 'cus we give 'em the ten shillings a week.' Now all the government had to do was pay for the pensions. That was not to prove easy (see pages 254–5).

(see pages 254–5).

Source D

Friday was the beginning of a new era for the aged poor of this country, as the first payment of old age pensions was made. In Norwich there were old people waiting for the doors to open at 8 am, and by 9 am the first pensioners produced their coupon books without a word, answered one or two routine questions, made their signatures, pocketed their money and walked out.

A report in the **Norwich Mercury,**
9 January 1909.

Source C

Pensioners queuing inside a post office for their pensions.

THINGS TO DO

1 Explain why 5 shillings a week pension was enough to make a difference to the lives of most pensioners.

2 (a) Would you say the *Norwich Mercury* was in favour of pensions? Explain your answer.

   (b) Would all newspapers agree with this view? Explain your answer.

3 What problems would the government face if pensioners were to 'go on livin' for ever?

Labour exchanges

To help the unemployed find work the President of the Board of Trade, Winston Churchill, pushed through the Labour Exchanges Act of 1909. The idea was to save unemployed people having to tramp from one factory to another in search of work. By 1913 there were 430 labour exchanges throughout the country. Today labour exchanges are called job centres.

National Insurance

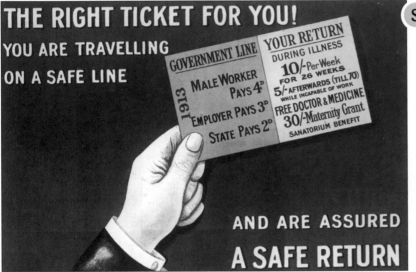

Source E

A government poster advertising the National Insurance Act.

The National Insurance Act of 1911 introduced an insurance scheme against ill-health and unemployment. Health insurance was only for manual and non-manual workers earning less than £160 a year. In this scheme the workman paid 4 pence into the scheme, the employer 3 pence and the state 2 pence, leading to the slogan '9d for 4d'. In return a worker was entitled to 'free' medical treatment and could claim 10 shillings (50 pence) a week for a maximum of 26 weeks if unable to work. After that a disability pension of 5 shillings (25 pence) could be awarded. The scheme itself was not available to women workers until 1920, but a male worker's wife was given a special payment of £1 and 10 shillings (£1.50) after the birth of a baby.

Unemployment insurance was introduced for men in industries such as building, engineering and shipbuilding, where short-term unemployment was common. A worker and his employer made contributions to the insurance fund and when unemployed a worker could claim 7 shillings (35 pence) a week for a limited period of 15 weeks. The scheme was extended to another eight million workers in 1920.

THINGS TO DO

How far had the welfare state been established by 1914?

How far did the government change as a result of events between 1905 and 1919?

The Liberal reforms were expensive and so the Chancellor, Lloyd George, proposed a range of tax increases in the 1909 budget to pay for them. This included an increase in income tax from 5p to 7p in the pound for those earning over £3000 a year (remember that health insurance was later to be set up for people earning less than £160 per year!) and an extra 2 pence in every pound for those earning over £5000. There was also an increase in death duties, a new land tax and increased duties on tobacco and alcohol. The proposals were very unpopular with many well-off people.

As the Liberals had most MPs in the House of Commons, the Finance Bill setting out the budget was easily passed. However, their opponents, the Conservatives, had more members in the House of Lords. Many of the Lords were angry at the proposed land tax which would be paid on any profit made on land sold. In November 1909 the Lords rejected the Finance Bill. Members of the Lords who did not usually attend were summoned to London to make sure the Bill was defeated. These 'backwoodsmen', as the Liberal press called them, even had difficulty in persuading the policeman at the door of the Lords to let them in as he did not recognise them. The Prime Minister, Herbert Asquith, called a general election to see if his plans had the support of the country.

Source A Liberal Party leaflet in 1909.

Mr Lloyd-George: What are you using this acre field for?
Owner: Agricultural purposes, I turn my pony in here!
Mr Lloyd-George: It can't be worth more than £50 for that purpose – couldn't you do something better with it?

Owner: There's no need for me to do anything – the builders over there are doing it all for me. They'll be wanting to build here soon. Why, I could get £500 tomorrow for this acre!
Mr Lloyd-George: Then, surely, it won't hurt you to pay tax of a halfpenny in the £ on an increased value which you had nothing to do with making!

The general election: January 1910

The election which some described as the 'Peers against People' was hard fought. The result was that the Liberals and Conservatives won nearly the same number of seats. However, the Liberals had the support of the Irish Nationalists and the Labour Party so they formed a new government.

They now set about getting the budget of the previous year passed. To make sure there would not be more obstructions they planned to reduce the power of the House of Lords through a new Parliament Bill. What was now known as the 'People's Budget' was eventually passed in April 1910, although the proposed land tax was dropped. The Lords and the Conservatives were more concerned about the proposed Parliament Bill. The opposition to it caused a constitutional crisis.

The constitutional crisis

The politicians now turned to the proposal to reduce the power of the Lords. The new king, George V, who had just succeeded to the throne and was almost immediately faced with this constitutional crisis, called for the parties to discuss the crisis at a conference in June. When talks broke down in November, the Liberal government called on the king to create 300 more Liberal peers for the House of Lords so that they would have more members than the Conservatives, making it possible to get the Parliament Bill passed. The king agreed, provided a general election was held to show that the people agreed.

In the second election of the year, in December, the result was almost identical to the first. Asquith knew that if the Lords rejected the Parliament Bill the king would create enough new peers for it to be passed. Eventually, in August 1911, the Lords passed the Bill by 131 votes to 114. As for the Conservatives, their leader, Balfour, resigned and the new leader, Bonar Law, continued the struggle against the Liberal government.

	1906	Jan 1910	Dec 1910	1918	1922
Liberal Party	377	275	272*	146*	117
Labour Party	53	40	42*	59	142
Conservative Party	157	273	272	338*	347
Irish Nationalists	83	82	84*	–	–
Asquith Liberals	–	–	–	26	–

* Liberal Government
(needing support from Labour and Irish Nationalists)

* Lloyd George Coalition Government
(Liberals and Conservatives)

General election results, 1906–22.

THE PARLIAMENT BILL

- established that all money bills (budgets) passed by the Commons had to be passed by the Lords;
- limited the power of the Lords over other bills;
- said that MPs should be paid;
- established that general elections take place every five years rather than every seven.

THINGS TO DO

1 Explain how the Liberals hoped to raise money to pay for pensions and why there was opposition to their proposals.

2 How reliable do you think **Source F** is in explaining why the government wanted to introduce a land tax?

3 Explain how the Liberal government was able to get its budget through the House of Lords.

Women's right to vote

The Parliament Act saw a change in the role of the House of Lords in passing laws, but there was a much more significant change in the way the country was governed during this period. Before the First World War women did not have a vote in general elections, could not be MPs or sit in the House of Lords. Many people, including Queen Victoria and the Prime Minister, Asquith, accepted this, but a campaign by suffragettes and the events of the First World War were to change that.

During the war the suffragettes suspended their campaign, changed their slogan to 'The Right to Serve' and committed themselves to the national effort to defeat Germany. Working on the land and in factories as well as serving in the armed forces, they proved their worth to the nation and in 1918 women aged 30 or over were given the right to vote. It was not until 1928 that women received the vote at the age of 21 on equal terms with men.

Source **G** Women fire-fighters.

The Suffragettes

The suffragettes were women who fought for the right to vote in general elections. From 1903 the fight was led by the Women's Social and Political Union (WSPU), founded by Emmeline Pankhurst and her daughters. At first they used peaceful methods of drawing attention to their cause: marches, petitions and publishing their own newspaper.

In 1909 the WSPU decided peaceful methods were not working as well as they wanted and they turned to violent ways of making the public aware of their demands.

Such action helped them gain publicity, but it also convinced some people that women were too 'unbalanced' to be given the vote.

Some of them went on hunger strike to highlight their case. Women who broke the law were arrested and some were imprisoned. To prevent them from dying the authorities force-fed them, but this was considered too brutal. So the Cat and Mouse Act of 1913 was passed. It allowed the prisons to release women on hunger strike and arrest them again once they had recovered from their ordeal.

In 1913 the suffragette Emily Wilding Davison, in a highly dangerous attempt to win the suffragettes widespread publicity, tried to disrupt the Epsom Derby horse race by throwing herself at the King's horse. She was seriously injured and died four days later. Her funeral was a massive public affair, giving the suffragettes huge publicity.

Keir Hardie and the rise of the Labour Party

Keir Hardie was leader of the miners. In 1888 he stood as a Labour candidate for Mid-Lanark. He came last. He then formed the Scottish Labour Party and other parts of the country formed local Labour parties. Four years later he won the West Ham seat as an Independent Labour candidate. In 1893 local Labour parties formed the Independent Labour Party (ILP) and although Hardie lost his seat in the 1895 election the new party was born.

An important milestone in the history of the Party came in 1903 when it made a pact with the Liberal Party agreeing that only one candidate (Liberal or Labour) should stand against the Conservatives in a general election, except in the case of Scotland.

In the 1906 election 53 Labour MPs were elected. The Parliament Act of 1911 provided MPs with an annual salary of £400, which was a benefit to Labour MPs, who had few other sources of income. Further help came from the Trades Union Act of 1913, which allowed union funding for the Labour Party. It could now campaign at election time on a more equal footing with the main parties.

The election of 1918 saw an increase in Labour seats to 59, although the Party leader, Arthur Henderson, failed to be re-elected.

Events between 1918 and 1922 were to prove beneficial for the Labour Party. A number of problems for the government, including a slump in the post-war economy, helped to persuade people that it was time for a change. In 1922 the Labour Party gained 142 seats (25 more than the Liberals) and became the main opposition party to the Conservatives. An increase to 191 MPs in the elections of 1923 saw the formation of the first Labour government under Ramsay MacDonald in January 1924.

SUMMARY

1909 Liberals introduce 'People's Budget'.

1910 Liberals win two general elections.

1911 Parliament Act passed.

1913 Trade Union Act.

1918 Women aged 30 and over given the vote.

1924 First Labour government.

1928 Voting age is reduced to 21 for women.

THINGS TO DO

1 How did women try to get the vote?

2 Why were women eventually given the vote in 1918 and 1928?

3 What were the main events in the rise of the Labour Party?

Source Keir Hardie

Why was there a General Strike in 1926?

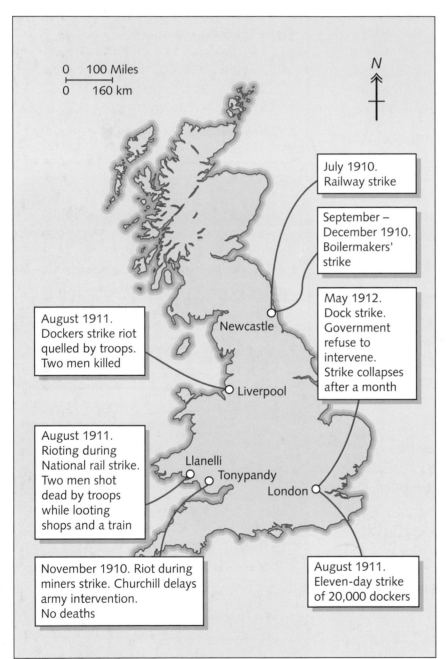

Industrial unrest in Britain, 1910–12.

July 1910. Railway strike

September – December 1910. Boilermakers' strike

May 1912. Dock strike. Government refuse to intervene. Strike collapses after a month

August 1911. Dockers strike riot quelled by troops. Two men killed

August 1911. Rioting during National rail strike. Two men shot dead by troops while looting shops and a train

November 1910. Riot during miners strike. Churchill delays army intervention. No deaths

August 1911. Eleven-day strike of 20,000 dockers

Newcastle
Liverpool
Llanelli
Tonypandy
London

Strikes, 1910–14

Although the Liberal government before the war was taking steps to improve living and working conditions in Britain, it still faced industrial unrest. Between 1910 and 1914 a series of official and unofficial strikes challenged the government. In 1910 railwaymen, boilermakers, miners and cotton workers all went on strike. In 1911, a dockers strike in Liverpool and a national rail strike were both ended by the government using troops. Four men died in street battles between strikers and soldiers. In February 1912, with over two million men unemployed, there was another miners' strike.

Some trade unions at this time believed that strike action was the most effective way of bringing about changes in society, in particular with trade unions taking over the running of industry. This was based on the idea that workers had the right to control the industries they worked in. This was known as syndicalism.

The British trade unions moved closer to realising this idea when they increased their power in 1913 through an alliance between miners, railwaymen, and transport workers – the Triple Alliance. This worried the government, but the outbreak of war in 1914 diverted people's attention from the issue.

Strikes, 1914-21

Although trade union leaders did agree in August 1914 to 'terminate all existing trade disputes' during the war, strikes in Glasgow, Clydeside and South Wales showed that many workers were still unhappy about their wages and working conditions. Union membership also doubled during the war.

During the war, new industrial giants, such as Japan and the USA, began selling goods into traditional British markets and so fewer British goods were being bought overseas. Exports of British coal, which before the war had been 100,000,000 tons a year, fell as British prices were too high to compete with the cheaper coal produced by countries such as America, Germany and Poland.

Although after the war the economy picked up, there were still problems in the coal industry. During the war the government had taken over the running of the coal mines. The miners wanted this to continue. But the mine owners wanted the mines back. Although a government inquiry, the Sankey Commission, recommended that the mines be nationalised, the mine owners persuaded the government to return the mines to them in 1921. Unfortunately, the export price of coal fell at this time from £4 a ton to £1.75 a ton, and the mine owners were forced to try to cut wages and lengthen the working day. The miners opposed this.

The Triple Alliance had been renewed in February 1919 and so the miners called upon the transport workers and the railwaymen to support them in a strike against the cut in wages. However, on Friday 15 April 1921 they said they could not support the miners on strike. This day became known as Black Friday by the unions.

The miners were eventually forced to accept a cut in wages. In the following months there were pay disputes involving the railwaymen, dockers, building workers and others. Unemployment rose to over 2 million by June and union membership fell by over 2.5 million to about 5.5 million.

Source

England this week is nearer revolution than it has ever been. Never before has there arisen a crisis which cancelled all naval leave and marshalled troops in our peaceful parks in peace time – just as though invasion were expected every hour.

An article in a British magazine, April 1921.

THINGS TO DO

1 Use the map on page 258 to explain the political problems which faced the government just before the First World War.

2 Explain how syndicalism and the Triple Alliance was a threat to the government between 1912 and 1926.

3 What effect did the First World War have on the coal-mining industry?

4 The article in **Source A** suggests that the Triple Alliance was a serious threat to the country. Do you agree?

Events leading to the General Strike

In 1925 falling prices forced the coal-mine owners to cut wages yet again and to increase the working day by one hour. The miners' leader, A. J. Cook, was furious. His reply, 'Not a penny off the pay! Not a minute on the day!' became the miners' slogan. This time it looked as if the Triple Alliance would hold together. The Prime Minister, Stanley Baldwin, thought so and on Friday 31 July 1925 he announced a government subsidy to keep wages at their current level and the setting up of a commission to be led by Sir Herbert Samuel to try to find a solution to the problem in the mines. Unions called this Red Friday and the disappointment of Black Friday seemed a thing of the past.

However, the subsidy was for only nine months. What would happen then? Some historians think that the government simply wanted time to build up stocks of coal and to plan what they would do if a general strike took place.

In the end the Samuel Commission failed to find a solution that could keep either side happy. It agreed with the owners' plan to cut wages, but not to lengthen hours, and also said that they should begin a programme of financial investment to modernise their mines.

Shortly after the Samuel Commission reported, Baldwin announced that the government subsidy would end on 30 April 1926. The owners then set wages lower than even Samuel had proposed. The miners refused to accept this and called on the other unions to support them by coming out on strike. The TUC (Trades Union Congress), the organisation which represents the unions, agreed to negotiate with the government on the miners' behalf and if necessary to call other trade unionists out on strike in support. The stage was set for the biggest industrial dispute of the 1920s.

Modern World History for AQA

Source B

Yesterday was the heaviest defeat that has befallen the Labour Movement within the memory of man. It is no use trying to minimise it. It is no use trying to pretend it is other than it is. We on this paper have said throughout that if the organised workers would stand together they would win. They have not stood together, and they have been beaten.

An article in the Daily Herald, 16 April 1921, commenting on Black Friday.

SUMMARY

1910 Series of strikes.

1913 Triple Alliance between miners, railwaymen and transport workers.

1919 Sankey Commission recommends mines stay under government control.

1921 Mines returned to mine owners. Black Friday.

1925 Red Friday. Government subsidy for nine months to keep up miners' wages.

1926 Samuel Commission fails to find solution.

Government withdraws subsidy.

Mine owners again reduce wages and increase working hours.

THINGS TO DO

1 The *Daily Herald* was a newspaper paid for by the trade unions. How useful therefore is **Source B**?

2 Why was Red Friday seen as a victory for the miners?

3 Why were both sides unhappy with the conclusions of the Samuel Commission?

Why did the General Strike fail after only nine days?

The strike begins

On the 30 April 1926 the employers made their final offer – a 13% cut in pay and a 'temporary' increase in the working day from 7 to 8 hours. It was rejected by the miners. Talks between the TUC and the government over how to resolve this situation broke down the following day when printers for the *Daily Mail* refused to print an article which described the proposed strike as 'a revolutionary movement intended to inflict suffering upon the great mass of innocent people'. The government called off the talks and the strike began at midnight on the 3 May 1926.

On the 4 May the people of many cities woke up to silence. Trains and buses were not running. (Later massive traffic jams replaced the silence as people tried to get to work by whatever means they could.) Even the TUC was surprised. Union members had followed their leaders' request and come out on strike. An estimated three million workers backed the miners.

Progress of the strike

At first the strike seemed successful and in the first few days the numbers on strike actually increased. The strikers were clearly well organised. They allowed essential supplies through and had no intention of bringing out on strike hospital workers or other key workers. There were even accounts that showed the good humour of both sides. In Plymouth and many other places there was a football match between strikers and police, and in Lincoln all the special constables were people already on strike!

However, the good humour was not evident everywhere, and some evidence suggests that it disappeared as the strike continued. In Glasgow and Doncaster strikers were arrested, tried and imprisoned. Fear of communism led to the arrest of two men in Wales for possessing communist literature.

Source **C** London's Waterloo station is deserted during the General Strike of 1926.

In Hull, the mayor called out the navy after attacks on trams and serious rioting that seemed to threaten the city. In London, food stocks were moved from the docks to Hyde Park protected by armoured cars.

Volunteers played an important part in keeping essential services going during the strike. Students, stockbrokers, and white-collar workers could act out their boyhood dreams as train drivers, firemen and lorry drivers. On one day alone 6000 men and women lined up outside the Foreign Office to sign up for the Organisation for the Maintenance of Supplies. Office workers even queued outside local police stations to be sworn in as special constables. If they were under 45 and with 'the required health, strength and vigour' they could join. Winston Churchill encouraged them to join to defeat 'the enemy'.

The attitude of both sides hardened as the strike went on and as it entered its second week violent clashes between the sides increased. Buses had their windows smashed, trams were turned over and trains were stopped when the tracks were blocked. There was even talk about the TUC bringing out their 'second line' of strikers, the electrical workers, which would have cut off electric light from the streets of major towns, but this did not materialise as the TUC took a different approach.

The TUC clearly felt that the situation could not continue. It had hoped simply to shock the government into surrender and had never intended to bring out on strike its second line, the electrical workers. It may have been afraid of not being able to control the demands and threats of the communists. It may have simply not been able to handle the pressures that the strike had brought, or it may have thought that Stanley Baldwin would still give the miners a fair deal despite his demands for unconditional surrender.

The end of the strike

Much to the surprise of the miners, the TUC did not extend the strike. Instead, on 12 May its leaders went to Downing Street and called off the strike! Why was this? Opinions on this are divided.

Source

1926
Even greater British invention – television. John Logie Baird demonstrates his 'pictures by radio' in London. Meanwhile there is a 'General Strike' of miners, transport workers and many others. The government appoints 140,000 special policemen to sort the strikers out. The special police don't have enough truncheons to go round so they sent a lorry-load of chair legs. Ouch!

A humorous modern view of the conflict between police and strikers from a book designed to make history amusing for children.

Why the strike failed

1 Government prepared

Shortly after Red Friday the government established the OMS, the Organisation for the Maintenance of Supplies. It was to make sure that food supplies were distributed and electricity and gas supplies maintained. It even set up a government newspaper, *The British Gazette*, to give people the government's view of events! Lists of volunteers to carry out vital jobs were drawn up and arrangements made to stockpile food just in case the strike dragged on for a long time.

2 Trade unions unprepared

Surprisingly, the trade union movement did not plan anything until five days before the strike started. By the time the talks collapsed the government was ready. When the TUC tried to re-open talks in the early hours of the 4 May 1926 the government ministers had gone home and the prime minister had already gone to bed.

3 Reaction of middle classes

An important factor in the defeat of the strikers was the reaction of many middle-class people. Protected by the army (and even the navy) they were gradually able to undermine the strike. For some people jobs such as driving a bus were 'good fun'.

It was important to maintain as normal a life as possible. As the secretary of the MCC (Marylebone Cricket Club), the governing body of English cricket, said, 'As far as we can see, we have no intention to allow cricket to be interrupted.'

Source **E**

We set out from Oxford early in the evening in a vintage Bentley, but from Doncaster onwards groups of strikers tried unsuccessfully to interrupt our progress by occasionally throwing stones or attempting to puncture our tyres.

On the following day those of us who were to work on the docks received our orders, while others went to drive trams or work the cranes. We were under the supervision of a Cambridge don, Mr Owen Morshead, now librarian of Windsor Castle.

Some of the old hands who drifted back to work were surprised by the speed with which we unloaded the ships, but we realised that it was a different story working for a few days as an adventure, compared to regular work over a period of years.

This is an account by an Oxford undergraduate of his experience as a volunteer working in the Liverpool docks during the General Strike.

Source **F** Women volunteer as postal workers during the General Strike.

4 Propaganda

The government's other weapon against the strike was the careful use of propaganda. *The British Gazette* was edited by Winston Churchill and took every opportunity to attack the strikers, whom Churchill called 'the enemy'. On the first day it was published, 5 May, it suggested that the 'strike was not so complete as hoped by its promoters'. Not surprisingly the TUC published its own newspaper, *The British Worker*, and began with the headline 'Wonderful response to the call.'

Source **G** The front page of *The British Gazette*, a government newspaper, covering the strike.

Although the TUC could print its version of events it had no way of challenging the BBC radio broadcasts, which reached the majority of homes in the country. The BBC chairman, Sir John Reith, decided to allow only broadcasts by the government and refused to allow Ramsay MacDonald, the Labour leader, to speak. So it was difficult for the TUC to put its case to the public, and, significantly, to other trade unionists.

5 Division among trade unionists

Many members of the TUC had been unhappy at the idea of a general strike. They feared that some revolutionaries in the union movement actually wanted to overthrow the government. They therefore refused to allow essential workers in health, water and sewerage to come out on strike and were determined to make sure that all picketing was done peacefully. So the TUC was looking for a way out from the start. On 10 May 1926 it asked the miners leaders to accept the Samuel Commission's recommendations. When the miners refused, the TUC met the prime minister and called off the strike, although the miners continued.

Immediately after this strike many employers cut the wages of their own workers even though the prime minister advised against such actions. The miners felt betrayed by the TUC. They remained locked out until November 1926, when hunger and the onset of winter forced them to accept the owners' terms.

THINGS TO DO

1 Explain how the government prepared for a general strike.

2 'Red Friday was only a plan by the government to buy time so they could think of ways to defeat the Triple Alliance.' Do you agree? Explain your answer.

3 **Source D** makes fun of the General Strike. Explain how and why the author does this.

4 (a) Write down five reasons why the strike ended after only nine days.

   (b) Which of the reasons do you think was the most important? Explain your answer.

The TUC had its own newspaper to give its side of the strike to the public.

THE BRITISH WORKER
OFFICIAL STRIKE NEWS BULLETIN
Published by The General Council of the Trades Union Congress

No. 1.   WEDNESDAY EVENING, MAY 5, 1926.   PRICE ONE PENNY

IN LONDON AND THE SOUTH

Splendid Loyalty of Transport Workers

EVERY DOCKER OUT

"London dock workers are absolutely splendid," said an official of the Transport and General Workers' Union.

"So far as they are concerned, it is a 100 per cent. strike. There is no trouble and everything is going smoothly."

POLICE HELP REFUSED

At Swindon the railwaymen are obeying Mr. Cramp's injunction to remain steady and to preserve order. The Great Western works are, of course, closed, and no trains are running.

It was stated at a mass meeting of the N.U.R. that Mr. Collett (the

The General Council suggests that in all districts where large numbers of workers are idle sports should be organised and entertainments arranged.

This will both keepa number

WONDERFUL RESPONSE TO THE CALL

General Council's Message : Stand Firm and Keep Order

The workers' response has exceeded all expectations. The first day of the great General Strike is over. They have manifested their determination and unity to the whole world. They have resolved that the attempt of the mineowners to starve three million men, women and children into submission shall not succeed.

All the essential industries and all the transport services have been brought to a standstill. The only exception is that the distribution of milk and food has been permitted to continue. The Trades Union General Council is not making war on the people. It is anxious that the ordinary members of the public shall not be penalised for the unpatriotic conduct of the mineowners and the Government.

Never have the workers responded with greater enthusiasm to the call of their leaders. The only difficulty that the General Council is experiencing, in fact, is in persuading those workers in the second line of defence to continue at work until the withdrawal of their labour may be needed.

WORKERS' QUIET DIGNITY

The conduct of the trade unionists, too, constitutes a credit to the whole movement. Despite the presence of armed police and the military, the workers have preserved a quiet orderliness and dignity, which the General Council urges them to maintain, even in the face of the temptation and provocation which the Government is placing in their path.

SOUTH WALES IS SOLID !

Not a Wheel Turning in Allied Industries

'MEN ARE SPLENDID !'

Throughout South Wales the stoppage is complete, and everywhere the men are loyally observing the orders of the T.U.C. to refrain from any conduct likely to lead to disturbance.

So unanimous has been the response to the call of the leaders, that not a wheel is turning in the industries affiliated to the T.U.C.

MONMOUTHSHIRE

Complete standstill of industries in the eastern valleys. Absolute unanimity prevails among the rank and file of the affiliated unions, and not a single wheel is turning in the allied industries.

Monmouth Education Authority—which has a majority of Labour representatives—has arranged to feed the school-children where required.

ABERDARE VALLEY

All railway and bus services are at a standstill. The miners' attitude indicates that they are absolutely loyal to the advice of their leaders to refrain from anything in the nature of riotous behaviour.

NEATH

Wages were cut, hours were extended and fewer men were employed. Union leaders were targeted for dismissal and many never worked again in the coal industry.

Impact of the strike on trade unions

In 1927 a new Trade Disputes Act was passed. This made any sort of general strike illegal. Workers could no longer come out on strike in sympathy with other workers, and it made it more difficult for trade unions to contribute money to the Labour Party. (This act was later repealed by a Labour Government in 1946.) Although trade union members had stood together and shown they could make a generally peaceful protest, the General Strike was a disaster for the unions. They had lost the strike and the leadership had shown that it feared that some of its members were revolutionaries. Now the government had banned any future general strikes. Not surprisingly, disillusioned workers left their unions in large numbers. Trade union membership dropped alarmingly in the years after the strike and it did not go up again for over seven years.

SUMMARY

Reasons for the failure of the strike.

- Government preparation.
- Middle-class opposition.
- Opposition from political parties and the Churches.
- Division in the TUC.
- Government propaganda.

THINGS TO DO

1 How reliable is **Source F** to historians studying the General Strike?

2 Study **Source E**. How useful are accounts like this for an historian studying the General Strike?

3 Study **Sources G** and **H**. Do these sources prove that historians should not rely on newspapers when studying the General Strike?

How far did Britain experience a depression in the 1930s?

The Wall Street Crash

The Wall Street Crash began on 24 October 1929. It brought the American economy to its knees. The Americans could no longer afford to lend European countries money to build up their industries or to buy goods. Consequently, economic depression soon hit Europe too and millions of workers lost their jobs.

Britain too followed the United States into economic depression, but in many ways the problems which brought economic depression in Britain had existed before the Wall Street Crash. Many British industries used out-of-date machinery and depended on the colonies for cheap raw material and export markets. As other countries began to develop their industries, British industries, such as coal mining, textiles, shipbuilding, and iron and steel began to suffer.

The declining industries

You have already seen how the coal-mining industry suffered in the 1920s. By the mid-1920s coal could be produced in America for 65p a tonne compared with £1.56 a tonne in Britain, and there was competition too from Poland and Germany. British mines could not compete with the superior technology being used in the mining industry of the USA and other countries.

It was the same in the textile industry. Japan's workers were paid a fifth of their British

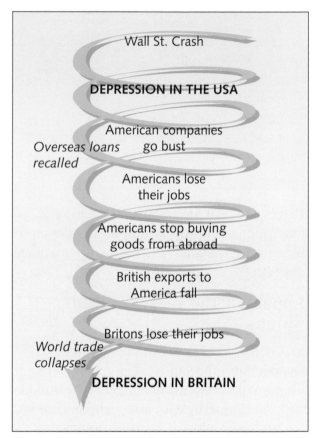

The American Depression hits Britain.

counterparts and worked in modern efficient factories. So Japanese cotton was much cheaper than that produced in the outdated British factories. Matters were not helped when synthetic fibres, such as rayon, were produced after the war and shorter skirts meant that less material was needed. In Britain about 1000 mills closed in the 1930s.

Shipbuilding also suffered. There was a post-war boom to replace the ships sunk in the First World War, but then a steady decline set in. As a result the iron and steel industry, which supplied shipbuilding with its raw materials, also suffered and like other industries faced competition from abroad. In the USA and Germany new efficient plants easily produced iron and steel more cheaply than their British rivals. In a world market Britain was finding it harder and harder to compete.

Source (A) A slum scene in the North in the 1920s.

Poor north, rich south?

The decline in British industries tended to affect the traditional occupations such as shipbuilding, coal mining and textiles. Areas of the country where these industries were based therefore were hardest hit by the decline. This applied particularly to Northern Ireland, Wales, Scotland and the North of England (see Source D). In the South East and the Midlands cities such as Coventry thrived while towns in the north, such as Jarrow, were in the words of its MP, Ellen Wilkinson, 'murdered'.

Why set up in the south?
The greater employment in the south encouraged owners and directors of new companies to set up their businesses there to be close to new customers who had the money to buy the washing machines, radios and cars they built. An example was the Ford Motor Company, which decided to move from Trafford Park in Manchester to an area close to London. Over 2000 Ford workers moved from the north to a new start in the south. Electricity provided the power to run the new washing machines and radios, as well as to make them. Factories no longer needed to be close to coalfields as they did in the days of steam power. And raw materials no longer needed to be close by; roads and railways could transport what was needed. It may have been that employers hoped for better industrial relations in the south after the northern industrial strikes of the 1920s.

SUMMARY

Reasons for the Depression in Britain.
- Wall Street Crash.
- Decline in old industries.
- Lack of investment in modern machinery.
- Competition from abroad.

THINGS TO DO

Explain how the following affected British industry after the First World War.

(a) Out-of-date machinery.
(b) Competition from abroad.
(c) New synthetic fibres.

How did standards of living change?

It is not possible to talk in general terms of how the standard of living changed for British people in the 1930s. For many unemployed people life was extremely difficult and hunger and despair was common. But for many of those in work times were good. The high unemployment throughout Britain meant that prices were kept low, so that those with a regular wage saw an increase in their standard of living.

Four million new houses were built in the 1930s. By 1939, 27 per cent of houses were owner-occupied. An income of £200 a year was enough to own your own home, with mortgages easy to get and interest rates low. With the houses came the schools, churches and cinemas needed to support the communities. New chain-stores, such as Marks & Spencer and Woolworth's, were built. The quality of food improved as branded foods, breakfast cereals and canned foods became available. The cost of a car halved between 1924 and 1935 because of mass production. So did the price of a vacuum cleaner. Those in work could afford new modern houses with electricity, and they could even consider buying a family car. Cheaper loans helped encourage a housing boom.

New electrical products, the motor car, and the boom in consumer goods and branded foods continued to make daily life more comfortable. Entertainment expanded with the growth in radio, cinemas and daily newspapers.

Northern Ireland	26.2%
Wales	24.3%
North-East England	19.1%
Scotland	15.2%
Lancashire	12.9%
Yorkshire	9.2%
London	8.2%
South East	6.1%
Midlands	6.0%

Unemployment figures for 1937.

The increase/decrease in output and employment in Britain in the period 1920–38.

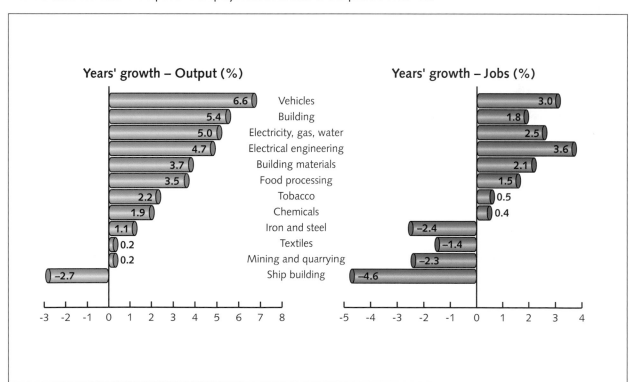

Years' growth – Output (%)

Industry	Output
Vehicles	6.6
Building	5.4
Electricity, gas, water	5.0
Electrical engineering	4.7
Building materials	3.7
Food processing	3.5
Tobacco	2.2
Chemicals	1.9
Iron and steel	1.1
Textiles	0.2
Mining and quarrying	0.2
Ship building	−2.7

Years' growth – Jobs (%)

Industry	Jobs
Vehicles	3.0
Building	1.8
Electricity, gas, water	2.5
Electrical engineering	3.6
Building materials	2.1
Food processing	1.5
Tobacco	0.5
Chemicals	0.4
Iron and steel	−2.4
Textiles	−1.4
Mining and quarrying	−2.3
Ship building	−4.6

Despair for others

While some workers, particularly in the south, prospered, others found it very difficult to maintain even a minimal standard of living. Areas which depended on shipbuilding or coal mining for employment were particularly badly hit with unemployment, poverty, malnutrition and ill-health common. In 1931 the national unemployment rate was 23 per cent, but this figure hid the real effects of the Depression. By the mid 1930s the worst hit areas like Jarrow on Tyneside and Merthyr Tydfil in South Wales had over 60% unemployment, whilst Birmingham and Oxford had less than 6%.

In an area of high unemployment everyone in the community felt the impact. Local shopkeepers were hit hard. In some towns half the shops closed, with the shopkeepers themselves joining the masses of the unemployed. For others the search for jobs in the richer south meant leaving their home town. Many hoped that better times were just around the corner and they would not have to leave the communities they had grown up in. Charities tried to ease the pain but found it difficult to make a difference when so many people needed their help.

Source **B**

This traffic jam in Britain shows how important motor transport had become in the lives of the people. Of course, for many others owning a car was little more than a dream.

THINGS TO DO

1 Why were some areas of Britain hit harder than others by the Depression?

2 Why was it possible for some people to live in prosperity even though Britain was hard hit by the Depression?

3 The traffic jam in **Source B** must have occurred in the south of England. Do you agree?

Jarrow: a town 'murdered'

One town which was particularly hard hit by the Depression was Jarrow, a small town on the south bank of the River Tyne. In 1930 nearby Hebburn colliery was closed and in 1931 one of Jarrow's major employers, the steel works, also shut down.

The government believed that the old industries needed reorganising. If some smaller factories and shipyards closed, the remaining fewer larger firms would be more competitive than many smaller ones. The National Shipbuilders' Security (NSS) was set up in 1930. It bought up shipyards and closed them down, hoping this would help other yards to stay in business.

For Jarrow this was disastrous. In 1934 the NSS closed Palmer's shipyard. By this time Jarrow was almost a one industry town, so the effect of closing the shipyard was devastating.

The Jarrow Crusade

The people of Jarrow decided to fight back. Public meetings were held. One desperate speaker even suggested going down to London with a bomb in his pocket to blow up the Houses of Parliament. The town council decided to draw up a petition demanding the right to work. They organised a march to London to present the petition to the government. Two hundred men were carefully selected by the council medical officer of health for the long journey to London. The men planned to walk between 15 and 25 miles a day carrying their petition from town to town.

Hunger marches were not new at the time of the Jarrow Crusade. They had taken place before, but were usually disorganised and frequently failed to win sympathy or support. Many people simply saw the marchers as beggars. What made the Jarrow march so different was that it was approved by the Jarrow town council and it was highly organised. The town council also allowed its headed notepaper to be used in making requests for food and shelter for the marchers as they marched south to London. The marchers were led on their journey by Miss Ellen Wilkinson, the town's Labour MP.

The Jarrow men captured the imagination of the country. They were accommodated each night along the route by sympathetic householders. The press gave them mouth organs so they could play music to march to and a rich lady in a fur coat handed out free cigarettes.

Source

I have seen nothing like it since the war. There is no escape anywhere from the prevailing misery. One out of every two shops appears to be closed. Wherever we went there were men hanging about, not scores of them but hundreds and thousands of them.

The writer J. B. Priestley describing the scene in the town of Jarrow in 1933.

Year	Unemployment
1927	2987
1928	3233
1929	3245
1930	3643
1931	6603
1932	6793
1933	7178
1934	6462
1935	6053
1936	4065

Unemployment in Jarrow, 1927–36. The total workforce in the town was 9700.

People in the more prosperous south began to understand the plight of those living in the old industrial towns and cities. Even the police in London praised the marchers for being well organised and disciplined. The government refused, however, to let them present their petition. This was left to their MP, Ellen Wilkinson, who was listened to sympathetically.

But the marchers failed to get the work needed for the town. Nevertheless, they returned home as heroes. However, when they arrived they discovered that their benefit had been stopped as they were not available for work while on their march. Some men did find work in a small trading estate that had been recently established. Others found work on the Team Valley Trading Estate in nearby Gateshead. Most had to wait for the upturn in the economy, which began with the rearmament programme for the Second World War. Still more had to wait for the war itself to find work.

 Jarrow men on their march to London, October 1936.

Source E

1936 First BBC television broadcasts – if you can afford the £110 for a set. The unemployed can't. Two hundred unemployed men march from Jarrow in north-east England to London with a petition asking the government to create jobs. After weeks of marching they reach London... and Prime Minister Baldwin refuses to meet them. They go home to houses without the new television sets – or even a loo.

At the time the first television broadcasts were made, and a television set cost £110, the Jarrow men were marching to London to protest at having no jobs.

A modern view of the contrast between the life of an unemployed Jarrow worker and the improvements taking place in society. It was written in a humorous book on history for school children.

Amongst the marchers was Robert Winship. He was 42 and worked in Hebburn Colliery from the age of 13 until it closed in 1930. He did not have another job until the war started in 1939. The year the colliery closed his wife was taken to a mental hospital and eventually died there in 1935. He had to bring up two daughters, Jean born in 1922 and Peggy born in 1925. His income was 95p a week. On one occasion he broke three ribs in a fall and was taken to hospital. He was there for fourteen days during which his dole was stopped as he was not available for work. The authorities insisted that he was brought home as soon as possible because it was costing £3 a week to keep his children in care. So he was brought home on a stretcher to fend for himself and his daughters as best he could.

An account of the life of one of the Jarrow marchers.

Source G

The policy of marches is, in my view, a revolutionary policy. It involves substituting organised mob rule for the proper constitutional way of doing things.

A letter from the Bishop of Durham to The Times in October 1936.

THINGS TO DO

1 Why did the town of Jarrow decide to send a march to London?

2 What does Priestley (**Source C**) find particularly sad about Jarrow?

3 What could a historian studying the effects of the Depression learn from the chart on page 270?

4 **Source E** is just a piece of fun and has no value to a historian studying the Depression in the 1930s. Do you agree?

5 Do you agree that **Source F** shows that the government in the 1930s were very hard-hearted?

6 Are you surprised by what **Source G** says? Explain your answer.

7 Was the Jarrow March really just a waste of time? Explain your answer.

How effective was the government in dealing with economic problems?

For those out of work there was a least unemployment benefit (dole money) which they could be given. Unemployment insurance had been established for some workers in 1911 and by 1920 it had been extended to include anyone earning less than £250 a year, with the exception of domestic servants, farm workers and civil servants. It was expected to pay for itself through the contributions received from those in work and their employers. But when unemployment rose dramatically, this did not happen. Originally, anyone on the dole for 15 weeks was not entitled to any further help as it was expected that an unemployed person would have found a new job before then and so further benefit would be unnecessary. This was not the case in the inter-war years. So in November 1922 the government had to extend benefit to all those unemployed for an unlimited period.

Source (H) Unemployed Welsh miners marching to London in 1932 to protest about the lack of job opportunities.

However, the slump after 1929 meant that more money was being paid out in benefits to the unemployed than was coming in from those still in work. So the government was under pressure to make changes to the scheme even before unemployment reached its highest in the 1930s.

Government spending cuts

The Labour government, elected in 1929, faced great difficulties in 1931 as exports had fallen by a half and 3 million people were out of work. The government was spending £2 million a day more than it had available and was having to look to the USA and France for loans. It could get the loans only if it cut its spending. The May Committee, composed of businessmen and trade unionists and headed by Sir George May, reported to the Labour cabinet with its suggestions to end the crisis. The prime minister asked for spending cuts but the government could not agree on them. The Prime Minister, Ramsay MacDonald, then formed an all-party National Government, at first seen as a temporary measure, to implement the cuts.

The government then began the unpleasant task of reducing public spending. Judges saw their pay cut by 10 per cent, and teachers by 15 per cent. The biggest saving however came from a 10 per cent cut in unemployment benefit.

The new National Government also decided to introduce a means test to make sure that payments were fair. Under the test a person's or family's sources of income were taken into account in deciding how much benefit they should be paid. Many claimed that the Means Test was more about the government trying to save money than providing a decent level of benefit.

The Means Test

The Means Test was carried out by officials from the local authorities' Public Assistance Committees which had been formed in 1930 to take over from the Poor Law. The unemployed claiming benefit had to reveal what everyone in their house, including grown up children and lodgers, had in savings and earnings. The test even looked at the value of things in the home that could be sold to raise cash. A family might have the father out of work and children in work. Under the Means Test the children were expected to feed and clothe their parents and even their younger brothers and sisters. This was very degrading for those who had to go through it.

The government was, however, able to introduce several measures which had a significant impact on the British economy. But it is true that, as in other countries, the economy did not really pick up until the demand for war goods brought about by the rearmament programme in 1937.

Import Duties Act, 1932

The government also tried to protect British industry by making the cost of foreign goods more expensive in Britain. They did this by taxing all imports by between 10 per cent and 20 per cent. They hoped this would encourage British industry to produce and sell more goods. The idea was that if more British goods were bought more would have to be produced, and so more people would be employed to produce them. This would mean that unemployment would fall.

However, the effect of the import tax on foreign goods was not as great as hoped. Nevertheless, British cars and electrical goods did sell well. But this tended to benefit the south of the country rather than the areas of high unemployment, such as in the north of England, Scotland and Wales, those areas where traditional industries were in decline.

Special Areas Act, 1934

The government realised that economic problems varied across the country. It attempted to address this problem by introducing an Act which appointed two commissioners with a budget of £2 million to try to attract some of the new industries to the old industrial areas. It had limited success. Some industrial estates were established, such as the Team Valley Industrial Estate in Gateshead, which is still a major source of employment today. But many companies still did not want to move to the north. Small industrial estates alone could not replace the coal-mining or shipbuilding industries which had made the region what it was.

THINGS TO DO

1 Why did the dole cause problems for the National Government?

2 What solutions were suggested? Why were they unpopular?

3 Why was the Means Test so unpopular?

Had the welfare state been fully established by 1951?

The Beveridge Report, 1942

This report was the result of the work of a committee set up during the war to suggest ways in which life in Britain could be improved after the war. It proposed that the state should support its citizens 'from the cradle to the grave', that is, from their birth until death. Beveridge identified five giant problems which had to be overcome to make progress and create a better society.

The first of the giants was *want*, which was the lack of the basic needs of life, especially food. It was proposed this could be defeated by a new system of national insurance. The second giant was *ignorance*, the lack of a proper education for everyone, which would be defeated by the building of new and better schools. The prevention of *disease*, or unnecessary illnesses, would be achieved by setting up a new health service for the whole nation. *Squalor*, or living in poverty, was to be remedied by a massive programme of house building. *Idleness*, or unemployment, was to be solved by the government helping industry create more jobs for everyone.

Conservatives	213
Labour	393
Liberals	12
Other parties	22

Result of the 1945 general election.

The general election, July 1945

During the war Britain had a coalition government led by Churchill. In July 1945, a general election was held. The Labour Party, led by Attlee, won a landslide victory. This was the first time they had ever won with a clear majority to govern on their own. The Conservative leader, Winston Churchill, himself was very popular, but his party was still seen by many people as the party of appeasement and the unemployment of the 1930s. The electorate also seemed to have decided that the Labour Party was more likely to implement the Beveridge Report and develop the welfare state.

The attack on want

To improve the standard of living, a family allowance was set up in 1945 and the first payments made in August 1946. A family received 5 shillings (25p) a week for each child after the first until each child reached the age of 16 or was employed full time. There was no means test, so all families received the benefit.

The Labour government's next step in the fight against want was the National Insurance Act of 1946. Employers, workers and the government all paid into the scheme which provided benefits to workers who were out of work through sickness, unemployment or pregnancy.

TACKLING THE FIRST GIANT

"WANT is only one of the five giants on the road of reconstruction" — The Beveridge Report.

Source (A) This 1942 cartoon shows Beveridge setting out to defeat the problems of British society.

If someone was sick, there was no limit to how long they could claim sickness benefit, but if they were unemployed they could claim unemployment benefit for only six months.

A further Act, the National Insurance (Industrial Injuries) Act of 1946, gave benefits to workers who were injured or disabled while at work and set up tribunals to decide the amount of compensation to be paid. The National Assistance Act of 1948 set up the National Assistance Board to provide for those in exceptional need, including those not covered by the National Insurance Act. The Board's purpose was to prevent extreme poverty and provide everyone with a minimum income. It was expected that only a few would need to apply for National Assistance, but demand was greater than expected.

The attack on disease

Aneurin Bevan, the Minister for Health, was responsible for improving the nation's health. Under the National Health Service Act of 1946 everyone received free medical, dental, hospital and eye treatment, and there was no charge for spectacles, false teeth and medicines. Most hospitals came under the control of the government as part of the National Health Service (NHS). Local councils provided midwives, home nurses, health visitors and ambulances. All this was paid for by taxation and National Insurance contributions. Doctors were paid under the National Health Service, which encouraged GPs (general practitioners) to practise in poorer areas without fear of not getting paid because people could not afford to.

Source (B)

The men and women of this country who have endured great hardships in war are asking what kind of life awaits them in peace. They need good homes, sufficient food, clothing and the amenities of life, employment and leisure, and social provision for accident, sickness and old age. For their children they desire an educational system that will give them the chance to develop all their faculties.

An excerpt from a radio election speech by Clement Attlee in 1945.